# The End of the Palestine Mandate

*Modern Middle East Series, No. 12*

*Sponsored by the Center for Middle Eastern Studies*
*The University of Texas at Austin*

# The End of the Palestine Mandate

*Edited by Wm. Roger Louis*
*and Robert W. Stookey*

 UNIVERSITY OF TEXAS PRESS, AUSTIN

First Edition, 1986

Requests for permission to reproduce material from this work
should be sent to Permissions, University of Texas Press,
Box 7819, Austin, Texas 78713.

Library of Congress Cataloging-in-Publication Data
Main entry under title:

The End of the Palestine mandate.

   (Modern Middle East series; no. 12)
   Bibliography: p.
   Includes index.
   Contents: Introduction / Wm. Roger Louis—The
president versus the diplomats / Peter Grose—The Soviet
role in the emergence of Israel / Oles M. Smolansky—[etc.]
   1. Palestine—History—Partition, 1947—Addresses,
essays, lectures.   2. Near East—Politics and government
—1945–     —Addresses, essays, lectures.   I. Louis,
William Roger, 1936–     .   II. Stookey, Robert W.,
1917–     .   III. Series: Modern Middle East series
(Austin, Tex.); no. 12
DS126.4.E63   1985     956.94′05     85-15109
ISBN 0-292-72052-1

# Contents

# Introduction

The historic episode of the end of the Palestine mandate is a turning point in Middle Eastern affairs. Almost four decades have passed since the climactic events of the late 1940s, yet no resolution is in prospect. The question in contemporary eyes was the ultimate demographic, political, and cultural character of Palestine. The termination of the British mandate ended an era and inaugurated a new phase. Britain relinquished responsibility for administration of the territory; the Yishuv, the Jewish community in Palestine, became an independent state in confrontation both with the neighboring sovereign Arab countries and with the indigenous Arabs of Palestine. Whether or not the Palestinian Arabs could be considered as an incipient nation, albeit without land to rule as their own, is one of the controversial issues raised in the essays of this book. In any case, the Arab-Jewish strife that had punctuated the mandate's history was transmuted after 1948 into recurrent wars between Israel and one or more Arab states. The outside powers continued to perceive in the eastern Mediterranean strategic and ideological as well as political and moral issues that transcended the highly charged local struggle between the Jews and Arabs. The end of the mandate is thus an important part of an unfolding conflict.

The broad lines of the struggle over Palestine emerged during World War I when the Western Allies, assuming that the Ottoman Empire would be dismembered upon its defeat, addressed the question of the fate of its non-Turkish territories. Palestine was the object of rival British and French aspirations. It was, moreover, the vital focus of the World Zionist Organization, which had already achieved considerable progress in rallying worldwide support for the objective of establishing a Jewish state in Palestine. Sharif Hussein of Mecca, on the other hand, had visions of an autonomous Arab state extending from the Taurus Mountains southward to the Indian Ocean, under the rule of his Hashemite dynasty; and he was in contact with the underground Arab dissident movement in Syria and Iraq.

Exigencies of the war prompted the British government to take two key actions affecting the future of Palestine. The British calculated that a public expression of support for the principle of a Jewish national home in Palestine would enable the World Zionist Organization to mobilize American Jews in support of the United States' entry into the war on the side of the Allied powers, that German Jews might shift their allegiance, and that Russian Jews might dissuade the new revolutionary regime in Russia from abandoning the conflict. Above all, the British aimed to keep the French out of Palestine. Quite apart from assisting "God's will," those were some of the underlying motives of the Balfour Declaration of November, 1917. Second, the British high commissioner in Cairo, Sir Henry McMahon, had been authorized to conduct a correspondence with Sharif Hussein sufficiently encouraging to the latter's aspirations to bring him into the struggle against the Ottoman Empire. In 1945 these were still tangled legacies. The British had made no progress in resolving the contradictions. If anything, the situation had been made worse because of the tension arising from two and a half decades of Jewish immigration into Palestine on one hand, and the plight of the postwar Jewish refugees in Europe on the other.

As part of the post–World War I settlement, Great Britain was awarded a League of Nations mandate over Palestine. The Balfour Declaration was written into the document as a charge on the mandatory power. The phraseology of the mandate failed to clarify the ambiguous term "national home." The mandate gave discretionary power to Britain to establish a separate administration in the portion of the mandated territory east of the Jordan River. Even before the mandate took effect, in September, 1923, the British had created a separate emirate there, headed by Sharif Hussein's son, Abdullah. Animosity between the Jewish and Arab Palestinian communities, furthermore, prompted Winston Churchill, then Britain's colonial secretary, to issue a White Paper in June, 1922, asserting that the status of Jews in Palestine under the existing British administration in fact constituted the "national home" called for by the Balfour Declaration and the mandate. The British were also attempting to refute the contention of Sharif Hussein and Arab nationalists that the McMahon correspondence had promised Palestine independence as part of a fully sovereign Arab state. The history of the British administration may be summed up by stating that no common ground could be found for the accommodation of the two nationalisms, whether by the partition proposed by the Royal Commission report of 1937 (the Peel report), or by the "binational" solution of the White Paper of 1939, which aimed to stabilize Palestine's population at a ratio of about two-thirds to one-third (with guarantees for the Jewish minority).

It is arguable that neither partition nor a binational state would have provided a workable solution before World War II. Certainly the events of the European war itself virtually guaranteed that there could be no resolution of the Palestine struggle without armed conflict. By 1939 there was increasing Arab resentment at Jewish immigration. Arab suspicion was barely assuaged by British "appeasement" in the famous 1939 White Paper. But it was the Holocaust that brought about the transformation. Hitler's attempt to exterminate the Jews created worldwide humanitarian concern for the refugees and gave a dynamism to Jewish nationalism that could not have been foreseen by the authors of the Balfour Declaration. By 1939, if not in 1919, the Jews and Arabs were on a collision course. By 1945 the Jewish sense of messianic inspiration appeared to be increasingly urgent as the scale of the Nazi atrocities became more widely known. From the Arab side the mounting Zionist crusade appeared as a sharply increasing challenge to the essentially Arab country of Palestine.

The essays of this book begin roughly at the end of World War II. In 1939 Britain had been the only "world power" directly involved in Palestine. By 1945 the United States could not be excluded. By 1947 the Soviet Union was actively participating in the Palestine controversy at the United Nations. Though the United Nations dimension of the problem does not form the subject of a separate essay, it is important to bear in mind that the issue was almost at once *internationalized*. The British referral of the Palestine question to the United Nations in early 1947 in effect signified that the British could not resolve the problem either by diplomatic ingenuity or by military action.

The first chapter by Roger Louis attempts to clarify British policy. It argues that the foreign secretary, Ernest Bevin, pursued the solution of a "binational state" in the hope that concerted action with the United States might guarantee Jewish minority rights without alienating the Arab majority, thereby allowing Britain to remain on good terms with the Arab world generally. The Anglo-American Committee of Inquiry of 1946 was, from the British point of view, intended to facilitate British aims by convincing the Americans of the inequity of creating a quasi–white settler community in Palestine. Zionist influence in the United States, together with the traditional American suspicions of British imperialism, frustrated Bevin's objective. The British were unable to persuade the Americans to check expansionist Zionist aims that appeared to jeopardize Britain's position in the Middle East and in the end were compelled to cut losses and evacuate.

Peter Grose's analysis of United States policy centers on the perspective of the presidents, Roosevelt and then Truman, toward a Palestine settlement. While the American foreign policy experts were closer to their British colleagues in opposing Zionist aspirations, the presidents repeatedly overruled their diplomatic advisors. Roosevelt was apparently moved by a naive belief that the Balfour Declaration had "promised" Palestine to the Jews, and that the Arabs would have to be bought off. For Truman, the essence of the problem was the practical matter of finding homes for Jewish refugees. Advised that he could win the 1948 election even without the Jewish vote, Truman never fully espoused the Zionists' political program, but his humanitarian idealism and support for the new United Nations coincided with the tactic of stealing a march on the Soviet Union as he rushed to grant *de facto* recognition to the state of Israel.

The chapter on the Soviet Union and Palestine by Oles Smolansky argues that in 1947 Stalin made a rational decision to support the establishment of the Jewish state. Though the documentary evidence about Soviet policy is far less copious than about the other powers, it is clear that Stalin aimed above all at the breakup of the British Empire in the eastern Mediterranean. Support of Zionist aims enabled him to stir up a maximum amount of trouble for the British with a minimum amount of expense and effort. Soviet policy can be explained on grounds of pure expediency in relation to shifting ideological and strategic preoccupations.

Michael Cohen argues in the chapter on the Zionist perspective that the diplomatic initiatives, the administrative preparation, and the military victories provide the historical explanation of the creation of the Jewish state. Against all odds the Zionists at the United Nations in November, 1947, succeeded in obtaining moral sanction for the Jewish state, but it was the military victories as well as the inspired belief in the "national home" that made the Zionist triumph comprehensible. The state of Israel was made possible by humanitarian sympathy for the sufferings of the Jews, but it was also born on the field of battle.

Walid Khalidi discusses the Arab dimension of the problem. The first great blow to the Arabs collectively involved in the Palestine problem was the realization that the White Paper of 1939 would not be enforced. There would be no guarantee limiting the numbers of Jewish immigrants. If the Arabs could not believe in the provisions of the 1939 White Paper, how could they be expected to subscribe to a further solution of, for example, the admission of the 100,000 refugees proposed by the Anglo-American Committee of Inquiry in 1946? Step by step, Arab faith in the goodwill of the West crumbled, until the Arab League became the only hope of concerted action against the Zionist threat. In the end the Arabs could rely only on themselves.

Essays written from such totally different perspectives cannot be intended to provide a consensus. Historical controversy will probably continue, because of different and conflicting interpretations of motive and reality from each angle of vision. Historical truth is complex and not necessarily harmonious. The Palestine question reminds us that historical forces with deep and enduring roots may be incompatible.

The dramatic events of the latter part of the 1940s are now almost forty years old. These issues can now be discussed dispassionately and objectively by professional historians who have had access to recent archival material, without muting the clash of perspectives. Such was the aim of a panel at the annual meeting of the American Historical Association in San Francisco in December, 1983. The present volume is the result of that exchange. The papers have been revised and elaborated for publication as a coherent volume. We as editors are grateful to J. C. Hurewitz for the concluding comment as well as to our fellow authors, who have borne with us each step of the way. We also wish to thank our colleagues in the Center for Middle Eastern Studies at the University of Texas, and, not least, an anonymous reader who enabled us greatly to improve the quality of the book.

Wm. Roger Louis
Robert W. Stookey

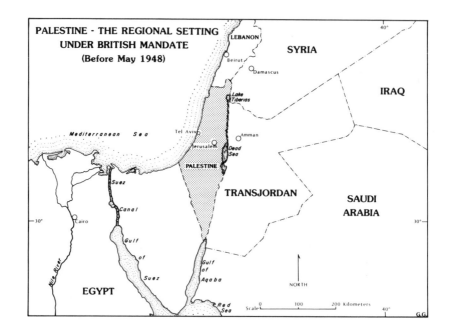

PALESTINE - THE REGIONAL SETTING
UNDER BRITISH MANDATE
(Before May 1948)

LEBANON

SYRIA

Beirut

Damascus

IRAQ

Lake
Tiberias

Mediterranean    Sea

Tel Aviv

Amman

Jerusalem

Dead
Sea

PALESTINE

TRANSJORDAN

SAUDI
ARABIA

Suez

Canal

Cairo

Gulf

of

Suez

Gulf
of
Aqaba

NORTH

EGYPT

Red
Sea

Scale    0    100    200 Kilometers

G.G.

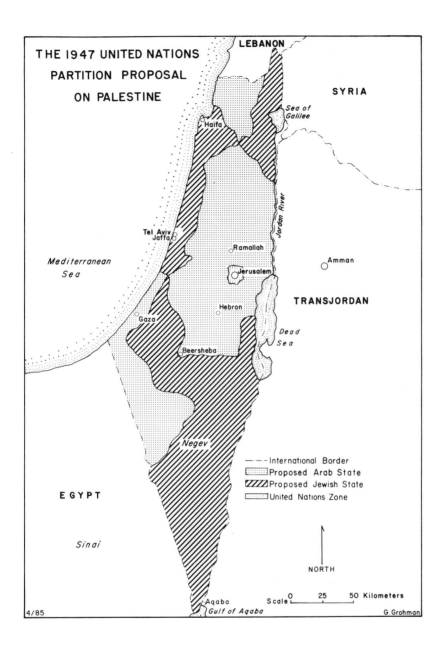

THE 1947 UNITED NATIONS
PARTITION PROPOSAL
ON PALESTINE

LEBANON

SYRIA

Sea of
Galilee

Haifa

Jordan River

Tel Aviv
Jaffa

Ramallah

Amman

Mediterranean
Sea

Jerusalem

TRANSJORDAN

Hebron

Gaza

Dead
Sea

Beersheba

Negev

International Border
Proposed Arab State
Proposed Jewish State
United Nations Zone

EGYPT

Sinai

NORTH

Scale  0   25   50 Kilometers

Aqaba
Gulf of Aqaba

4/85

G. Grohman

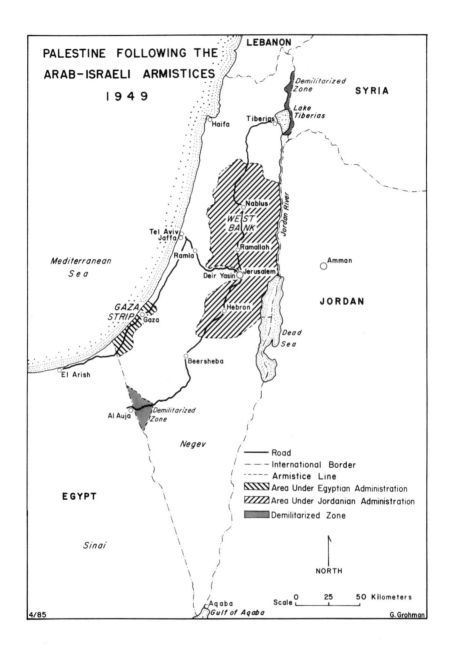

PALESTINE FOLLOWING THE
ARAB-ISRAELI ARMISTICES
1949

LEBANON

*Demilitarized Zone*

SYRIA

*Lake Tiberias*

Haifa    Tiberias

*Jordan River*

Nablus

WEST BANK

Tel Aviv
Jaffa

Ramla

Ramallah

*Mediterranean Sea*

Deir Yasin    Jerusalem

Amman

GAZA STRIP    Gaza

Hebron

JORDAN

*Dead Sea*

El Arish

Beersheba

Al Auja    *Demilitarized Zone*

*Negev*

EGYPT

—— Road
—·— International Border
----- Armistice Line
▨ Area Under Egyptian Administration
▨ Area Under Jordanian Administration
▨ Demilitarized Zone

*Sinai*

↑
NORTH

Scale  0    25    50 Kilometers

4/85

Aqaba
*Gulf of Aqaba*

G. Grohman

# The End of the Palestine Mandate

# British Imperialism and the End of the Palestine Mandate

*Wm. Roger Louis*

The key to the problem of Britain and the end of the Palestine mandate lies in an understanding of the thought and motivation of the foreign secretary, Ernest Bevin. He often referred to British Palestine policy as "his" policy, and he was right in doing so, even though the contributions of the prime minister, the Chiefs of Staff, and the colonial secretary were substantial. Bevin was in overall control, and he followed developments with a grasp of detail and force and personality unrivaled by his British contemporaries. He has often been denounced as anti-Semitic. As Lord Bullock has pointed out, however, Bevin reached the age of sixty-four before anyone suspected him of harboring an anti-Jewish prejudice.[1] It was rather the reverse. Bevin's "anti-Semitic" reputation developed from policy, not personal sentiment. He consistently attempted to avert partition. He wished to create a binational state in which Arabs and Jews would live and work together as equals. He temperamentally tended to regard those who disagreed with him as enemies. Thus the Zionists from the beginning became his adversaries. When he was frustrated, he often became angry, and he sometimes rose in wrath against the Americans as well as the Zionists. For example, at a Labour party conference in June, 1946, he exclaimed that the Americans supported the proposal to admit 100,000 Jewish refugees into Palestine because they did not want any more Jews in New York. Bevin's outbursts must not be allowed to obscure the creative thrust and coherence of his purpose. Paradoxically, there is truth in the view that his "pro-Arab" disposition helped to bring about the creation of the state of Israel. Zionists throughout the world were able to unite in vilifying him.

Bevin had in mind Commonwealth precedents for the "binational" state in Palestine. It was a common British view, in the words of W. K. Hancock, who helped to build part of the theory that the Labour government attempted to put into practice, that "the experience of Canada and South Africa is written into the mandate."[2]

Toward the end of his life, Bevin referred to Lord Durham's solution of responsible self-government for the French and British in Canada and to Sir Henry Campbell-Bannerman's peace of reconciliation with the Boers as two of the three "milestones" in the history of the Commonwealth. To Bevin "partition" symbolized a bankruptcy of policy, the end of the road, and an admission of failure—though sometimes unavoidable, as in the case of India. The granting of freedom to India and Pakistan was the third of Bevin's milestones.[3] In Palestine he pursued the goal of the binational state with such tenacity that one wonders what might have happened if he had become secretary of state for India in 1945 rather than secretary of state for foreign affairs. In the view of his principal critic on Palestine in the House of Commons, Richard Crossman, the result might have been disastrous. "It is a crowning mercy," Crossman once stated, "that Bevin did not have a hand in India. He would have messed it up as he did Palestine."[4] One will never know. The point of the comparison is that the original goal was the same, a unified India on the one hand, a binational state in Palestine on the other. A divided India would split the Indian army and erode Britain's power in Asia. With a divided Palestine, Arab nationalism would continue to fester and would bring about the end of Britain's paramount position in the Middle East. In sum, Bevin's motivation must be found in areas of military power and economic resources as well as the idealism of the Commonwealth.

Bevin believed that the answer to the problem of Jewish refugees and displaced persons should be sought in Europe rather than in Palestine, which he regarded as a predominantly Arab country. He found himself caught between Jewish nationalism supercharged by the emotions of the Holocaust, and the anti-Zionism of the Arabs, without whose goodwill the British Empire in the Middle East would be doomed. The British could not support a Jewish state without alienating the Arabs. Nor could the British impose a settlement acceptable to the Arab countries without antagonizing the United States. The Middle East in Bevin's view was second in importance only to Europe; but, in order for Britain to remain the dominant regional power, both Arab cooperation and the support of the United States were vital. Without them Britain's influence would decline, and not only in the Middle East. Britain would sink to the status of a second-class European power such as the Netherlands. That apprehension helps to explain the emotional energy that Bevin and other British leaders expended on the regeneration of the British Empire in the Middle East and Africa. Palestine in this larger context represented the principal stumbling block. In view of the overriding priorities of Arab collaboration and American assistance, the accusations against Bevin—for example, that he was callous to Jewish suffering—become more comprehensible. In short he was pursuing a grand "imperial" strategy in which Palestine played only a small but most irritating part.

Churchill once described Bevin as "a working class John Bull." Like all good caricatures there was an element of truth in this. With his working-class background and his concern for the welfare of common people, Bevin saw no contradiction between the development of the oil and other resources of the Middle East and what he hoped would be the future prosperity of the British Commonwealth. He believed, as did many English of his generation, that the British Empire was a beneficent force in world affairs, though the word "Empire" would have to be replaced in the Middle East with something that suggested less exploitation and more equal partnership. The British and the Arabs could work together to develop the region to mutual advantage. Economically the Middle East together with Africa offered just as alluring a prospect as India had in the past. Militarily the countries of the Middle East could be brought into a system of defense that would help to offset the manpower and military potential of the Soviet Union. Such in brief was Bevin's vision. He combined political, economic, and military strands of thought into a coherent general policy that sought to preserve Britain as a great power. The Middle East was the principal pillar of Britain's position in the world.

Bevin could not systematically have pursued his Middle Eastern aims without the effective partnership of the prime minister, Clement Attlee. Bevin was careful to square his ideas with Attlee's before Cabinet meetings. Together the two of them often made an unbreakable combination, though Attlee was much more skeptical about Britain's economic and military capacity to remain a "great power" in the Middle East. To a far greater extent than Bevin, Attlee was willing to acknowledge the diminution of British power, to contemplate general withdrawal from the area, and specifically to cut losses in Palestine.[5]

Apart from those in the military chain of command, the other figure who requires a brief comment is Arthur Creech Jones, who was parliamentary under-secretary for the colonies from July, 1945, until October, 1946, and then colonial secretary until his defeat in the general election of February, 1950. Both Attlee and Bevin respected Creech Jones and listened to his advice, though Attlee lamented his political ineffectiveness and came to regard his appointment as a mistake. "Creech Jones despite much hard work and devotion," Attlee wrote in 1950, "had not appeared to have a real grip of administration in the Colonial Office."⁶ "Creech" (as he was known to his friends) was sympathetic to the aims of the moderate Zionists (though he himself never endorsed the idea of a state so large as the one that came into existence in 1948). He was over-shadowed by both the prime minister and the foreign secretary, and his ability to work harmoniously with them explains why the Pal-estine issue within the Labour government remained relatively non-controversial. The Colonial Office and the Foreign Office, the two offices of state mainly concerned with Palestine, often clashed over many issues, but when ministerial policy was agreed upon by Creech Jones and Bevin as well as Attlee, then it was virtually invulnerable to challenge by other members of the Cabinet or by the Chiefs of Staff. The Bevin/Attlee/Creech Jones combination helps to explain why the pro-Zionist voices in the Cabinet—including those of Hugh Dalton, Aneurin Bevan, and Emmanuel Shinwell—remained ineffec-tive, and why the policy of the Labour government in practice ap-peared to be at variance with the Labour party's publicly proclaimed sympathy with the Zionist cause.

In getting a bearing on the tacit as well as the spoken British postwar assumptions about Palestine, it is useful to dwell briefly on the relationship between Creech Jones and Bevin and the responsi-bilities of the Colonial Office and Foreign Office. Throughout his ca-reer Creech Jones was associated with Bevin, first in the Transport and General Workers' Union and later as Bevin's parliamentary under-secretary at the Ministry of Labour during the war. The facts of that connection, however, fail to do justice to Creech Jones's passionate and long-standing interest in colonial affairs. In 1940 he founded the Fabian Colonial Bureau with Rita Hinden. In terms of knowledge about the colonies, especially the ones in Africa, he came to his position as colonial secretary with thorough preparation. He was re-sponsible for endorsing the Labour government's new direction in colonial policy that later culminated in the transfer of power in Af-rica. He is remembered as the epitome of British decency and good-will toward "colonial" peoples. It is therefore ironic that he had to devote so much of his time to Palestine, which was by no means a typical colonial dependency. At first he was not unoptimistic, but eventually he came to believe that it was impossible realistically to come to terms with the Zionists. He later took pains to emphasize that he and Bevin were ultimately at one on Palestine.⁷

Since 1922 Palestine had been a Colonial Office responsibility. In the late 1930s its relatively minor significance as a mandated territory of the League of Nations was transformed because of the crisis in Europe. Palestine became a major political and strategic concern of the Foreign Office and Chiefs of Staff as well as the Colonial Office. In 1945–48 the Foreign Office and Colonial Office shared responsibility for Palestine, the former for the international dimension of the problem, the latter for the mandate's administration. Both departments responded to the strategic demands of the Chiefs of Staff, the Colonial Office in relation to Palestine as a strategic territory (and as a fallback from Egypt), the Foreign Office in regard to broader aspects of the defense of the Middle East and global security of the Empire and Commonwealth. In these intricate relationships Creech Jones played a critical part. During his tenure as colonial secretary he favored partition as a solution, but on this and other important issues he eventually yielded and followed Bevin's lead. On the whole Bevin found in Creech Jones a supporter as faithful as he could have expected in the head of another major, and in some senses rival, government department.

In Parliament Bevin confronted Churchill, who was not only his most powerful and persistent adversary in imperial and foreign affairs, but also his principal critic on the tactics and timing of withdrawal from Palestine. Churchill was important in the background of the Labour government's policy toward Palestine because after World War I he himself as colonial secretary had penned the official elaboration of the Balfour Declaration. The declaration of 1922 established Transjordan as an Arab territory distinct from Palestine. Palestine itself, in words that followed the Balfour Declaration, was not to be a Jewish "national home," but there was to be a national home *in* Palestine. Jewish immigration would be allowed, in Churchill's own phrase, up to the limit of "economic absorptive capacity," which was to be judged by the mandatory power. The declaration of 1922 served as the basis of British policy for nearly two decades. When the White Paper of 1939 attempted to curtail and stabilize the Jewish population of Palestine at one-third of the Arab majority (with further immigration after five years dependent on Arab acquiescence), Churchill denounced it as a breach of faith with the Jews. Throughout his career, with varying degrees of enthusiasm and skepticism, Churchill remained a moderate Zionist. As prime minister during the war he became the moving spirit behind the solution of partition and its possible corollary of an independent Jewish state. But he always kept his Zionism subordinate to his imperial priorities. He never became a convert to the idea that Palestine might be substituted strategically for Egypt. And he always believed that a relatively minor conflict or "wars of mice" between Arabs and Jews (in comparison with the struggle in India) should never disrupt the Anglo-American "alliance." In August, 1946, he summarized his indictment of the Labour government's handling of the Palestine problem: "it is our duty . . . to offer to lay down the Mandate. We should . . . as soon as the war stopped, have made it clear to the United States that, unless they came in and bore their share, we should lay the whole care and burden at the foot of the United Nations organisation."[8]

Anglo-American cooperation over Palestine proved to be perhaps the single most frustrating and elusive goal of the Labour government. A major disagreement developed in August, 1945, when President Truman requested the admission of 100,000 Jewish refugees into Palestine. This issue is discussed in the next section of this essay. It is mentioned here because to the British it constituted the point of departure for the postwar controversy. Bevin later reflected that, "had it not been for a succession of unfortunate actions on the part of the United States" following the demand of the 100,000, the question might have been settled. His point was that if the United States and Britain had acted together immediately and decisively at the end of the war, the Palestine drama might have had an entirely different denouement.

One might question whether it was not rather late in the day for the British to make such bold assertions about decisive chronology. For the British, at least, was not the White Paper of 1939 the turning point? Could not its constitutional provisions, which for better or worse were never developed, have led to a binational state? Or, for that matter, what of the recommendations of the Royal Commission of 1937? Might they not have prepared the way in the opposite direction for the creation of a Jewish state at a much earlier date? To pursue the chronology still further, Bevin might have lamented the lost opportunity of 1922, when the Arabs rejected measures that might have started Palestine down the path of self-government, as in the case of other British dependencies. The British were entirely willing to share the blame for failure in Palestine with the Arabs as well as with the Jews, and with the Americans as well as with the Russians. On the question of chronology and points of departure in the story, Bevin was emphatic on one subject. The Balfour Declaration, in his view, was no more than "a unilateral declaration" that "did not take into account the Arabs & was really a Power Politics declaration."[9] It was the source of all the trouble. In Bevin's opinion it was the greatest mistake in Britain's imperial history.[10]

### The 100,000 and the Anglo-American Committee of Inquiry

When President Truman called for the admission of 100,000 Jewish refugees into Palestine in August, 1945, the population of the country itself, according to British estimates, was 550,000 Jews and 1,200,000 Arabs. It could be that the British made a tactical blunder by not accepting the additional 100,000 as a final quota. In any case, the Foreign Office believed that a sudden influx of Jewish immigrants would destroy any last chance of reconciling the two communities. It is important to emphasize the thrust of Foreign Office thought, which upheld the principles of the White Paper of 1939 and the solution of the binational state, rather than the consensus of Colonial Office opinion, which tended to support the opposite solution—partition—recommended by the Royal Commission in 1937 and reaffirmed by Churchill during the war. The Foreign Office predominated, not least because of Bevin. One is struck by the continuity of official sentiment, which responded to the White Paper of 1939 not as "appeasement" of the Arabs (and still less, at least by implication, of the Nazis) but rather as the basis of a constructive and just solution. The head of the Eastern Department of the Foreign Office, C. W. Baxter, wrote about "the constitutional proposals envisaged in the 1939 White Paper":

> It was then considered essential that Jews and Arabs should learn to work together as part of a single Palestine State. It was realised that the Jews would never attempt to work with the Arabs in a joint Arab-Jewish State, so long as they hoped that, by the continuance of Jewish immigration, the Jews would eventually become a majority in Palestine, and be able to press for a Jewish State. There must therefore be some finality as regards Jewish immigration and the size of the Jewish National Home. . . .
> Unhappily, owing to the war, the White Paper's constitutional proposals were never put into force. The 1939 policy has thus not been given a fair trial. If it is now decided to pursue the idea of a joint "bi-national" State, it would seem necessary to decide now, once and for all, what the size of the Jewish National Home in Palestine is to be.[11]

The phrases "finality as regards Jewish immigration" and "the size of the Jewish National Home" (as opposed to "Jewish State") are thus keys to official British thought.

Bevin is sometimes accused of having fallen captive to the prejudices of the permanent officials of the Foreign Office after July, 1945. This was not the case (the accusation could be more accurately leveled against Creech Jones in 1946 in regard to general colonial policy). The archival records reveal that he took a strong and independent line from the beginning, that he was influenced by the Chiefs of Staff as well as the prime minister, and that his natural sympathies flowed toward the Arabs. He regarded them as an indigenous people who were being dislodged by the equivalent of white settlers in Algeria and Kenya. He was quick to remind his critics in the House of Commons that he was not lacking in sympathy for the Jews. But he wished to find a solution to the problem of the survivors of the Holocaust elsewhere, in other words, in Europe, the United States, and "other countries" besides Palestine.[12] He was convinced that he could persuade the Americans of the reasonableness of that point of view. He also had great confidence in his own ability to resolve difficult problems by negotiation, as he believed was apparent from his success in the trade union movement in Britain. This sense of assurance, some would say arrogance, helps to explain his incautious statement, when he announced the appointment of the Anglo-American Committee of Inquiry in November, 1945: "I will stake my political future on solving the problem."[13] Churchill was right in saying later that "no more rash a bet has ever been recorded in the annals of the British turf."[14]

Bevin's preconceived ideas help to explain his later policy. He labored under certain misapprehensions, as did many of his contemporaries. He believed, for example, that there would be, to use his own words, "a certain amount of re-emigration" of Jews from Palestine back to Europe.[15] A record of his thoughts in September, 1945, also reveals his conviction that, if the Palestine question were submitted to the General Assembly of the United Nations, "the Arabs would have a chance to state their case."[16] The United Nations would endorse British policy. These of course proved to be misguided judgments. But he was not far wrong in believing that an independent committee of inquiry might recommend the creation of a binational state. One of the major conclusions of the Anglo-American Committee of Inquiry, which was composed of six Englishmen and six Americans, was that the Palestinian state should be neither Arab nor Jewish. On the other hand, the other principal recommendation of the committee, which reported in April, 1946, came as a jolt to the British. It called for the immediate admission of the 100,000 Jewish refugees.[17] President Truman precipitately and publicly accepted this part of the report without referring to its "binational" recommendations. He made this announcement unilaterally, without discussing it with the British. Bevin had assumed that the British and American governments would be able to work closely together on the Palestine question and that there would be a correlation between the policies endorsed by the White House and the State Department. Both those assumptions proved to be false. In the year following the end of the war, Bevin learned that the Americans would not follow his lead in resolving the Palestine issue and that President Truman would respond to the pressures and opportunities of American politics more than to the dilemmas of the British.

To preserve British paramountcy in the Middle East, Bevin needed the economic underwriting and, if necessary, the military support of the United States. The Jews, in his eyes, threatened to poison his relations with both the Arabs and the Americans. The report of the Anglo-American Committee of Inquiry and Truman's further demand for the 100,000 made things worse, not better. A minute by Sir Walter Smart, the Oriental secretary at the British Embassy in Cairo, reveals the Arab side of the dilemma:

> I am much struck by the superficiality and intellectual dishonesty of this Report. . . . the Committee demands the admission within less than a year of 100,000 immigrants (i.e. a larger number than have ever been brought in within such a short period at any time in the past) without making any mention of the question of Palestine's economic capacity to absorb them. It must have been perfectly obvious to the members of the Committee, as it is to all of us, that their proposals must result in acute political and military conflict between the Arabs and the Jews in Palestine and the Arab countries round it.[18]

On the other hand, if the British refused to yield on the issue of the 100,000, then the Zionists would be able to exploit the volatile anti-imperialist sentiment of the American public. According to Sir Nevile Butler, who had served as head of the North American Department during World War II, "The American 'anti-imperialist' feeling . . . is traditional and profound and it is in these areas that the Russians are trying to drive their wedge."[19] He wrote that minute in April, 1946, a critical time in the development of the cold war as well as in the Palestine conflict. It was also the time of the British Cabinet Mission to India. A false step in Palestine could lead to disaster in the larger areas not only of Anglo-Arab relations but also of American support of the British Empire, the transfer of power in India, and the confrontation with the Soviet Union.

It was a perilous time. Most British officials and statesmen,

including Attlee and Bevin, would probably have agreed with the
analysis, though not the sentiment, of an American critic of the British Empire who was a member of the Anglo-American Committee,
Frank Buxton (editor of the *Boston Herald*): "There was a time . . .
when England was so strong that muddling-through and stupidity
were not especially harmful to her; she had so much reserve strength
that she could retrieve her blunders. But now . . . stupidity and
shortsightedness are unforgivable sins and may inflict wounds from
which she cannot recover."[20] The quotation is significant because
the unpublished British records yield the overall impression that, far
from "muddling-through," the policy of the Labour government on
the Palestine question was a painstaking attempt to keep in balance
the vital Arab and American parts of the equation. It was the need for
American as well as Arab support that explains the British retreat to
a position of evenhanded withdrawal.

### The Critical Period: Summer, 1946, through February, 1947

Zionist terrorism offers a basic explanation of why the British were
forced to retreat. On July 22, 1946, the Irgun Zvai Leumi blew up the
British military headquarters at the King David Hotel in Jerusalem,
with heavy loss of British, Arab, and Jewish life. It is a melancholy
fact that the explosion polarized the Palestine conflict. Everyone in
the British civil administration or army had a friend or acquaintance
who had been killed at the King David. It stirred up powerful and
conflicting emotions among the British that terrorism should be re-
pressed and, at the same time, that they should withdraw because of
Jewish ingratitude. The chief of the Imperial General Staff, Field
Marshal Bernard Montgomery, wrote two days after the incident,
"We shall show the world and the Jews that we are not going to submit tamely to violence."[21] Churchill, on the other hand, represented
a wide current of public thought when he questioned the wisdom of
further loss of British life in Palestine. The blowing up of the King
David explains much about the public mood on Palestine in the
summer of 1946. Emotions were running high.

The explosion at the King David occurred at the same time that
officials in the British and American governments were attempting
to salvage the recommendations of the Anglo-American Committee
of Inquiry by implementing a scheme of provincial autonomy. It
would have provided an ambiguous compromise between the two extreme solutions of partition and a binational state. There would have
been a large measure of Arab and Jewish autonomy, with certain

powers reserved to the central administering authority. Britain would continue indefinitely as the trusteeship power. It is not important to dwell on the details, because the scheme was unacceptable to both Arabs and Jews. It might have been remotely feasible if both the United States and Britain could have agreed upon it. In the event, according to the dominant British interpretation, President Truman became apprehensive about Palestine as a campaign issue in the 1946 congressional elections and feared that he would be accused of "ghettoizing" the Jews in Palestine. So ended the plan for provincial autonomy, which, if it had been implemented decisively, might eventually have led to a binational state or, perhaps, to a more peaceful partition. Yet one can only agree with one of the first authorities who wrote dispassionately on the subject, J. C. Hurewitz, that by 1946 it was too late.[22]

British leaders, then and later, recognized President Truman's statement on the eve of Yom Kippur as a turning point. On October 4, 1946, he expressed the hope for a compromise between the British and Zionist proposals. The Zionists, however, publicized the part of the statement in which the president appeared to support "the creation of a viable Jewish state." Attlee and Bevin at this time correctly believed that the Zionist movement was in disarray, at odds with itself over the extremist demand for a Jewish state in all of Palestine. They still hoped that the Zionist "moderates" might negotiate if the Americans would support the solution of a binational state. Then came news of the "Yom Kippur statement." Attlee had attempted to prevent another unilateral move on the part of the president, but Truman refused to wait. He drew a rebuke from Attlee that must rank high in memorable exchanges between British prime ministers and American presidents. The flawless handwritten draft of Attlee's letter, which is among his papers at the Public Record Office, still radiates white-hot anger:

> I have received with great regret your letter refusing even a few hours' grace to the Prime Minister of the country which has the actual responsibility for the government of Palestine in order that he might acquaint you with the actual situation and the probable results of your action.
>
> These may well include the frustration of the patient efforts to achieve a settlement and the loss of still more lives in Palestine.
>
> I am astonished that you did not wait to acquaint yourself with the reasons for the suspension of the Conference with the Arabs. You do not seem to have been informed that so far from

negotiations having been broken off, conversations with leading Zionists with a view to their entering the Conference were
proceeding with good prospects of success.[23]

It did not amuse Attlee and Bevin to learn that Truman had made the
statement on the eve of Yom Kippur (with no mention of the congressional elections) for the reason that the Jewish people on their
day of atonement "are accustomed to give contemplation to the lot
of the Jewish people" and that he therefore hoped to relieve "their
feeling of depression and frustration."[24]

The conference mentioned in Attlee's letter to Truman was the
London conference on the Middle East, which met sporadically from
September, 1946, to February, 1947. The Arabs stood by the letter
and spirit of the assurances of 1939 and would yield to nothing less
than Palestine as an Arab state. The Jews boycotted the proceedings
because of the denial of the opposite premise of a Jewish state. They
conducted unofficial simultaneous negotiations with the British.
Bevin and Creech Jones provided the basis of discussion by presenting in essence the plan for provincial autonomy. It was as close as
British ingenuity could come to reconciling Arab and Jew and preserving British influence. The Arabs rejected the British plan because they believed it to be a move toward partition. The ghost of the
1930s haunted the conference. Since the British had proclaimed finality in 1939, why should the Arabs believe them in 1946?

For the British the hardening in the Jewish position was symbolized by the fall from formal political power of Chaim Weizmann at
the Zionist Congress in Basel in December. When David Ben-Gurion
met with British officials shortly thereafter, he stated that Weizmann
was "still first in moral standing" but that his political defeaʳ had
come about because of "his blind trust in Britain."[25] Those who now
led the Zionist movement did not believe that the British would
leave Palestine unless they were pushed out, though Ben-Gurion
made it clear that he hoped for a nudge as peaceful as possible. The
Jews judged the plan for provincial autonomy in exactly the opposite
way than did the Arabs. To the Zionists it was a step in the direction
of an Arab Palestinian state.

In November, 1946, Bevin paid a visit to New York in order to
attend the meeting of the Council of Foreign Ministers. Dock workers refused to handle his luggage. He was booed at a football game by
a crowd who remembered his statement about Americans not wanting any more Jews in New York. During this time he met with President Truman, who, though sharing a common sense of humor at the
expense of the Jews, unfortunately was struck by Bevin's resem-

blance to John L. Lewis, the leader of the United Mine Workers of America. Bevin also had a conversation with Rabbi Abba Hillel Silver, the anti-British leader of the American Zionist movement. He told the rabbi that, if the Jews pressed the issue of partition, the British "would give up the mandate" and hand it over to the United Nations. "At this," Bevin reported to Attlee, "Doctor Silver showed signs of distress."[26] This was more than a warning. It was an articulation of what might be called the British "United Nations strategy."

The game at the United Nations was one that the British believed they could win. In the autumn and winter of 1946, when Bevin's ideas crystallized in New York against the background of discussion in the Council of Foreign Ministers and the United Nations, it would have been a bold prophecy to have anticipated Zionist success in mobilizing two-thirds of the members of the General Assembly in support of the creation of a Jewish state. It would require the unlikely combination of the American and Russian voting blocs and what seemed to British and American officials alike to be the flouting of a fundamental principle of the organization itself—the imposition of a form of government against the wishes of the majority of the inhabitants. With such thoughts in mind, Bevin and his advisors hoped that the United Nations might endorse the solution of a binational state. Bevin himself continued to be skeptical about partition, because he believed that the Arab opposition would be so great that it would undermine Britain's entire position in the Middle East.[27] Nevertheless, at this time he began to give serious thought to the possible military and strategic consequences of the division of Palestine as well as to a possible political solution through the United Nations. "Partition" was generally in the wind in the British Cabinet. A meeting of October 25, 1946, concluded, "several Ministers said that they were glad that the possibility of Partition was not excluded . . . and expressed the view that this would in the end be found to be the only practicable solution of the Palestine problem."[28]

The Chiefs of Staff held that Britain could not successfully impose a solution by force if it were actively resisted by both communities. If compelled to choose between Arab and Jew, there could be no doubt whatsoever of the imperative need to preserve Arab goodwill. The Chiefs of Staff wrote in the aftermath of the publication of the "disastrous" report by the Anglo-American Committee of Inquiry: "All our defence requirements in the Middle East, including maintenance of our essential oil supplies and communications, demand that an essential feature of our policy should be to retain the co-operation of the Arab States, and to ensure that the Arab world does not gravitate towards the Russians. . . . We cannot stress too strongly the importance of Middle East oil resources to us both in peace and war."[29] When it became clear in mid-1946 that British military, air, and naval forces might be withdrawn from Egypt, the Chiefs of Staff attached emphatic importance to the retention of strategic rights in Palestine.

The Chiefs of Staff believed that Jewish terrorism could be quelled. Police and military authorities attempted to break the back of Jewish resistance by searching for arm caches and interning prominent leaders of the Jewish Agency. The British army hoped at the minimum to neutralize the Jews' ability to attack. Those tactics had the opposite of the intended effect on Jewish morale, though the military effectiveness of the Haganah was no doubt weakened. After the King David Hotel explosion, the British commanding officer, Gen. Sir Evelyn Barker, ordered British troops to have no "social intercourse with any Jew" and to punish the Jews "in a way the race dislikes as much as any, by striking at their pockets and showing our contempt for them."[30] He accused prominent Jews of "hypocritical sympathy" with the terrorists. By August the Colonial Office feared that Palestine would be plunged into a bloodbath.

The prime minister himself steadied British nerves. Attlee believed that firmness against terrorism would strengthen the "moderates," with whom it might be possible to work out a political solution. He stuck by his maxim of trying to accommodate the more "sensible" of the leaders of the Jewish Agency in order to prevent the extremists from precipitating, in Jewish eyes, a war of liberation. Curfews and house-to-house searches were relaxed. Barker was reprimanded for his nonfraternization order and eventually replaced (before his departure he urinated on the soil of Palestine as if in symbolic disgust). Attlee's "appeasement" did not please the chief of the Imperial General Staff, Montgomery, who continued to believe that military force would and should prove to be the only answer in Palestine. Montgomery stated in late 1946: "The policy of appeasement which had been adopted during the last few months had failed. Searches had been discontinued and internees had been released with no consequent improvement in the position, which in fact had deteriorated. The police and military forces were placed in a most difficult position. . . . He felt that what was required was a clear directive by His Majesty's Government to the High Commissioner to use all the forces at his disposal to maintain strict law and order. . . ."[31] Montgomery had a high opinion of British capability of imposing a peace with bayonets. His memoirs veil only slightly his contempt for Attlee's and Bevin's capitulation to the Jews, and for

Creech Jones's "spineless" handling of Palestine he reserved a special rancor.[32]

In London the Palestine crisis gained momentum in December and January of 1946–47 and reached a climax in February. The decisions took place against the background of the great emotional debate about India, the general deterioration of Britain in the Middle Eastern "northern tier," the collapse of new defense arrangements with Egypt, a sense of impending economic disaster, and one of the worst winters in British history. Two great offices of state, the Foreign Office and the Colonial Office, clashed over the interpretation of "trusteeship." Trusteeship for whom? Arab or Jew? The Chiefs of Staff continued to answer that question in terms of "the British" and to press for the retention of Palestine as a permanent strategic possession. The salient feature of this period was the persistent effort on the part of the British, especially Ernest Bevin, to support the Arabs and thereby to sustain British power in the Middle East. As a case study in decolonization, Palestine demonstrates the convergence of ethical sympathy for the Arabs and political calculation of how best to maintain British influence.

The two men making the critical decisions about timing and cutting losses were Bevin and Attlee. There was tension between them. "I do not think," Attlee wrote to Bevin in December, 1946, "that the countries bordering on Soviet Russia's zone viz Greece, Turkey, Iraq and Persia can be made strong enough to form an effective barrier. We do not command the resources to make them so."[33] When the two of them agreed that British troops should be withdrawn from Greece, Attlee viewed this problem above all as one of economic and military retrenchment. Bevin, by contrast, regarded the crisis in the eastern Mediterranean not only as an economic and military emergency but also as an opportunity to win American commitment to a "northern tier" that would provide a shield enabling the British to carry on with the defense and development of the "British" Middle East. By late 1946 Bevin and his advisors had begun to devise a strategy whereby referring Palestine to the United Nations might win international support for both the British and the Arabs.

The Greek and Palestine crises interlocked. The "Bevin Papers" now accessible at the Public Record Office in London make clear an important point of chronological detail that previously remained elusive. Two days after Christmas of 1946 Attlee and Bevin not only agreed on the question of withdrawal from Greece but also on the issue of submitting the Palestine problem to the United Nations.

Bevin had become disillusioned not only with the Greeks and Jews but also with the Egyptians. His grand design for a defense arrangement about the Canal Zone now lay in shambles because of nationalist sentiment in Egypt. The more precarious the British position in the eastern Mediterranean appeared to be, the more attractive was the potential of Libya as the future linchpin of the British Empire. The following note recording a consensus between the prime minister and the foreign secretary after the latter's return from New York is revealing: "The Prime Minister agreed [with Bevin] that if we had Cyrenaica, there would be no need to stay in either Egypt or Palestine."[34]

The Chiefs of Staff continued to advise that British troops could impose a solution by force upon one community in Palestine but not both. In their view the extreme solution of partition would, in bluntest terms, destroy Britain's position in the Middle East. The Chiefs of Staff presented their case in a Cabinet meeting of January 15, 1947:

> It was essential to our defence that we should be able to fight from the Middle East in war. . . . In future we should not be able to use India as a base for . . . deployment of force: it was the more essential, therefore, that we should retain other bases in the Middle East for this purpose.
>
> Palestine was of special importance in this general scheme of defence. In war, Egypt would be our key position in the Middle East; and it was necessary that we should hold Palestine as a screen for the defence of Egypt.[35]

Far from wishing to relinquish Palestine for mere reasons of political discontent, the Chiefs of Staff wished to retain a naval base at Haifa, at least two army garrisons, and a major air base. Dividing Palestine would create indefensible borders. To the traditional British military mind, treaty rights with a binational state would provide, under the circumstances, the best answer to the strategic problems of the British Empire in the eastern Mediterranean.

Creech Jones presented the Colonial Office's case for partition. The chancellor of the exchequer, Hugh Dalton, observed that the Palestine issue was now being discussed mainly in relation to the United Nations. Dalton is of interest because before the Labour landslide victory in 1945 he had been the moving spirit behind the Labour party's endorsement of the Zionist cause. He wrote in his diary in mid-1947 about the Cabinet deliberations: "On Palestine a number of us have been shouting for partition—Creech Jones is very good on this and much more decisive than his predecessor. E.B. and the P.M. try to tangle up the merits of various solutions with hypothetical conclusions of who would vote for this or that at U.N.O. I have been trying to keep these disentangled and have been urging that partition is the least objectionable of all policies."[36] If Dalton had been colonial secretary in 1947, the solution of partition might have stood a better chance. Creech Jones could not stand up to Bevin. Nor could the colonial secretary conduct skillful enough negotiations with the Jews in order to put a more persuasive case before the British Cabinet. In the end he reconciled himself to Bevin's policy as "inevitable." Bevin for his part took care not to make it difficult for Creech Jones. The foreign secretary used the effective argument that partition was untenable because of overriding reasons of British security.

Bevin argued the case relentlessly in the discussions of the Cabinet. He emphasized the repercussions of partition on the Arab states. One of his deputies perhaps pressed the argument to its fullest global dimension:

> To how great an extent partition would result in an estrangement between Great Britain and the Arab peoples it is not possible to estimate. But the consequences of such an estrangement would be so grave that the risk of it should be a major consideration in the examination of partition as a possible policy. The loss of Arab good will would mean the elimination of British influence from the Middle East to the great advantage of Russia. And this in turn would greatly weaken the position of the British Commonwealth in the world.[37]

In the end the argument about "the British Commonwealth in the world" was one that Attlee as well as Bevin had to bear in mind.

The key to Attlee's (and Bevin's) thought lies in a statement he made to the Cabinet in late November, 1946. Though partition might have a powerful attraction as an immediate and decisive solution, Attlee said, "His Majesty's Government should not commit themselves to support of this solution before all the alternatives had been fully discussed in the . . . proceedings of the Palestine Conference."[38] The Jews and Arabs would be given the chance to agree or disagree with all reasonable proposals, including the extremes of partition and a unitary state. If no solution were found, then they and not the British would bear the main brunt of failure. Attlee and Bevin independently arrived at the same conclusion. They did not want to be held responsible in Arab eyes for a policy of partition. If there could be no agreement, then the British government would continue to play the same hand at the United Nations, where a showdown could not be avoided (if only because of the indeterminate status of the mandate in international law). The British would appear to assume an impartial position, but in fact they would allow the pro-Arab majority of the General Assembly to decide the issue for them. That calculation explains Dalton's comment in mid-January, 1947, about Attlee's and Bevin's preoccupation with UN votes.

In the last stages of the London conference, which still dragged on formally and informally until mid-February, Bevin continued to guide the discussions on the basis of the plan for provincial autonomy. With an ostensibly even hand he exhausted possibilities of concessions that might be interpreted as a step toward either partition or a binational state. The more the details of partition were examined, the more the problem seemed to be insuperable. With impending stalemate Bevin and Creech Jones then put forward last proposals in the form of a binational Arab-Jewish state. In what became known as the "Bevin plan" there would be a five-year trusteeship regime supervised by the United Nations that would prepare Palestine for independence as a binational state. Instead of provincial autonomy there would be "cantons" determined by the size of Jewish or Arab majorities. Bevin had in mind alliances of Jewish and Arab groups based on a community of economic interest. As Sir Harold Beeley has written, "Bevin's plan was in essence a return to the White Paper of 1939," though close to 100,000 Jewish immigrants would be admitted within a period of two years. Jewish and Arab local and self-governing institutions would be "rooted in the lives of the people." The Bevin plan represented the last effort to solve the problem of Palestine in the tradition of British trusteeship, in which ethnic differences could be resolved within the framework of a single state.[39]

At the end of the London conference, the Arabs refused to consider Jewish self-government in any form or further Jewish immigration. Thus the British confronted one impasse. The Jews regarded the boundaries of the "cantons" that the British were prepared to allocate to them as totally unacceptable and would not agree to any scheme not based on the premise of an eventual Jewish state. Thus the British presided over final deadlock.

Bevin and Creech Jones together in mid-February, 1947, submitted to the Cabinet a report anticipating difficulties at the United Nations. They emphasized that once the British made the decision to refer the Palestine controversy to the United Nations, they would have to act with all possible speed to bring about a final solution, because otherwise the administration in Palestine itself would face

renewed outbreaks of terrorism and possible civil war. At this stage
the British considered, but rejected with a ring of self-confidence,
the possibility of evacuation. They did not wish to leave the Arabs,
the Jews, the Americans, and the United Nations stewing in their
own juice. Such an abnegation of responsibility, according to Bevin
and Creech Jones, would be ignoble and would amount to a repudiation of the "sacred trust" of the mandate: "We do not recommend the
adoption of this humiliating course."[40] Creech Jones reemphasized
that point in the subsequent Parliamentary debate: "We are not
going to the United Nations to surrender the mandate."[41]

## Evacuation and the End of the Mandate

The rapid deterioration of British moral suasion and military power
in Palestine took place against the background of political drama in
the United Nations. It was accompanied by the rising danger of anti-
Semitism in England and by increasingly virulent anti-British sentiment in New York. In Palestine Jewish "terrorism" and British "op-
pression" reached symbolic heights. In July the Irgun brutally hanged
two British sergeants and placed booby traps on their bodies. They
became martyrs. Bevin told the American secretary of state, General
Marshall, that the executions "would never be forgotten" and that as
a result "anti-Jewish feeling in England now was greater than it had
been in a hundred years."[42] The Jews also had symbolic figures, and
they appealed to a much greater public conscience. In the same
month British authorities turned away some 4,500 Jewish refugees
aboard the *Exodus 1947*. In one of his "black rages" Bevin decided
"to teach the Jews a lesson." The passengers aboard the *Exodus*
would be returned to their port of embarkation in France. As it trans-
pired, the Jews refused to disembark and the British, blundering from
one position to another, wound up sending these survivors of the
Nazi murder camps back to Germany.[43]

When the members of the United Nations Special Committee
on Palestine (UNSCOP) visited Palestine in the summer of 1947,
they found the British community in a state of siege. Wives and children had been evacuated. The number of British police and military
forces together with contingents of the Arab Legion now rivaled the
symbolic figure of the 100,000 Jewish refugees who were still in-
terned in European displaced person camps. The United Nations
committee observed "Bevingrads," the British redoubts in the center
of Jerusalem and other places where British personnel were biv-
ouacked behind barbed wire. One-tenth of the armed forces of the
entire British Empire now occupied a territory the size of Wales.

There was one soldier for every eighteen inhabitants in the country, or, as one observer calculated, one for every city block. The drain on the economy for military upkeep alone amounted to close to £40 million per annum. "There is the manpower of at least 100,000 men in Palestine," Churchill stated in Parliament, "who might well be at home strengthening our depleted industry. What are they doing there? What good are we getting out of it?"[44] When Britain moved into severe economic crisis in 1947, a broad consensus of public, parliamentary, and Cabinet opinion developed that recognized military withdrawal as an economic as well as a political and ethical imperative.

The general crystallization of British sentiment in favor of withdrawal did not necessarily contradict the Foreign Office's hope of preserving Britain's political and strategic position by relying on the probable action of the United Nations. It was a rational and indeed ingenious calculation, as the Zionists at the time recognized. It was based on the assumption that even biased or obtuse observers would not endorse partition, because the creation of a Jewish state would precipitate civil war. The Foreign Office also assumed that the Soviet Union and the United States on this issue as on others would gravitate into opposite camps and that such influences as Catholicism would militate against the Jews. The British, in short, hoped that the United Nations would support an independent binational state in which Jewish rights would be guaranteed and the promise of a national home more or less fulfilled. As it turned out, the British merely reconfirmed that United Nations special committees as well as the United Nations General Assembly did not operate on British rational assumptions.

The struggle for the Jewish state, as the British discovered, was fueled not only by a sense of historical necessity deriving from the Holocaust, and by genuine humanitarian sentiment, but also by worldwide animosity against British imperialism. Anticolonialism, as it has been traditionally understood, was a conspicuous force in the summer and autumn of 1947. The opportunity to disrupt the British Empire in the Middle East certainly helps to explain Russian motivation. Though the American aim was the opposite, a tacit alliance emerged between the United States and the Soviet Union in favor of the Jews. The anticolonial movement found vociferous representation on UNSCOP, which, the British could later sadly reflect, was the first of many United Nations bodies dedicated to the exposure of the evils of colonialism. The UNSCOP majority voted in favor of partition. This development triggered the British decision in September, 1947, to evacuate.

Montgomery and a few others continued to believe that a Pax

Britannica could be maintained by British bayonets. On the whole, however, the British by this time were ready to quit. They were responding to a combination of international, local, and domestic pressures. From the United Nations, and from the United States, they were subjected to demands for the creation of a Jewish state. In Palestine itself they faced a skillful campaign of Zionist terrorism. In England a certain current of public protest guided by Richard Crossman, who was assistant editor of the *New Statesman* as well as a Member of Parliament, expressed revulsion against suppressing a .people who had suffered unspeakable atrocities under the Nazis.[45] All of this was occurring at a time when the British feared the impending collapse of their economy. Decisions on Palestine were being made during the convertibility crisis. Underlying economic anxiety thus provides a key to the mood of September, 1947. By then the British had concluded that the only way to resolve the international, local, and metropolitan tensions was to evacuate Palestine. The same interaction of similar forces in other circumstances in Asia and Africa triggered transfers of power. In the case of Palestine the Labour government decided that the crisis could be resolved only by evacuation pure and simple.

What inspired the actual decision to evacuate? There can be no doubt that the UNSCOP report precipitated it, but the international annoyance only acted as a catalyst for more fundamental discontent. The minutes of the Cabinet meeting of September 20, 1947, only starkly convey the sense of relief at arriving at a firm decision that marked the end of years of frustration. "This," Dalton wrote in his diary, "if we stick to it, is a historic decision."[46]

The foreign secretary again stated the case against endorsing partition. He was not willing, Bevin reemphasized in a remark that became his public theme in the coming months, "to enforce a settlement which was unacceptable" to either side.[47] The colonial secretary, who by now was thoroughly embittered at Jewish terrorism, had resigned himself to "leaving Palestine in a state of chaos." Creech Jones would instruct the staff of the Colonial Office to begin making plans for the withdrawal of some 5,200 British subjects in the civil administration.[48] The minister of defense, A. V. Alexander, was not hopeful about maintaining law and order over the whole of Palestine for an indefinite period of time. The army could, however, protect the oil installations and the airfields without additional military reinforcements.[49] The minister of health, Aneurin Bevan, hoped that British withdrawal would finally demonstrate to other powers, notably the United States, that the British "did not wish to retain forces in Palestine for imperialist reasons." The Labour government would at last live up to its pledges. The minister of fuel and power, Emmanuel Shinwell, stressed the importance of an "orderly" evacuation in order to avoid the impression of British "weakness." There was apprehension that leaving Palestine in "chaos" might not be compatible with British "dignity." The chancellor of the exchequer emphasized that the continuing presence of British troops "merely led to a heavy drain on our financial resources and to the creation of a dangerous spirit of anti-Semitism." Dalton, moreover, introduced the theme of a timetable. "He . . . felt that a date for the withdrawal of British administration and British forces should be announced as soon as possible."[50] This was the key to the problem as it had also crystallized in the mind of the prime minister.

Attlee was determined to liquidate Palestine as an economic and military liability. In the aftermath of the transfer of power in India, he began more and more to apply the same formula to Palestine. He wrote, for example, three days before the decision on evacuation by the Cabinet, "We should . . . state that we will withdraw our administrative officers and troops from Palestine by a definite date which should not be longer than six months, even if no other mandatory has been appointed and no agreement has been come to between the Arabs and the Jews."[51] Only by imposing a definite time limit would there be any hope of forcing the Arabs and the Jews to make arrangements for their own political future, as had been proved, Attlee believed, in the analogous case of India. The minutes of the meeting of September 20 record Attlee's train of thought: *"The Prime Minister* said that in his view there was a close parallel between the position in Palestine and the recent situation in India. He did not think it reasonable to ask the British administration in Palestine to continue in present conditions, and he hoped that salutary results would be produced by a clear announcement that His Majesty's Government intended to relinquish the Mandate and, failing a peaceful settlement, to withdraw the British administration and British forces."[52] The Indian solution thus played a prominent part in the evolution of the thought of the prime minister. It was duly applied to Palestine, with sanguinary results, only on a smaller scale.

After September, 1947, the influence of the British diminished. They stayed on, of course, for some eight months, until the expiration of the mandate on May 14–15, 1948. It would be possible to examine in detail the circumstances of the end of the mandate by drawing attention to such memorable episodes as the singing of "Auld Lang Syne" as well as "God Save the King" when the Union Jack was hauled down for the last time in Jerusalem. But such a recounting of events leading to the end of formal British rule might detract from the larger continuity of postwar British imperialism. The termination of the mandate was only part of the story. The paramount aim was to remain on good terms with the Arabs as well as the Americans. The British could not do so as long as Palestine continued to poison the atmosphere. Arab nationalism, frustrated in Palestine, could not be appeased. It was the American failure, in British eyes, to curb militant Zionism that was at the heart of the trouble. The actual struggle for military and political control from the autumn of 1947 on is dealt with in other chapters of this symposium. These concluding remarks focus on a few of the salient British perceptions and misperceptions about the motives of the other powers, the nature of Zionism, and the responsibility of the United States for the outcome.

Before the historic vote by the United Nations in favor of partition on November 29, 1947, Ernest Bevin wrote one of his rare personal letters, in which he discussed Soviet motives. Among other things it reveals that he shared the belief, not uncommon in British official circles, that the Jewish state would eventually become Communist:

> I was not surprised when the Russians supported partition. . . . There are two things operating in the Russian mind. First of all, Palestine. I am sure they are convinced that by immigration they cạn pour in sufficient indoctrinated Jews to turn it into a Communist state in a very short time. The New York Jews have been doing their work for them.
>
> Secondly, I shall not be surprised if Russia, to consolidate her position in Eastern Europe, does not break up all her satellite States into smaller provinces, reaching down to the Adriatic. Thus partition would suit them as a principle. . . . You must study very carefully Stalin's work on nationalities to realise how his mind works, and then you will learn that he would have no compunction at all in exploiting these nationalities to achieve his object by means of a whole series which Russia could control.[53]

On another occasion Bevin used the phrase "international Jewry," with its connotation of conspiracy, as an explanation of what had gone wrong.[54] If he did not implicitly subscribe to the equivalent of a conspiracy theory, at least he believed that the Jews might be fitting into Stalin's plan for eventually absorbing Jewish Palestine into the system of Soviet satellites. Bevin's ideas on this subject were not idiosyncratic. British apprehensions about the Jews and Communism can be traced to the time of the Russian revolution in 1917. The world of the early twentieth century abounded in conspiracy theories about Freemasons, Papists, international financiers, and not least Jews. Revolutionary Jews were believed to have been decisive in the overthrow of the czar. There later appeared to be a similarity between the collective farms in the Soviet Union and the *kibbutzim* in Palestine. Stereotyped ideas, absurd as they may seem in retrospect, help to explain British attitudes toward the Zionists in 1947–48. During the 1948 war Czechoslovakia supplied arms and ammunition to the Jews. British intelligence reports indicated that refugees from Eastern Europe included indoctrinated Communists.[55] Thus Bevin's attitude and his suspicions, though misguided in retrospect, are at least comprehensible.

Bevin twice attempted to influence the territorial outcome of the struggle. In early 1948 he encouraged King Abdullah of Jordan to take over most of "Arab Palestine." In the last stage of the 1948 war, in an episode discussed later, he attempted to secure part of the Negev as a connecting strip between Egypt and the other Arab states. At no time did he consider the possibility of an independent Arab Palestinian state, which the Foreign Office feared would be too small to be viable and moreover would probably fall under the control of extremists led by the anti-British leader of the Palestinian Arabs, the Mufti, Hajj Amin al-Husseini. The head of the Eastern Department of the Foreign Office, Bernard Burrows, wrote of "the disadvantages of a separate Arab state under the Mufti" during the 1948 war: "It would be a hotbed of ineffectual Arab fanaticism and after causing maximum disturbance to our relations with the Arabs would very likely fall in the end under Jewish influence and be finally absorbed in the Jewish state, thereby increasing the area of possible Russian influence and excluding the possibility of our obtaining strategic requirements in any part of Palestine."[56] Bevin pinned his hopes on the takeover of most of "Arab Palestine" by the Arab Legion of Transjordan led by Sir John Bagot Glubb. Glubb acted as interpreter between Bevin and the foreign minister of Transjordan, Tawfiq Pasha Abul-Huda, in a critical meeting in March, 1948. "I can to this day almost see Mr. Bevin sitting at his table in that splendid room" at the Foreign Office, Glubb recalled later. Commenting on Transjordan's intention to occupy the West Bank, Bevin said, "It seems the obvious thing to do," then repeated, "It seems the obvious thing to do . . . but do not go and invade the areas allotted to the Jews" under the United Nations partition plan.[57] The British records do not sustain the view that Bevin intended to reduce the Jewish part of Palestine into a "rump state" that would be forced to throw itself on British mercy, though it is clear that he wished to salvage, in the retrospective words of one of his lieutenants, "the dismal wreck of Arab Palestine."[58]

The long-range goal was the preservation of as much as possible  of "Arab Palestine," mainly by its absorption into Transjordan. The short-range aim was to hold the ring for the Arabs from September, 1947, until mid-May, 1948, so that "Arab Palestine" would not be overrun by the Zionists before the expiration of the mandate. The fall of Haifa on April 22, 1948, was a critical blow, militarily and psychologically, to both the British and the Arabs. Bevin complained angrily that he had been "let down by the Army," which led to a row between him and Montgomery.[59] The political purpose was at variance with the military risk of British casualties. Bevin was not merely concerned with the loss of military position. He was also alarmed at the Arab mass exodus that had been precipitated earlier in the month, on April 9, by the Irgun's massacre of the Arabs of a village called Deir Yasin. The high commissioner, General Sir Alan Cunningham, had written three days afterward of "that brutal Jewish attack on Deir Yassin where 250 Arab civilians were butchered, half being women and children." He went on to explain to the colonial secretary the reasons why the British had not intervened, in Deir Yasin and in other places, against the Zionist offensives: "This village is still in the hands of the Jews as I write. I wanted the soldiers to attack it, if necessary with all the power they can produce and turn out the Jews. But I am told that they [the British army] are not in a position to do so, or indeed do anything which may provoke a general conflict with either side as their troops are already fully committed. This is only one example out of many where the Civil Government has to stand idle while its authority is flouted in all directions."[60] From the point of view of the high commissioner, the tragedy of the massacre was matched by the calamity of British impotence during the last weeks of the mandate. To some British officials, though not to all by any means, the atrocity at Deir Yasin came as a revelation about the nature of the new Jewish state. Sir John Troutbeck, the head of the British Middle East Office in Cairo, wrote that "Deir Yassein is a warning of what a Jew will do to gain his purpose."[61]

On the eve of the Arab-Israeli war the British were apprehensive about its outcome, but virtually no one anticipated the extent of the Arab collapse and the Israeli victory. The British associated themselves with the Arab cause as one that was ultimately compatible with their own sense of mission in the Middle East, and during the course of the war they became convinced that a grave injustice was being perpetrated because of American support of the Israelis. The resentment toward the United States still smoulders in the files at the Public Record Office. It existed as the main sentiment underlying official policy, and it was perhaps most indignantly expressed by Troutbeck, who held that the Americans were responsible for the creation of a gangster state headed by "an utterly unscrupulous set of leaders."[62] Even if one disregards such intemperate and indeed unbalanced comments, the anti-Israeli and anti-American tone of the telegrams, dispatches, and minutes cannot be ignored. This sense of moral outrage reached a climax in late 1948 with the collapse of the "Bernadotte plan." A brief concluding comment on this episode serves to place some of the more controversial issues concerning the birth of the state of Israel into British perspective.

The Bernadotte plan essentially would have given the Negev to the Arabs in return for a Jewish Galilee. The British believed this to be a geographically sound solution that would at least help to placate the Arab world. They argued that a Jewish "wedge" driven between Egypt and the Arab countries would give the Soviet Union the opportunity to exploit Arab discontent. They held that only by American pressure could militant Zionism be curbed and Arab irredentism be mitigated. The long and the short of the interlude is that there was an abrupt change of American policy from supporting the Bernadotte plan to championing the Israeli claim to the Negev. President Truman wrote to President Weizmann to this effect in a letter written on the anniversary of the United Nations vote, on November 29, 1948. The British believed, in the words of Hector McNeil (who was then acting as Bevin's lieutenant on Palestine affairs), that they had been "double-crossed." This was not the first time he had used that phrase to describe the reversal of State Department policy by the president. Furthermore, he used the expression passionately and angrily. The Jews would now hold on to the Negev *and* Galilee. Nevertheless, it was McNeil who wrote to Bevin in early 1949 that the time had come to face realities. The British would have to recognize that the Israelis held frontiers that they had the military capacity to defend, and that the United States would refuse to rein in militant Zionism.

"This is not a happy situation for us," McNeil wrote to Bevin. "Indeed it is so unhappy, that whenever some new offence or indignity is given to us, or some further disadvantage is imposed upon the Arabs, we are tempted to act unilaterally." By pretending still to be the masters of the Middle East, the British tended to neglect the overriding importance of retaining American goodwill. American collaboration in the Middle East and the rest of the world remained the paramount consideration. "It is essential even when the Jews are most wicked and the Americans most exasperating not to lose sight of this point." It was irritating to reflect that, each time the British had attempted to work in concert with the Americans, the president had intervened—to repeat McNeil's phrase, had "double-crossed" them: "Each time the Americans have shifted. One way of explaining this is to point to the undoubted weakness of their President. Another way of explaining it is that each time the Jews have been permitted too much time so that they have been enabled to put the screw on Truman."[63] Whatever the explanation, it always led McNeil to the same conclusion, which he now pressed on Bevin: "As long as America is a major power, and as long as she is free of major war, anyone taking on the Jews will indirectly be taking on America." Since the Americans would not cooperate, the only alternative would be for the British themselves to fight in the Negev. McNeil ruled out this possibility for a simple and compelling reason: "Our public would not stand for it."[64] British policy had thus led to a dead end. There was nothing left but to accommodate the Jews on their own terms.

Bevin's tempestuous response to the events of late 1948–early 1949 sums up his exasperated thoughts as well as what might be called the final "British perspective" on the Palestine problem. He wrote that the American attitude appeared to be not only "let there be an Israel and to hell with the consequences" but also "peace at any price, and Jewish expansion whatever the consequences."[65]

## Notes

1. Bevin's attitude toward the Jews and Palestine is discussed at length in Alan Bullock, *The Life and Times of Ernest Bevin: Foreign Secretary, 1945–1951* (London: Heineman, 1983), and in my own book, *The British Empire in the Middle East 1945–1951: Arab Nationalism, the United States and Postwar Imperialism* (Oxford: Clarendon Press, 1984). The present essay draws from the latter work, though not without a fresh examination of the archival records and reflection on the specific issues of concern here.

2. W. K. Hancock, *Survey of British Commonwealth Affairs 1918–1939*, 2 vols. (London: Oxford University Press, 1937, 1940), I, p. 473.

3. Bevin's concluding speech at the Colombo conference, January 14, 1950, as recorded in the minutes of the Commonwealth Meeting on Foreign Affairs at Colombo, January 15, 1950, F[oreign] O[ffice] 371/84818. All FO,

C[olonial] O[ffice], CAB[inet] Office, W[ar] O[ffice], and PREM[ier] papers under reference are to records at the Public Record Office, London.

4. Quoted in the New York tabloid *P.M.*, October 26, 1947.

5. For an extensive discussion of Attlee and Palestine, see Kenneth Harris, *Attlee* (London: Weidenfeld and Nicolson, 1982), chap. 22.

6. Attlee's notes, 1950, ATLE 1/17, Attlee Papers (Churchill College, Cambridge).

7. See Creech Jones to Elizabeth Monroe, October 23, 1961, Creech Jones Papers (Rhodes House, Oxford).

8. *Parliamentary Debates* (Commons), August 1, 1946, col. 1253. For Churchill and Palestine, see especially Michael J. Cohen, *Churchill and the Jews* (London: Frank Cass, 1984).

9. Minute by Bevin, *c.* February 1, 1946, FO 371/52509/E1413/G. For an interpretation, with which Bevin himself might have agreed, of the motives and meaning of the Balfour Declaration, see Mayir Vereté, "The Balfour Declaration and Its Makers," *Middle Eastern Studies*, 6/1 (January, 1970), 48–76.

10. Sir Harold Beeley, "Ernest Bevin and Palestine" (unpublished Antonius Lecture, St. Antony's College, Oxford, June 14, 1983), p. 9. This was in fact a common British view. See Elizabeth Monroe, *Britain's Moment in the Middle East* (London: Chatto and Windus, 1963), p. 43: "Measured by British interest alone, it was one of the greatest mistakes in our imperial history"; and, in a slightly different vein, "Arnold Toynbee on the Arab-Israeli Conflict," *Journal of Palestine Studies*, 2/3 (Spring, 1973), 3: "I will say straight out: Balfour was a wicked man." For the opposite tradition, that of defending the commitment to the Jews, see N. A. Rose, *The Gentile Zionists: A Study in Anglo-Zionist Diplomacy* (London: Frank Cass, 1973).

11. Minute by Baxter, January 14, 1946, FO 371/52504/E389/G.

12. The words "other countries" were those that Bevin himself scrawled onto a Foreign Office memorandum on the subject (see note by Robert Howe, October 6, 1945, FO 371/45380/E7479/15/G).

13. *Parliamentary Debates* (Commons), November 13, 1945, col. 1934.

14. Ibid., January 29, 1949, col. 948.

15. Foreign Office minutes, September 6, 1945, FO 371/45379/E6954/G.

16. Ibid., September 10, 1945.

17. For detailed assessment of the committee's work based on full use of archival sources, see Amikam Nachmani, "British Policy in Palestine after World War II: The Anglo-American Committee of Inquiry" (Oxford, D.Phil. thesis, 1980); see also William Travis Hanes III, "Year of Crisis: British Policy in the Palestine Mandate January 1946–February 1947" (University of Texas, M.A. thesis, 1983), which is based in part on the papers of the American chairman, Joseph C. Hutcheson, at the Humanities Research Center at the University of Texas.

18. Minute by Smart, May 2, 1946, FO 141/1090 (Cairo Embassy files).

19. Minute by Butler, April 5, 1946, FO 371/51630.

20. Buxton to Felix Frankfurter, June 6, 1946, Frankfurter Papers, Library of Congress. This quotation is taken from a file in the Frankfurter Pa-

pers that I was not able to study while writing *The British Empire in the Middle East*, and I am glad to be able to provide an excerpt from it.

21. Montgomery to Dempsey, "Personal and Top Secret," July 24, 1946, WO 216/194.

22. See J. C. Hurewitz, *The Struggle for Palestine* (New York: W. W. Norton, 1950), chaps. 18 and 19.

23. See PREM 8/627/5, Attlee to Truman, October 4, 1946, *Foreign Relations of the United States 1946* (Washington: U.S. Government Printing Office, 1969), VII, pp. 704–5.

24. Truman to Attlee, October 10, 1946, enclosed in memorandum by Acheson to Truman, President's Secretary's Files Box 170, Truman Papers (Independence, Missouri); *Foreign Relations 1946*, VII, pp. 706–8.

25. "Note of Interview with Mr. Ben Gurion at the Colonial Office," January 2, 1947, copy in FO 371/61762.

26. Memorandum of conversation, November 14, 1946, FO 371/52565.

27. Although Bevin was consistent in his opposition to partition, the records in London, Washington, and Jerusalem make it clear that he did not have a closed mind. In an especially revealing conversation with Nahum Goldmann of the Jewish Agency in August, 1946, he talked about partition as a "possibility" but added that he was troubled about the prospect of a Jewish "racial state" ("I got annoyed at that," Goldmann noted, and he pointed out to Bevin that 300,000 Arabs would be included "with equal rights"). Bevin emphasized several times that he "never ruled out partition." Goldmann for his part believed that he detected a more fair-minded attitude than the one usually attributed to Bevin. But he told him, "you have treated us abominably." Bevin responded by saying that he had always wanted to be fair to the Jews, and that "he knew the Jewish tragedy and their sufferings" (Memorandum by Goldmann, August 14, 1946, Central Zionist Archives [Jerusalem] Z6/17/21).

28. Cabinet Conclusions 91 (46), October 25, 1946, CAB 128/6; see minutes in FO 371/52563.

29. C.P. (46) 267, July 10, 1946, CAB 129/11; see also minutes in FO 371/52563.

30. For extensive discussion of British army policies, see Michael J. Cohen, *Palestine and the Great Powers 1945–1948* (Princeton: Princeton University Press, 1982), chap. 4.

31. Chiefs of Staff (46) 169, November 20, 1946, copy in FO 371/52565.

32. Montgomery's contentious discussion of his part in the Palestine controversy is in *The Memoirs of Field-Marshal the Viscount Montgomery of Alamein* (Cleveland: World Publishing Co., 1958), chap. 29.

33. Attlee to Bevin, "Private & Personal," December 1, 1946, FO 800/475. These are the "Bevin Papers," that is, Private Office Papers.

34. Note by J. N. Henderson, December 28, 1946, FO 800/475.

35. Cabinet Minutes (47) 6, Minute 3, Confidential Annex, January 15, 1947, CAB 128/11.

36. Dalton Diary, January 17, 1947, Dalton Papers (London School of Economics).

37. Memorandum by Robert Howe, January 21, 1947, FO 371/61858.

38. Cabinet Conclusions 101 (46), November 28, 1946; see also CO 535/1787.

39. Beeley, "Ernest Bevin and Palestine," treats the "Bevin plan" with sympathetic insight.

40. Memorandum by Bevin and Creech Jones, February 13, 1947, C.P. (47) 59; for minutes, see CO 537/2327–2328.

41. *Parliamentary Debates* (Commons), February 25, 1947, col. 2007.

42. See *Foreign Relations 1947*, V, pp. 1285–87.

43. For the *Exodus* episode from the British vantage point, see especially Nicholas Bethell, *The Palestine Triangle: The Struggle between the British, the Jews and the Arabs, 1935–48* (London: André Deutsch, 1979), chap. 10.

44. *Parliamentary Debates* (Commons), January 31, 1947, col. 1347.

45. See especially Khalid Kishtainy, *The New Statesman and the Middle East* (Beirut: Palestine Research Center, 1972), chaps. 6 and 7.

46. Dalton Diary, September 20, 1947.

47. Cabinet Minutes (47) 76, September 20, 1947, CAB 128/10; PREM 8/859/1; see also C.P. (47) 259, September 18, 1947, CAB 129/21.

48. The dilemmas facing the Colonial Office and other ministries are outlined in a memorandum by the Official Committee on Palestine, D.O. (47) 83, November 5, 1947, Creech Jones Papers; CAB 134/4.

49. See memorandum by Alexander, "Military and Strategic Implications," September 18, 1947, C.P. (47) 262, CAB 129/21.

50. C.M. (47) 76, September 20, 1947, CAB 128/10.

51. Minute by Attlee, September 17, 1947, FO 371/61878.

52. C.M. (47) 76, September 20, 1947, CAB 128/10.

53. Bevin wrote that letter to his minister of state, Hector McNeil, and designated it "Confidential and Personal." "Please burn it after you have read it," Bevin instructed him (October 15, 1947, FO 800/509). Fortunately the carbon copy was not destroyed. As will be seen, McNeil played an important part in discussing unpleasant but unavoidable facts about Palestine with Bevin.

54. See minutes of Foreign Office Middle East conference, July 21, 1949, FO 371/75072.

55. This point is established by Bullock, *Bevin: Foreign Secretary*, chap. 16, sec. 6.

56. Minute by Burrows, August 17, 1948, FO 371/68822/E11049/G.

57. John Bagot Glubb, *A Soldier with the Arabs* (London: Hodder and Stoughton, 1957), pp. 63–66.

58. Michael Wright to Ronald Campbell, March 30, 1949, FO 371/75064.

59. See *Memoirs of Field-Marshal Montgomery*, pp. 424–26.

60. Cunningham to Creech Jones, "Private and Personal," April 12, 1948, Cunningham Papers (Middle East Centre, St. Antony's College, Oxford).

61. Troutbeck to Wright, "Personal and Secret," May 18, 1948, FO 371/68386/E8738.

62. Troutbeck to Bevin, "Secret," June 2, 1948, FO 371/68559/E7376.

63. Minute by McNeil, January 14, 1949, FO 371/75337/E1881. The permanent under-secretary, Sir Orme Sargent, added to this assessment that Truman was "a weak, obstinate and suspicious man" (minute by Sargent, January 17, 1949, FO 371/75336/E1273).

64. Minute by McNeil, January 14, 1949, FO 371/75337/E1881.

65. Bevin to Franks (draft), February 3, 1949, FO 371/75337.

# The President versus the Diplomats

*Peter Grose*

On May 15, 1948, the day after he granted *de facto* recognition to the newly proclaimed Jewish state of Israel, President Harry S Truman sent off a brief letter. "I think the report of the British American Commission of Palestine [*sic*] was the correct solution," he wrote, "and, I think, eventually we are going to get it worked out just that way."[1]

That laconic and, on examination, absurd presidential sentiment encapsulates a blunt reality about American policy toward Palestine on the collapse of the British mandate: with all the other interested forces at work on all sides of the dilemma, the chief executive himself had virtually no comprehension of the implications of his actions. For the Anglo-American Committee of Inquiry (to call it by its correct name) had recommended in 1946 the precise opposite of the course Truman took in 1948.

Of all the major decisions in America's early postwar years, none was taken with as little intellectual underpinning and as far-reaching consequences as the recognition of a Jewish state in partitioned Palestine. To be sure, the decision responded to a deep-seated visceral reaction within American intellectual history and, despite the protests of the practitioners of statecraft, it was immensely popular. Almost four decades later, a new generation of Americans has difficulty imagining that the United States could have done otherwise.

Yet at the time virtually all foreign policy experts of the government were arrayed against the president's policy and were dumbfounded—some still remain so—that a responsible political leader could so flout their considered counsel.

The attempt to untangle the threads of American policies toward Palestine immediately encounters a particular difficulty, beyond those that confront the chronicler of any recent historical episode. The body of hard documentary evidence for the decisions of these years is in the files of the State Department and other appropriate executive agencies, which convey primarily the views and perspectives of the diplomats. These archives have been thoroughly studied by careful scholars (see the bibliographic note at the end of this chapter). The diplomatic record is one of repeated warnings about the dangers to American national interests of any espousal of the Zionist program for a separate Jewish state, the disruption of friendly relations with emerging Arab nationalism that such an espousal would provoke, the potential for unending warfare in the region, and the competition between Soviet Russia and Western democracy that a Zionist victory would bring. [4]

But these warnings were not heeded in American policy, as it developed in fact. Clearly, the diplomats were not the ones making the decisions that counted. In search of the mainsprings of policy, where else can a diligent researcher turn? The answer lies in the workings of the presidency. What little was put on paper in the casual atmosphere of Truman's White House is fragmented and disparate, though the well-catalogued collections at the Harry S Truman Library certainly help. An effort at conjecture and supposition is necessary to reconstruct the real factors at work.

This chapter focuses on the presidential perspective, not the more reasoned arguments of the foreign affairs experts, whose views have been analyzed elsewhere. From such a perspective on the arena where policy was actually decided, it was not the facts that mattered; it was what the key individuals understood to be the facts. For the coming decades of international politics, 1948 was remembered, not as the year when the Palestine mandate ended, but as the year when an acute regional hostility, a superpower rivalry, and the state of Israel began.

Alongside the difficulty of assembling documentary evidence comes the inevitable circumstance that the memories of the key participants are naturally colored by all that came after. Truman himself, in his memoirs, provides a prime example of one who remembered things just the way he wanted to remember them. Finally, though the years 1945–48 are but one professional lifetime away, the unstated assumptions and fundamental outlook in the period were significantly different from those of today, leading to judgments and attitudes that seem almost inexplicable in retrospect:

- Two issues, the Holocaust in Europe and the political future of Palestine, have been blurred in historical memory as aspects of the same problem, the survival and destiny of the Jews. Yet in the early post–World War II years, these issues were considered separately and even in isolation from each other. Only militant Zionists sought to link them.

- Popular fervor came to be directed against wartime ally Soviet Russia as the cold war set in, but in 1945 and 1946 it was another ally, imperial Britain, that drew popular scorn. Longshoremen at the port of New York, who would later make arrival at the United Nations unpleasant for Soviet diplomats, took their first job action against the foreign secretary of Great Britain, Ernest Bevin, after one of his particularly tactless remarks about New York Jews.
- Among the corps of professional diplomats, the Zionism building in Palestine still smacked menacingly of Bolshevism. Those Jewish settlements called *kibbutzim* were openly socialistic, a proudly communal life style; the Balfour Declaration and the Bolshevik revolution had come upon the world in the same fortnight in November, 1917. Though obviously a linkage of the two ideologies could never stand up to analysis, Bolshevism and Zionism were cited in the same breath as threats to the traditional order.
- Idealistic American Protestant missionaries had long built up an educational presence in the Arab Near East, but the number of Arab Americans was small, and they were reticent about asserting a group interest. As Charles Crane, an American champion of Arab interests who did not shrink from anti-Semitism in the interwar decades, put it, Arab Americans were good and loyal citizens; "they did not try to run our politics or anything else."[2] Parallel to this sort of analysis, however, was the deeper stream of American intellectual life that, from the days of the New England Puritans, regarded the restoration of the Jews in Palestine as a holy event, the realization of an age-old prophecy, with the American republic playing a decisive role in righting the wrongs of Old World prejudice over centuries past.

Options for the political structure of Palestine upon the collapse of the British mandate divided into two broad categories: separate homelands for the Jews and (if they wanted it) the Arabs, rival claimants to the same land; or a unitary binational society in which political power would be shared by rival communities. The first option derived, in American thought, from the progressive ideals of Louis D. Brandeis, who—late in a highly successful career—came to a form of Zionism that was eventually repudiated by the mainstream European Zionists at work establishing a Jewish state. The second, binational, option was the choice of the academic and diplomatic Middle East experts. Deriving, with modifications, from the King-Crane report of 1919, this option acknowledged the dangers of Zionism as an ideology and preferred to maintain the Arabs of Palestine in a majority role that would support American interests throughout the Middle East.

At the dawn of 1945 a particular vision for Palestine was alive in the mind of the most important American, Franklin D. Roosevelt.

A White House functionary named David Niles, whom Truman inherited from Roosevelt, once confessed to "serious doubts in my mind that Israel would have come into being if Roosevelt had lived."[3] The conventional portrait of the thirty-second president as an aloof patrician unmoved by the plight of the Jews omits a consistent theme in his mental bearing whenever he turned—more often than commonly supposed—to the political future of Palestine.

In relaxation, Roosevelt loved to turn loose his political imagination, spinning out instincts and hunches in mellow moments with trusted intimates, in effect testing the intellectual waters for policy ideas that later might—or might not—emerge to public view and action. Through the scattered records of these unguarded conversations emerges a special Rooseveltian vision for Palestine, for a Jewish restoration more ambitious than the British allies or even mainstream contemporary Zionism dared to advocate. As a factor in policy determination, Roosevelt's extravagant notions evaporated with his death in April, 1945. But they are highly revealing of premises that American idealists brought to consideration of Palestine for the coming postwar era.

As early as 1938 Roosevelt had complained to Secretary of State Cordell Hull that, in the Balfour Declaration, "the British made no secret of the fact they promised Palestine to the Jews. Why are they now reneging on their promise?"[4] This was the first element in the Roosevelt vision: Britain, and by extension the world, had promised Palestine to the Jews.

A plan began taking shape in his mind, aimed at nothing less than the transfer of the entire Arab population of Palestine to a nearby land. Two hundred thousand to three hundred thousand Arabs should be resettled, at a cost of some $300 million. Britain and France should together put up one-third of that, the United States another third, and wealthy Jews of the Western democracies the rest. Twice he raised this notion with British representatives, only to be firmly told that no amount of financial inducement would move the Palestinian Arabs.[5]

The president was unconvinced and told Zionist friends early in 1939, as they reported, that "as soon as he was somewhat relieved from the pressure of other affairs, he might try to tackle the job."[6]

Thus emerged a second theme in Roosevelt's Palestine vision: once the pressures of war were lifted from his shoulders, he would himself move in to resolve the dilemma that had resisted the efforts of statesmanship before.

In February, 1940, when Roosevelt first met Chaim Weizmann, he pressed his Zionist visitor on the economic absorptive capacity of Palestine. "What about the Arabs?" Roosevelt asked breezily. "Can't that be settled with a little baksheesh?" Weizmann patiently explained to the president that uprooting the entire Arab population would not be quite as simple as that.[7]

As the 1942 Christmas season set in, the Roosevelt imagination turned naturally to mellow thought of the Holy Land. His Hyde Park neighbor, Treasury Secretary Henry J. Morgenthau, Jr., remembered Roosevelt's rambling words vividly:

> What I think I will do is this. First, I would call Palestine a religious country. Then I would leave Jerusalem the way it is and have it run by the Orthodox Greek Catholic Church, the Protestants and the Jews—have a joint committee run it. . . . I actually would put a barbed wire around Palestine, and I would begin to move the Arabs out. . . . I would provide land for the Arabs in some other part of the Middle East. . . . Each time we move out an Arab we would bring in another Jewish family. . . . But I don't want to bring in more than they can economically support. . . . It would be an independent nation just like any other nation. . . . Naturally, if there are 90% Jews, the Jews would dominate the government. . . . There are lots of places to which you could move the Arabs. All you have to do is drill a well, because there is this large underground water supply, and we can move the Arabs to places where they can really live. . . .[8]

Such notions for Palestine matured in the back of Roosevelt's mind during the years of war with Germany and Japan, and during the electoral campaign for an unprecedented fourth presidential term, in which the president won 90 percent of the Jewish vote. The vague pro-Zionism of his public utterances was put down as merely electoral tactics, and even the private musings were generally spun out in the presence of Jewish friends. Was Roosevelt simply soothing these colleagues with talk he thought they wanted to hear? (In fact, many of the Jewish New Dealers, Judge Samuel I. Rosenman, for example, were not Zionists.)

The most revealing portrayal of the Roosevelt vision, however, came after—not before—the election. It was reported by a new associate totally aloof from any possible ethnic aspirations, Edward R. Stettinius, a genial business executive soon to replace Hull as secretary of state.

Tracing one of his impressionistic *tours d'horizon*, Roosevelt turned to the lands of the Middle East and spelled out his thinking in no uncertain terms. "Palestine should be for the Jews and no Arabs should be in it," he said flatly, as Stettinius noted in his diary entry of November 10, 1944. "He has definite ideas on the subject. . . . It should be exclusive Jewish territory."[9] In a confidential chat, after an election, there was no need for the president to dissemble or disguise his true sentiments—and these, as relayed to Stettinius, envisaged a Jewish Palestine in the original meaning of the Balfour Declaration as he understood it.

Among many Zionists at the time, it had become prudent to speak of coexistence with the Arab population of Palestine under a Jewish government; some Zionists even spoke of the possibility of a binational state in which Arabs and Jews would share political power. Roosevelt would have none of it. In his vision, the Arabs must be moved out of Palestine, whether they liked it or not; whether with "baksheesh" or resettlement funds, Palestine should be made "exclusive Jewish territory."

In the last months of his life, Roosevelt set out upon an audacious mission to test the ground for realizing this vision. Against advice from all the experts who knew the Arab world, Roosevelt decided to try selling his plan for a Jewish Palestine in a face-to-face meeting with Ibn Saud of Saudi Arabia.

"The President said he desired to take with him a map showing the Near Eastern area as a whole and the relationship of Palestine to the area," Stettinius noted on January 2, 1945. He intended "to point out to Ibn Saud what an infinitesimal part of the whole area was occupied by Palestine and that he could not see why a portion of Palestine could not be given to the Jews without harming in any way the interests of the Arabs."[10]

Of all the men Franklin D. Roosevelt met in his entire life, it was this iron-willed desert monarch who gave him the least satisfaction—Roosevelt admitted as much to Bernard Baruch.[11] Reporting to Congress on March 1, Roosevelt ad-libbed a phrase that sent shivers through the American Jewish community and puzzled even his own advisors. "On the problem of Arabia," he said, "I learned more about that whole problem, the Moslem problem, the Jewish problem, by talking with Ibn Saud for five minutes than I could have learned in the exchange of two or three dozen letters."

The only thing he learned, Harry Hopkins wrote, "which all people well acquainted with the Palestine cause knew, is that the Arabs don't want any more Jews in Palestine."[12] But until he heard it himself, Roosevelt could not believe it. Stettinius noted in his diary that Roosevelt "was now convinced that if nature took its course there would be bloodshed between the Arabs and Jews. Some formula, not yet discovered, would have to prevent this warfare."[13] The sixty-three-year-old president was failing in health, and many around him began to wonder if time would be left to discover what a new formula might be.

To several visitors in these last days, the president threw out hints. Postwar responsibility for Palestine might be beyond his and Churchill's power after all. Instead, it would be the new United Nations Organization that would create the Jewish state and underwrite its survival with an international police force. Clearly, normal diplomatic procedures of sovereign states would not suffice. Perhaps Palestine would become the first test of the community of nations; Roosevelt approved Zionist participation in the conference at San Francisco opening on April 25 to organize the United Nations.

But he had not given up on a personal role. "When I get through being President," the dying Roosevelt told Frances Perkins, "I think Eleanor and I will go to the Near East and see if we can manage to put over an operation like the Tennessee Valley system that will really make something of that country. I would love to do it. . . . I don't know any people who need someone to help them more than the people in the Near East."[14]

Nowhere in Roosevelt's record is there an indication that the president envisaged the unilateral proclamation of a sovereign Jewish state such as occurred in May, 1948. Indeed, the foreknowledge would surely have filled him with apprehension, as it would have most other Americans in the early 1940s, Jews and non-Jews alike.

Roosevelt's Middle Eastern policy implied coexistence between Jews and Arabs. This sounds like the binationalism that became the banner of the State Department and of all who opposed the notion of a Jewish state. But Roosevelt was thinking not of Palestine alone when he thought of Arab-Jewish cooperation. Like the most extreme Zionists, he determined that Palestine itself would be secure and exclusive for Jewish nationalism. Arab nationalism, the other side of the "baksheesh," would find its full expression in the newly independent Arab states of Syria, Lebanon, Jordan, and Iraq. Together these new nations of the Middle East—the Jewish state and the Arab states—would form a wide binational federation to promote their mutual economic development.

How could such harmonious cooperation be achieved among the restive societies of the Middle East? What could the United States do to promote it? What could Arab nationalists and Jewish nationalists do to strive toward their own aspirations without crushing the aspirations of others? These are questions that Roosevelt was pondering when his days came to an end and the problem became the responsibility of another.

Often overlooked in the eighty-two-day record of Roosevelt's fourth term is an offhand proposal that never came to anything. The president one day asked Vice-President Harry S Truman to consider a tour of the Arab Middle East, the sort of orientation visit that Roosevelt himself hoped to make when he retired. Planning was started for a vice-presidential mission in April, the month of Roosevelt's death. Truman disclosed this shortly after he assumed the presidency, and he "regretted immeasurably" that it never came about.[15]

Instead, President Truman's first official encounter with the problem of Palestine came in an innocuous memorandum from his own State Department, in effect warning him against any public statements on Palestine until he had been fully briefed. In their patronizing tone, appropriate from a board of senior prefects to a new boy in the lower forms, the diplomatic officers committed an indiscretion they would never live down in Truman's mind. "In those days nobody seemed to think I was aware of anything," Truman recalled some twenty-five years later. His memory of that memorandum was still vivid, "a communication from some of the 'striped-pants' boys warning me . . . in effect telling me to watch my step, that I didn't really understand what was going on over there and that I ought to leave it to the 'experts'. . . ."[16]

With all the burdens of world leadership thrust unexpectedly upon his shoulders—the climax of war in Europe and Asia, the awesome decision to use a terrifying new atomic weapon—Truman did in fact leave the politics of Palestine to his experts in the first year of his presidency.

On the initiative of a moderate Zionist leader, Nahum Goldmann, some interest was generated in the State Department and Pentagon for the partition of Palestine between a Jewish and an Arab state. The Anglo-American Committee of Inquiry rejected such a departure and offered instead the possibility of a binational state in which "Jew shall not dominate Arab and Arab shall not dominate Jew." Subsequent Anglo-American talks between Herbert Morrison and Henry F. Grady refined the formula further, but the diplomatic subtleties were not closely followed in the White House. "I don't even know what the latest plan is," Truman snapped in one encounter with pro-Zionist petitioners.[17]

Critics in Britain and America charged that Truman could follow only the partisan politics of the United States—as, for example, the Yom Kippur statement of 1946 in which the president offered soothing assurances of fidelity to American Jewry on the eve of their solemn holy day. Prime Minister Attlee and Foreign Minister Bevin were furious when word of this statement reached London at a delicate moment of diplomatic maneuver; in their complaints of political opportunism, they missed the careful ambiguity with which the statement was crafted (as, it must be said, did American Jews who cheered Truman on). Principal drafter of the statement was Dean Acheson in the State Department, and for all its comforting tone, it most specifically did not endorse the Zionist demand for a Jewish state in Palestine.[18]

Through the first postwar years it was another aspect of the Jewish fate that dominated Truman's concern. The occupation armies in Europe were confronting, along with all their other problems, a homeless mass of refugees, largely Jews from Eastern Europe who had no desire to return to the anti-Semitism of their former homes. The Middle Eastern experts of the State Department considered this problem remote from their calculations of statecraft, but to Truman it quickly became the heart of the matter.

Raising this situation to the forefront of the president's attentions was an episode that remains one of the great unresearched turning points in the formulation of America's Palestine policy, the Harrison fact-finding mission to Europe.[19]

Treasury Secretary Morgenthau had urged Truman during his first month in office to raise the problem of the displaced persons before the Cabinet. But the new president had little more fondness for Morgenthau than for his striped-pants diplomats, and he let the suggestion drop. A short time later he agreed to a proposal—he did not know that it was Morgenthau who had initiated it—to send an emissary on an investigation of the DP camps.

The State Department succeeded in vetoing Morgenthau's pro-Zionist candidate for this mission and nominated instead Earl G. Harrison, dean of the University of Pennsylvania Law School, commissioner of immigration and naturalization during World War II, and director of the wartime census of enemy aliens, a proven administrative professional. Harrison had demonstrated experience in politically sensitive situations, and he had no preconceptions about the problems of Jews in Europe or Palestine. From this modest beginning, the Harrison mission in the summer of 1945 developed into an enduring influence upon Truman's Palestine policy. More than anything else that happened early in his presidency, it defined the issue for three years to come.

Certain alert Zionists spotted the potential of the Harrison mission from the start. To Weizmann and his American associate, Meyer W. Weisgal, Harrison was an objective but idealistic law professor who, though not their first choice for the job, could become an instrument for combining the political aspirations of Zionism with the plight of the surviving Jews of Europe. Weisgal was frequently in touch with Morgenthau. Early in June, as the treasury secretary was quietly discussing the DP problem with State Department colleagues, Weisgal reported to Weizmann that Morgenthau had been "very kind and cooperative in a certain important matter he was asked to do." (With censorship and uncertain international mails, indirection was the norm for sensitive correspondence.)[20] Shortly thereafter, Harrison was summoned to Washington for briefings, and on June 21 he accepted the mission "to ascertain the needs of stateless and non-repatriables, particularly Jews, among the displaced persons in Germany."

Recognizing in Harrison a man completely unacquainted, for all his general experience, with the particular subtleties of this mission, Weisgal suggested to Morgenthau that the envoy be accompanied by someone "thoroughly steeped in the Jewish situation." He proposed the name of Joseph J. Schwartz, European director of the Joint Distribution Committee, foremost among the voluntary organizations in aiding the Jewish homeless. This was an inspired choice. Aside from Schwartz's clear expertise in refugee matters, his organization had been distinctly non-Zionist, sometimes even anti-Zionist, from the days of its founder, Felix Warburg. With a man from "the Joint," no one could suspect an improper Zionist influence on the American fact-finding mission. Yet Weisgal knew his man. Speaking for himself and Weizmann, Weisgal wrote confidentially that "although Dr. Schwartz is on the staff of the JDC, we have absolute faith in his integrity *and Zionist convictions*" (italics added).[21]

Harrison was not unaware of the interests converging on him. The head of the War Refugee Board, John Pehle, told him frankly that his investigation had been urged by "political Zionists." While Morgenthau himself was "primarily concerned with the problem of the needs of these displaced people," Pehle said, "the Zionist groups are primarily interested in obtaining information concerning the desire of these people to emigrate from Europe."[22]

Harrison arrived in Europe early in July. On his first night in

Munich, another influence bore down on him, an encounter as helpful to the Zionist cause as the companionship of Schwartz, but spontaneous in its origin. A young American rabbi named Abraham J. Klausner took it upon himself to call on Harrison, and the two men sat up all night long in earnest discussion. Klausner was a chaplain in the American army. Never much interested in Zionism before, he had become a militant in helping the surviving remnant of European Jewry organize itself and prepare to migrate to Palestine. Klausner took Harrison in hand and showed him the full horrors of the situation of the Jewish survivors in Europe.[23]

Harrison's report to Truman, submitted late in August, 1945, conveyed the DP plight in vivid terms. "We appear to be treating the Jews as the Nazis treated them except that we do not exterminate them," Harrison noted (Truman underlined the passage). "They are in concentration camps in large numbers under our military guard instead of S.S. troops. One is led to wonder whether the German people, seeing this, are not supposing that we are following or at least condoning Nazi policy." Then Harrison moved beyond administrative and logistical reforms to make a judgment about the ultimate fate of this problematic populace. He concluded that "Palestine is definitely and pre-eminently the first choice."[24]

Harrison's report created a sensation when Truman made it public in September, and the occupation authorities were hard pressed to respond to specific criticisms of administrative mistreatment. But it was Harrison's political conclusions that made the lasting impact: for the first time and against all the arguments of Britain and the State Department, Truman was shown that the difficulties of Europe's surviving Jews and the political future of Palestine were aspects of the same problem.

Harrison was sailing close to the wind in his conclusions. In a confidential report to White House aide David Niles a few months after the Harrison mission, a senior American relief worker, a committed Zionist, admitted that Harrison could not have substantiated his belief that Palestine was the sincere choice of the mass of Jewish survivors.[25] Zionism was not the only political movement at work in the DP camps, and among Polish Jews, in particular, the anti-Zionist Socialist Bund was strong. The Bundists called for return to their homes in Poland, whereas those who articulated their views to Harrison refused repatriation. The politics of the survivors often depended on previous origin. In the camps of the American occupation zone, for example, survivors of the Lithuanian ghettos had seized control, and they had been strongly Zionist before the war. At Bergen-Belsen, on the other hand, a struggle was under way between pro- and anti-Zionist factions, and Harrison apparently did not sense it during his brief visit.

A month after publication of Harrison's report, the Zionist Labor leader from Palestine, David Ben-Gurion, toured the camps; his mere presence on the sordid scene raised Zionist hopes. More discreetly, Ben-Gurion met with his loyalists and mobilized a network of agents for a massive Jewish migration. From the wreckage of the East European ghettos, where the Western occupation forces held no sway, clandestine migrants embarked upon the course of "illegal immigration" through the British blockade to Palestine. Under the oft-averted eyes of the U.S. Army, and sometimes with the open cooperation of the corps of Jewish chaplains, a second wave of DPs swelled the reception centers of the American occupation zone to a population almost double 100,000.

In short, the Harrison report may not have been defensible at the time he wrote it, but the dynamics of postwar Europe soon made the reality correspond. "It is not safe to make a single simple statement as to the nature of a concentration camp survivor as a human being," wrote the American relief worker to David Niles. "Many of these people cannot be expected to make normal judgments or moral decisions." But, several months after Harrison and Ben-Gurion had come and gone, he concluded "to the extent that . . . personalities are intact and decisions can be made, these Jews want to go to Palestine."[26]

Truman was not a man to be troubled by the subtleties. What he saw in the Harrison report was a moving portrait of human beings. "The misery it depicted could not be allowed to continue," he wrote.[27] If Palestine was what they wanted and no other country was coming forward with resettlement offers—least of all the United States—then Palestine it should be. Truman sent a copy of the Harrison report to British Prime Minister Attlee, bypassing all the avenues of diplomacy and saying, "the main solution appears to lie in the quick evacuation of as many as possible of the non-repatriable Jews who wish it, to Palestine. If it is to be effective, such action should not be long delayed."[28]

Truman did not bother consulting his State Department about this personal venture into Anglo-American diplomacy. Indeed, just as the president was accepting Harrison's assessments, the State Department was preparing to oppose the suggestion of moving 100,000 refugees to Palestine. But, as Truman saw it, "the State Department continued to be more concerned about the Arab reaction than the sufferings of the Jews."[29]

Once the president decided to "have a go" at Palestine negotiations, wrote one officer, "I see nothing further we can appropriately do for the moment except carry on our current work, answering letters and telegrams, receiving callers, etc., as best we can, pending the time (which will come soon) when the whole thing will be dumped back in our laps."[30]

Truman's policy was not as mindless as the weary desk officers supposed. On November 10, 1945, he made a revealing admission to a gathering of American ambassadors posted to the Arab world. "If Palestine could only take some refugees from Europe to relieve the pressure," he said, according to the official transcript, "it might satisfy some of the demands of the 'humanitarian' Zionists and give us an opportunity to turn our attention to a permanent solution of the political problem."[31] The "political problem" was not Truman's first concern. "My only interest," he wrote an old Senate colleague, "is to find some proper way to take care of these displaced persons, not only because they should be taken care of and are in a pitiful plight, but because it is to our own financial interest to have them taken care of because we are feeding most of them."[32]

Through 1946 Truman was content to let the State Department pursue all the various programs, the Anglo-American Committee of Inquiry, the Morrison-Grady venture, even the Yom Kippur statement of October, 1946, which he signed but probably did not really care about or understand (see discussion above).

On February 25, 1947, the British government admitted failure in Palestine by turning the entire problem over to the United Nations. Even as he tried to lay blame everywhere else, Bevin acknowledged his blunder in refusing to heed the Truman initiatives. "I say this in all seriousness," he told the House of Commons. "If it were only a question of relieving Europe of 100,000 Jews, I believe a settlement could be found." For once he sounded almost contrite: "If I could get back to the contribution on purely humanitarian grounds of 100,000 into Palestine, and if this political fight for a Jewish state could be put on one side, and we could develop self-government by the people resident in Palestine, without any other political issue, I would be willing to try again."

But that, of course, was just what Truman had been trying to do from the start.

The twenty-eighth and last year of Britain's Palestine mandate found the United States government divided, frustrated, and confused in its policy. Suspicions of British imperial designs, rife within the diplomatic establishment at the end of World War II, faded as statesmen sought to mobilize the "special relationship" of the English-speaking world for a cold war against Stalinist Russia. Distrust of Whitehall had long since been superseded among American diplomats by frustration at the undisciplined forays into diplomacy by a president from the Middle West who clearly cared little about the Middle East.

The diplomatic service viewed domestic politics with distaste. Somehow, whenever Arab crowds gathered in the streets or the Arab press editorialized in wrath, diplomatic envoys saw promising expressions of democracy. But when Zionist "pressure groups" made themselves heard or, even worse, when the president of the United States paid more heed to campaign advisors than to diplomatic experts, this was seen as an improper intrusion of politics into foreign affairs.

Truman's impatience at Zionist pressures and his confusion over the Palestine issue were amply demonstrated through 1947.

### The UN Debate on the Partition of Palestine

Truman had not followed all the maneuvers at Lake Success when he reluctantly agreed to meet Chaim Weizmann on November 19. Weizmann, veteran of the Balfour Declaration, knew the state of play exactly. He persuaded the president that it was crucial to include the desert wastes of the Negev in the proposed Jewish state and not allow the original plan to be altered to the advantage of the Arabs.

No one recorded exactly what Truman said when he picked up the telephone to his UN delegation a few minutes after 3 P.M. that day (a call placed, it need hardly be added, without the knowledge of his State Department), but it was something about doing nothing to "upset the apple cart." Only three hours later did Under Secretary of State Robert A. Lovett get through to the president and discover to his dismay that Truman had overruled the Department's considered judgment that it would be prudent to assign the Negev to the Arabs.[33]

### Pressure on Uncommitted UN Delegations

Truman always professed ignorance of any pressure tactics to persuade small countries far from the scene to vote for partition; indeed, in his memoirs he expressed outrage that any such cynical, undemocratic techniques could have been contemplated. Yet at a Cabinet meeting on November 11, just a fortnight before the final vote, there was discussion about which delegations might swing over to support partition, if they were "encouraged" to do so. Four UN members were the target of the most intense pressure, much of it from individuals high in the United States government, over the

Thanksgiving holiday that preceded the vote: Haiti, the Philippines, Liberia, and Greece. Each had announced opposition to partition on Wednesday. Each of them was susceptible, in one way or another, to American influence. If just three could be persuaded to change their votes—and everything else held firm—partition would carry. Three changed their vote, and partition carried.[34]

The publicity campaigns of the American Zionist organizations stimulated debate and a good deal of sympathy among the general public, but they were often counterproductive with Truman personally as he faced specific decisions over the winter of 1947–48. At one moment of irritation, he brushed aside their electoral pressures in a testy private conversation with an old Senate colleague: "I don't know about that [the Jewish vote], I think a candidate on an anti-semitic platform might sweep the country," said Truman.[35] He acquiesced in the enforcement of an official embargo on arms shipments to Palestine from December 5, 1947, ignoring the likelihood that the ban would hamper the Jewish militias far more than the Arabs, who could claim secure supply arrangements with Britain. Against all the Zionist and, later, Israeli pressure this embargo remained in effect until August 4, 1949.[36]

### Retreat from Partition

Of all the decisions in the final months of the British mandate, the American announcement on March 19, 1948, that partition would not be workable and that there should be an international trusteeship instead was the most inexplicable to commentators at the time and in retrospect.

The concept of a trusteeship over the Holy Land was not novel, of course. It had figured in the Roosevelt vision; it emerged as the favored course of the State Department, since the diplomatic analysts doubted that either Arabs or Jews of Palestine were mature enough to manage their own sovereignty. Some Americans suspected that the referral of the Palestine issue to the United Nations by the British was but a ploy aimed at a rewriting of the original mandate and the assignment of trustee powers to Britain without the inhibitions of the Balfour Declaration.

Not all British experts saw it quite this way. From the eminence of the Royal Institute of International Affairs, Arnold Toynbee came to the Council on Foreign Relations in New York to expound his analysis of the Palestine dilemma. The Council's archives contain a digest of a fascinating round-table discussion—off the record—on

April 20, 1948, at which Toynbee declared the partition of Palestine to be "the *reductio ad absurdum* of territorial nationality." His counter-proposal: "a despotic government over Palestine by a third party, for the indefinite future." Since Britain had clearly botched the job, Toynbee said, the United States would be the ideal candidate for despot. He added that an absolute prerequisite for effective third-party rule would have to be the firm and final halt to all Jewish immigration for generations ahead.[37]

The Americans present showed no eagerness to take up the job "botched" by Britain, but the notion of an international trusteeship was steadily gaining ground in the State Department. Truman's involvement in the reversal of March has been hotly debated, but the record is clear.[38]

Early in March, while relaxing on the presidential yacht between Key West and Saint Croix, Truman had given routine approval to a Palestine position paper submitted by the State Department. If partition turned out to be unworkable, the Department proposed that the United States accept an international trusteeship to enforce peace between Jews and Arabs. It was a hypothetical position, as Truman saw it; he told one friend on that vacation trip that he had not given up on partition, despite the experts' advice.[39] Moreover, a week or so earlier, the president had sent specific instructions: "nothing should be presented to the Security Council that could be interpreted as a recession on our part from the position we took in the General Assembly"—that is, in favor of partition. But he let the hypothetical position paper go through and thought nothing more about it.

The State Department was promoting the trusteeship plan, for it had believed from the start that partition was unworkable. On March 16 the United States delegation at the UN was instructed to turn to the alternative position paper. Two days later, Truman saw Weizmann again in an unannounced meeting and assured him of America's reliability in support of partition. The State Department knew nothing of that meeting, and Truman knew nothing of all the seemingly routine instructions passing from the Department to the UN delegation in New York.

Thus on March 19 the United States ambassador to the United Nations, Warren Austin, assumed that he was acting with the full authority of the president when he sought recognition in the Security Council to declare the United States' judgment that partition was no longer a viable option and that an international trusteeship should therefore be established over Palestine.

It was an international and domestic bombshell. "Almost every major paper in the country has commented on recent developments concerning Palestine," acknowledged the State Department's press office. "Ineptness," "weakness," "vacillating" seemed to be the words most frequently used.[40] Did the United States have a policy—any policy at all—on Palestine?

Contradictory advice bore down on President Truman in the final months of the Palestine mandate.

From the corps of diplomatic experts came the solemn warnings of George F. Kennan, head of the State Department's newly created Policy Planning Staff. "US prestige in the Moslem world has suffered a severe blow, and US strategic interests in the Mediterranean and Near East have been seriously prejudiced," Kennan concluded on January 19, 1948. "Our vital interests in those areas will continue to be adversely affected to the extent that we continue to support partition." Kennan argued that the whole matter should be reopened at the General Assembly. Instead of a Jewish state and an Arab state, which would be bound to go to war and call for outside military support, something like the old British mandate should be renewed under more modern auspices.[41]

Kennan's views went the rounds, with each appropriate division adding its embellishments, and by the time the agreed-upon State Department text went to the White House, it had become sobering indeed:

> We are deeply involved . . . in a situation which has no direct relation to our national security, and where the motives of our involvement lie solely in past commitments of dubious wisdom and in our attachment to the UN itself. . . . If we do not effect a fairly radical reversal of the trend of our policy to date, we will end up either in the position of being ourselves militarily responsible for the protection of the Jewish population in Palestine against the declared hostility of the Arab world, or of sharing that responsibility with the Russians and thus assisting at their installation as one of the military powers of the area. In either case, the clarity and efficiency of a sound national policy for that area will be shattered.[42]

This was only the beginning. A new agency set up to coordinate all American intelligence services against the growing Communist menace, the Central Intelligence Agency, weighed in with an estimate that seemed detached, for the intelligence community had played little role in the Palestine debate up to this point. Its findings were clear-cut. "The partition of Palestine . . . cannot be implemented," the CIA declared. "The Arabs will use force to oppose the establishment of a Jewish state and to this end are training troops in Palestine and other Arab states. Moreover, the United Kingdom has stated repeatedly that it will take no part in implementing a UN decision not acceptable to both Jews and Arabs. . . . Even among Jews there is dissatisfaction over the partition plan."[43]

Then, from the new Department of Defense and the Joint Chiefs of Staff, alarmist messages reached Truman's desk warning that a Jewish state would surely be a potential outpost of Soviet Communism. As late as March 16, 1948, the Joint Chiefs of Staff believed that the dominant Labor party of the Jewish Agency "stems from the Soviet Union and its satellite states and has strong bonds of kinship in those regions, and ideologically is much closer to the Soviet Union than to the United States."[44]

From another source came advice that Truman found more palatable: his own White House counsel, Clark Clifford, a street-smart Missouri lawyer who knew next to nothing of Jews, or of Palestine. But he knew American politics; he understood the humanitarian impulses that moved the American public and, most particularly, the American president. And he knew how to "pull it all together" for a harried chief executive who, after all, had a number of other things on his mind.

"The policy of the United States must be to support the United Nations settlement of the Palestine issue," Clifford began an important memorandum of March 6. "This government urged partition upon the United Nations in the first place and it is unthinkable that it should fail to back up that decision in every possible way." Then followed a step-by-step proposal of how the United States should respond to the tactical decisions:

- pressure upon Britain and the Arabs for partition; if that failed, the Arabs should be branded as aggressors and American arms should be allowed to flow to the defending Jewish forces;
- private American citizens should not be penalized if they chose to go to Palestine to defend partition, Clifford argued; "American citizens were not barred from joining the British Air Force or the Chinese Flying Tigers in the last war";
- special danger, Clifford warned, attached to the Holy City of Jerusalem. Christian holy places must not be allowed to fall under the control of "fanatical Moslems."[45]

Two days later Clifford sent another memorandum to the president, dealing with the domestic politics of the issue. It is interesting that the two aspects were not contained in the same note; a good staff aide normally discusses all facets of the problem in one communication. Perhaps, with an eye on the historical record, Clifford did not want the two considerations bunched together, though this is doubtful; more likely, Truman asked Clifford to pursue the politics when they talked during those intervening two days.

A nagging fact in March, 1948, was that Truman was not an elected president. Many Democrats were urging that a more popular candidate be chosen in his place. On March 8 Truman announced that, though he might have become president by chance, he was now ready to run on his own. In this mood he sought high-toned political position papers on which he could stand. Clifford obliged, and Palestine seemed one of the central issues.

"At the outset, let me say that the Palestine problem should not be approached as a Jewish question, or an Arab question, or a United Nations question," he began his second memorandum. "The sole question is what is best for the United States of America. Your active support of partition was in complete harmony with the policy of the United States. Had you failed to support partition, you would have been departing from an established American policy and justifiably subject to criticism."

Clifford tried to answer the objections of all the bureaucrats' studies. The Arab oil threats were empty, he argued, for "the fact of the matter is that the Arab states must have oil royalties or go broke. . . . Their need of the United States is greater than our need of them." Then there were those, Clifford said, who believed that partition could not work. "This comes from those who never wanted partition to succeed, and who have been determined to sabotage it." Clifford concluded: "The United States appears in the ridiculous role of trembling before threats of a few nomadic desert tribes. This has done us irreparable damage. Why should Russia or Yugoslavia or any other nation treat us with anything but contempt in light of our shilly-shallying appeasement of the Arabs."

Building to a rhetorical climax, Clifford noted "a complete lack of confidence in our foreign policy from one end of this country to the other and among all classes of our population. This lack of confidence is shared by Democrats, Republicans, young people and old people. There is a definite feeling that we have no foreign policy, that we do not know where we are going, that the President and the State Department are bewildered, that the United States, instead of furnishing leadership in world affairs, is drifting helplessly. I believe all of this can be changed." The way to start the national reversal would be to "promptly and vigorously support the United Nations actions regarding Palestine." Only thus could America's reliability and leadership be confirmed; only thus could Soviet Russia be prevented from exploiting Middle East tensions; only thus could full-scale war between Jews and Arabs be averted upon the termination of Britain's Palestine mandate on May 15, just two months hence.[46]

With this guidance from his own trusted political aide, Truman developed his own agenda as the diplomats fretted over this or that trusteeship proposal. After the stunning reversal of March 19, Truman's anguish was that he had unwittingly misled kindly old Chaim Weizmann, who had sat in his office just one day before the bomb burst. Trivial, perhaps, against the sweep of history, but important to the mind of the moment.

The very morning of the dismal headlines, Judge Sam Rosenman came in for one of his regular, off-the-record meetings among political professionals. The old Roosevelt loyalist had no official position in the Truman White House by this time, but he was happy to be of help in brainstorming the coming political campaign. On this occasion, Truman had something more specific to ask of him: did Rosenman know how to get in touch with "the little doctor," Weizmann? Could he convey the assurances that the president meant every word he had said two days before, his fullest support for the partition of Palestine? And further, would Weizmann please accept his word that, at the time they spoke, the president did not know of the statement that was about to be delivered at the United Nations? Rosenman had not expected such a mission, but he promptly passed Truman's message to Weizmann at the Shoreham Hotel.[47]

Weizmann understood that events, not words, would determine the Jewish fate. Since the Jews of Palestine were themselves about to proclaim the long-awaited Jewish state, and defend it with their lives, the issue for politicians and diplomats far from the scene was not yet another plan of partition or trusteeship or mandate or whatever. It was rather whether the United States would recognize the Jewish state once the Jews brought it into being.

Weizmann directed his next efforts toward the goal of American recognition. Over the next few weeks, Weizmann and Rosenman held some most discreet discussions, and Rosenman talked of the recognition problem with Truman. The public flap over the trusteeship proposal had long since been explained away, but Truman had told Rosenman, "I have Dr. Weizmann on my conscience." Would the judge once again approach the little doctor and tell him in the highest secrecy that if a Jewish state were declared, and if the United Nations remained stalled in its drive to establish a trusteeship, the president of the United States would recognize the new state immediately?[48]

These exchanges were never reported to the State Department. Even Weizmann kept his silence, for he understood that if he conveyed reassurance to any of the Zionist factions agitating through Palestine, Europe, and the United States, the aura of confidence would be broken and the assurance would be worthless. The move was typical of Truman, a statement of personal integrity and intent, uncluttered by bureaucratic options and provisos. It was the word of one amiable citizen to another, one from Independence, the other from Pinsk. In the context in which it was given, it was as binding as an act of state.

American diplomats who hoped Weizmann would raise a voice of moderation during the final weeks of frenzied effort to head off the unilateral proclamation of a Jewish state were puzzled at the old man's confidence in the face of overwhelming Arab numbers.[49] Even his more radical Zionist rival in Palestine, David Ben-Gurion, seemed surprised when word came that Weizmann was urging him on in the early proclamation of the state.[50] For his part, Truman delayed raising United States options with his diplomatic advisors, but he let drop a casual word of the decision he had already made for himself. Bartley Crum, a pro-Zionist member of the Anglo-American Committee of Inquiry, had occasion to see the president early in May, and he asked what Truman anticipated for Palestine if the Jews went ahead and proclaimed their state. Crum reported that Truman replied without a pause, "What would I do? I would recognize the state, of course."[51]

Secretary of State George C. Marshall urged caution upon the Jewish Agency when he met the unofficial Zionist foreign minister, Moshe Shertok, on May 8; nothing was said about American recognition, for, as far as Marshall was concerned, no decision had been made. On May 10 Crum managed to see Truman again, and word came back to the Zionists that their friend was "fairly optimistic."[52] Clifford's office was producing memoranda warning against unquestioning acceptance of State Department forebodings. Indeed, recognition of the Jewish state, one insisted, "might bring our country a useful ally and supporter, diminish violence, help the United Nations."[53]

During his final session with Shertok, Under Secretary Lovett had made veiled reference to an option the Department was considering: to appeal to American public opinion against the Zionists and produce a documented record of pressure tactics. He repeated the threat in more forceful terms to Nahum Goldmann on May 11, pointing to a dossier on his desk, saying, "You see those files? That is all evidence of the violent, ruthless pressures exerted on the American government, mostly by American Jews. I wonder to whom they feel they owe their primary loyalty."[54]

By May 12 Truman could delay confronting the issues no longer. His staff advised him that within three days the British would abandon their Palestine mandate, the Zionists would declare their own state in accordance with the UN partition plan, and the Arab armies would invade to crush Jewish nationalism and declare Palestine an undivided Arab state. What would the United States do? Truman's own mind was evidently made up, and, if he insisted upon it, he could impose that decision upon his administration without further ado. But no chief executive could be so callous to the considered recommendations of his expert advisors, particularly advisors of the stature of General Marshall, in an election year, when the pressures against his candidacy were intense and a single defection of prominence could be fatal.

At 4 P.M. Marshall and his team of advisors came to the White House for the showdown with Truman. To the secretary's distaste, Clifford joined the group, though the diplomats considered him to have no proper standing in the matter. Only Clifford knew that Truman's purpose in calling the meeting was to gain concurrence in the decision that he, as president, had already made. As the meeting was being scheduled a day or two before, Truman had told his counsel, "I want you to get ready for this as if you were presenting a case to the Supreme Court. You will be addressing all of us present, of course, but the person I really want you to convince is Marshall."[55]

Familiar arguments were rehearsed by both sides in the course of the next hour, with the State Department urging last-ditch diplomacy to forestall a proclamation of a Jewish state, and Clifford arguing for letting partition proceed by the decisions of the Jewish authorities in place. Tension was high in the White House circle, and at one point Truman reverted to banter to try breaking a little of the ice. "Well, General," he said, "it sounds to me as if even you might vote against me in November if I go ahead to recognize." George C. Marshall was not a man to banter. "Yes, Mr. President, if I were to vote at all, I might do just that."[56]

In jest, perhaps, or possibly in all seriousness, Marshall was threatening to break politically with Truman. This was not what the underdog from Missouri needed in May, 1948, two months before a Democratic convention he did not yet control, six months before a presidential election in which he looked like a sure loser. Nothing more could be accomplished in such a mood, and Truman ended the meeting. He authorized the State Department to continue the diplomatic efforts at the UN and put aside the draft statement promising recognition that Clifford had prepared. But he gave the departing officials no further clue about what he would do on May 15. "I'm sorry, Clark," said Truman quietly as Clifford lingered behind. "I hope you understand." "That's all right, Mr. President; this isn't the first time

I've lost a case." But Truman did not consider the case closed. Let everyone sleep on it, he told Clifford, and then "we will get into it again."[57]

Direct confrontation was not Marshall's style, certainly not confrontation with his commander-in-chief on an issue like Palestine in which he had so little interest. The secretary was still bruised by the unseemly misunderstandings of the March trusteeship proposal, and he was comfortable leaving the matter to Lovett. As he left the White House that Wednesday, it apparently dawned on the under secretary that Clifford had argued with an air of authority that eluded the career diplomats. Had the president's thinking advanced further than the Department knew? Lovett telephoned Clifford the next morning to convey his uneasiness; he and the others at State would be talking it all out among themselves that day, he said. Perhaps it would be a good idea if just the two of them, Lovett and Clifford, had a private little lunch.[58]

Truman maintained a holding pattern at his Thursday news conference, ignoring the recognition text that Clifford had proposed. When a reporter asked what he intended to do about the imminent declaration of a Jewish state, he said simply, "I will cross that bridge when I get to it."

Both Clifford and Lovett saw the bridge in front of them when they sat down to lunch at the 1925 F Street Club at noon on Friday. Clifford made it as easy as he could for the State Department. There would be no need for Marshall to give the president a formal retraction of his Wednesday advice; indeed, Clifford assured Lovett that Truman had been very much impressed by the Department's arguments against recognition in advance of the Jewish state's proclamation and had followed that advice at his news conference. By 6 P.M. (midnight in Tel Aviv), however, the circumstances would be different. "There would be no government or authority of any kind in Palestine," Clifford said. "Title would be lying about for anybody to seize and a number of people had advised the President that this should not be permitted." A Jewish state would be declared, its boundaries defined, and the composition of its provisional government announced.

Lovett listened with ever fuller understanding of the imminence of the act. The question was no longer whether to recognize the Jewish state, but how soon. Lovett regrouped his arguments to urge only against "indecent haste." Even a day's delay would help the diplomats prepare the ground. Clifford agreed that key officials should be forewarned—but he would not concede even a twenty-four-hour delay. Advisory cables must go out immediately. Timing was "of the greatest possible importance to the President from a domestic point of view," he admitted; "the President was under unbearable pressure to recognize the Jewish state promptly." Lovett remembered the words and put them down in a formal memorandum for the Department's files. They became the authoritative basis for the diplomats' case that Truman had acted only to grab the Jewish vote.

"My protests against the precipitate action and warnings as to consequences with the Arab world appear to have been outweighed by considerations unknown to me," Lovett wrote archly, "but I can only conclude that the President's political advisers, having failed last Wednesday afternoon to make the President a father of the new state, have determined at least to make him the midwife."[59]

The actual record of those spring days of 1948 does not enhance Truman's stature, even among Israelis. One of the ironies of the Jewish restoration, as it came about in fact, is the imbalance of credit apportioned between Roosevelt and Truman. Roosevelt's sorry record in refusing to face the Holocaust has blotted out his radical vision for a Jewish Palestine. But as for Truman, as he himself admitted sheepishly years later, "Those Israelites have placed me on a pedestal alongside of Moses."[60] Except for occasional musings about Cyprus and the Near East of the Bible, Truman showed little interest in the Jewish restoration. The notion of a Jewish state held no mystery for him; the Zionist politicians agitating for that dream were, to him, nothing short of repugnant.

"The little doctor," Weizmann, was the only Zionist leader who seems to have really touched Truman. On Israel's first day in the modern world, May 15, 1948, Truman wrote Weizmann a letter. Surely this was a natural opportunity for any expression of historical sentiment or appreciation that Truman might have felt. There was none. He told Weizmann simply, "I sincerely hope that the Palestine situation will eventually work out on an equitable and peaceful basis." Four months later, Truman still displayed no signs of appreciation for the Jewish restoration then unfolding amid war and disruption. "I hope that peace will come to Palestine," he wrote Weizmann in September, 1948—not even using the word "Israel"—"and that we will eventually be able to work out proper location of all those Jews who suffered so much during the war." These letters were typewritten, presumably drafted by a correspondence secretary. But Truman signed them, without adding any of the handwritten messages through which he carried on such an unguarded personal correspondence on matters of real import to him.[61]

From his first days in office, he had regarded the problem of Palestine as a practical matter of finding homes for miserable people ravaged by war, not as any political revolution or act of statecraft following two thousand years of exile. All the various diplomatic formulas of those years were but legalistic doubletalk that kept the striped-pants boys busy. As late as March, 1948, he could refer blithely to the Anglo-American Committee report and the UN partition plan in the same breath, ignoring the fact that these international bodies had come to quite opposite political conclusions.

Most revealing of all was the letter Truman wrote on the very day of Israel's rebirth to Bartley Crum. "I think the report of the British American Commission on Palestine [*sic*] was the correct solution," Truman wrote, "and, I think, eventually we are going to get it worked out just that way."[62] Just twenty-four hours before telling one friend what he thought was the "correct solution" for Palestine, Truman had set in motion the final official acts toward a quite different solution.

American politicians and historians charged Truman with crude political pandering in his recognition of Israel. Was politics a factor? "Of course it was," acknowledged Clifford many years later. "Political considerations are present in every important decision that a President makes."[63] But Clifford insisted that the Jewish vote was neither compelling nor decisive. The issue of Palestine lurked on the margins of the 1948 campaign to the very end, but, faced with Zionist entreaties and threats, Truman remained stubborn. Some 65 percent of America's Jews lived in the three large states of New York, Pennsylvania, and Illinois, with 110 electoral votes among them. Truman lost all three—and won the election.

So-called Jewish issues broke down into several facets. First was the quality of America's recognition of Israel: accorded on May 14 was *de facto* recognition of a living reality, not the *de jure* recognition that would acknowledge legal legitimacy.

After their first expressions of gratitude, the American Zionist leaders grasped the halfhearted nature of Truman's action. Truman insisted that *de jure* recognition could come to Israel only after elections in the new state and the installation of something more than a provisional government. Not until January, 1949, did that come about—and only then, when the domestic American political factor was no longer relevant, did Truman upgrade the diplomatic recognition.

Of more tangible importance was the American arms embargo to Palestine. This remained in effect even against the sovereign Jewish state. Through all the fighting of Israel's first months, the months of

America's election campaign, Truman refused to lift the restrictions against supplies for the Jewish forces. Against Zionist pressures, he let the diplomats pursue their quest for compromise between warring Jews and Arabs. A United Nations mediator, Count Folke Bernadotte of Sweden, proposed new boundaries that would once again turn the Negev over to the Arabs. Marshall promptly accepted the Bernadotte plan; American Zionists protested another "betrayal of American policy." Bernadotte was assassinated by Israeli irregulars in September. Truman refused all demands that he repudiate Marshall and the Bernadotte plan. As late as October, on the whistle-stop tour of America that reversed his electoral fortunes, Truman resisted the temptation to make political capital of his Palestine decisions. Only when his Republican opponent, Governor Thomas E. Dewey of New York, accused him of betraying pledges to Israel did Truman declare his full support for the Jewish state as defined by the United Nations.

By election day, Israel had become too confusing a problem for the American electorate to contemplate. Truman's own interest had waned—as far as he was concerned, the problems of the homeless refugees had been solved. The voters had moved on to other things; Israel and the Jewish vote were not decisive.

## Notes

This paper is adapted, after further research and review, from Peter Grose, *Israel in the Mind of America* (New York: Alfred A. Knopf, 1983), in which additional references may be found.

Any writers on this period are indebted to the careful scholarship of the late Evan M. Wilson, whose *Decision on Palestine: How the U.S. Came to Recognize Israel* (Stanford, Calif.: Hoover Institution Press, 1979) remains the best dissection of the American diplomatic documents at the close of the Palestine mandate. In what was perhaps his last essay before his death on March 13, 1984, a review of my above-mentioned book in the *Middle East Journal* (Spring, 1984), Wilson warned against any simpleminded judgment that professional American diplomats in 1948 were motivated by sentiments of anti-Semitism. I concur in this admonition, for, as he himself showed me, the diplomatic officers of the late 1940s brought to their task sensitivities quite different from those of their predecessors of the

late 1930s. Another invaluable analysis of the diplomatic documents
of the period is Zvi Ganin, *Truman, American Jewry, and Israel,
1945–1948* (New York: Holmes and Meier, 1979).

1.  Harry S Truman Library, Independence, Mo. (HSTL), OF204*d*, Misc.
May 15, 1948.
    2.  Harry N. Howard, *The King-Crane Commission* (Beirut: Khayats,
1963), p. 99.
    3.  Alfred Steinberg, *The Man from Missouri* (New York: G. P. Put-
nam's Sons, 1962), p. 304. The following portrayal of Roosevelt's thinking
about Palestine after World War II is conveyed in much greater detail in my
book cited above. See particularly the source notes (pp. 329–32), with specific references to the Franklin D. Roosevelt Library, Hyde Park, N.Y. (FDRL).
    4.  *Foreign Relations of the United States (FRUS) 1939*, IV, pp. 748–58.
    5.  Central Zionist Archives, Jerusalem (CZA), S25/237*b*, Goldmann
to Weizmann, June 20, 1939.
    6.  Ibid.
    7.  CZA, Z4/15463, "Note of Conversation."
    8.  John Morton Blum, ed., *From the Morgenthau Diaries, Vol. III,
Years of War, 1941–45* (Boston: Houghton Mifflin, 1967), p. 208.
    9.  *The Diaries of Edward R. Stettinius, Jr., 1943–1946* (New York:
New Viewpoints, 1975), p. 170.
    10.  Ibid., p. 211.
    11.  Cited in Joseph B. Schechtman, *The United States and the Jewish
State Movement: The Crucial Decade, 1939–1949* (New York: Herzl Press,
1966), p. 110.
    12.  Robert E. Sherwood, *Roosevelt and Hopkins* (New York: Harper and
Bros., 1948), pp. 871–82.
    13.  Edward R. Stettinius, *Roosevelt and the Russians* (Garden City,
N.Y.: Doubleday, 1949), pp. 289–90, cited in Samuel Halperin and Irvin
Oder, "The United States in Search of a Policy: Franklin D. Roosevelt and
Palestine," *Review of Politics*, 24 (1962), 338.
    14.  George Martin, *Madame Secretary* (New York: Houghton Mifflin,
1976), p. 89.
    15.  *FRUS 1945*, VIII, p. 18.
    16.  Merle Miller, *Plain Speaking* (New York: G. P. Putnam's Sons,
1974), p. 215.
    17.  CZA, Z4/20276, July 28, 1946.
    18.  *FRUS 1946*, VII, pp. 703–5; Dean Acheson, *Present at the Creation*
(New York: W. W. Norton, 1969), p. 169.
    19.  The account of the next few pages is only the start of what I hope
will be a serious effort at "investigative scholarship" on the Harrison mission. His diaries of the Holocaust camps appeared only, as far as I could find
them, in *Survey Graphic* (December, 1945), 469–73. Beyond my sources
cited below, Leonard Dinnerstein, *America and the Survivors of the Holocaust* (New York: Columbia University Press, 1982) is helpful. But my contention is that a few alert Zionist activists spotted the Harrison mission as a
useful instrument in their campaign, and his conclusions were helpful to

them even though they were not justified by the facts at the time of his investigation. I await convincing refutation of the evidence presented. Considering the impact of his report on the presidential policy-making process, I argue that it is an essential point to be pursued.

20. FDRL, WRB Box 9, June 27, 1945.

21. CZA, Z5/967, June 28, 1945.

22. FDRL, WRB, June 12, 1945.

23. Yehuda Bauer, *Flight and Rescue: Brichah* (New York: Random House, 1970), pp. 57–62, 76–77; Abraham J. Klausner, "A Jewish Chaplain at Dachau," reproduced in *American Jewish Memoirs: Oral Documentation* (Jerusalem: Institute of Contemporary Jewry, Hebrew University, 1980), pp. 73–80.

24. Department of State, *Bulletin* (September 30, 1945), 455–63.

25. Niles papers, Brandeis University, Waltham, Mass., n5.195.

26. Ibid.

27. Harry S Truman, *Years of Trial and Hope* (Garden City, N.Y.: Doubleday, 1956), p. 138.

28. *FRUS 1945*, VIII, pp. 737–39.

29. Truman, *Years of Trial*, p. 140.

30. *FRUS 1945*, VIII, footnote, pp. 745–46.

31. Ibid., p. 17.

32. HSTL, OF204 Misc., letter to George, October 17, 1946.

33. The best analysis of all the conflicting documentation about this episode is in Zvi Ganin, *Truman, American Jewry, and Israel, 1945–1948* (New York: Holmes and Meier, 1979), pp. 138–41.

34. A more thorough account of the various pressure tactics can be found in Grose, *Israel in the Mind of America*, pp. 248–54, with references on p. 343.

35. Jules Abels, *Out of the Jaws of Victory* (New York: Henry Holt and Co., 1959), p. 17, cited in Ganin, *Truman*, p. 182.

36. An excellent study, with detailed references, is Shlomo Slonim, "The 1948 American Embargo on Arms to Palestine," *Political Science Quarterly* (Fall, 1979).

37. Archives of the Council on Foreign Relations (New York), Digest of Discussion, April 20, 1948, Study Group on "The Near and Middle East," vol. XXVII-A.

38. Much of the record, with additional references noted below, is spelled out in Zvi Ganin, "The Limits of American Jewish Political Power: America's Retreat from Partition, November 1947–March 1948," *Jewish Social Studies* (Winter–Spring, 1977), 1–36.

39. Israel State Archives, *Political and Diplomatic Documents (PDD)*, December, 1947–May, 1948 (Jerusalem, 1979), no. 269.

40. Department of State, Office of Public Affairs, "U.S. Opinion on Recent U.S. Policy Statements Concerning Palestine," April 2, 1948, National Archives.

41. *FRUS 1948*, V, pp. 545–54ff.

42. Ibid., pp. 655–57.

43. Ibid., pp. 666–75.

44. RG319, P&O 091 Palestine, TS Sect. I, Part I, Modern Military Branch, National Archives.

45. *FRUS 1948*, V, pp. 687–89.

46. Ibid., pp. 690–96.

47. *PDD*, nos. 263, 452.

48. Ibid.; Abba Eban, in *Chaim Weizmann: A Biography by Several Hands* (New York: Atheneum, 1963), pp. 308–11; Abba Eban, *An Autobiography* (New York: Random House, 1977), pp. 109–11; *PDD*, no. 452.

49. *FRUS 1948*, V, pp. 823–24.

50. Vera Weizmann, *The Impossible Takes Longer* (New York: Harper and Row, 1967), pp. 230–32; Eban, *Autobiography*, p. 111; see also Zeev Sheref, *Three Days* (London: W. H. Allen, 1962).

51. Emanuel Neumann, *In the Arena* (New York: Herzl Press, 1976), p. 776.

52. *PDD*, p. 776.

53. See memo by Owen S. Stratton, Clifford papers, HSTL, April 9, 1960, items 10, 11.

54. *PDD*, no. 483; see also Dan Kurzman, *Genesis 1948* (New York: World Publishing Co., 1970), pp. 212–13, for Goldmann's account.

55. Clark M. Clifford, "Recognizing Israel," in *American Heritage* (April, 1977), 8.

56. *FRUS 1948*, V, pp. 972–76; see also note in Grose, *Israel in the Mind of America*, p. 346.

57. Clifford, "Recognizing Israel," p. 10; Kurzman, *Genesis*, p. 216.

58. HSTL, Charles G. Ross papers, "Notes re Palestine, etc.," March 29, 1948, p. 6; Clifford, "Recognizing Israel," p. 10.

59. *FRUS 1948*, V, pp. 1005–7.

60. Robert Ferrell, ed., *Off the Record: The Private Papers of Harry S. Truman* (New York: Harper and Row, 1980), p. 402.

61. HSTL, OF204d, Misc. May 15, 1948, September 10, 1948.

62. HSTL, OF204d, Misc. May 15, 1948.

63. Clifford, "Recognizing Israel," p. 11.

# The Soviet Role in the Emergence of Israel

*Oles M. Smolansky*

At the conclusion of World War II, the victorious USSR confronted a number of military, political, and economic problems. For the sake of convenience, they can be grouped in three major categories: domestic, regional, and international. On the home front—a subject outside the scope of this chapter—the war-torn areas of the Soviet Union had to be rebuilt. Not surprisingly, the gigantic task of postwar reconstruction was given top priority, since Moscow's claim to "superpower" status rested on the twin pillars of military and industrial strength.

In areas adjacent to the Soviet frontiers—Eastern Europe, the Far East, and the Middle East—the Kremlin, in the name of countering "capitalist encirclement" and of protecting the country's national security, set out to consolidate and, in some instances, to expand the territorial gains made during the war. It should be noted parenthetically that the above three regions have been ranked in accordance with their respective military-strategic and political importance to the USSR. Specifically, there can be no doubt that, to Stalin, Eastern and Central Europe (including much of the Balkans) was indeed the "catch" of World War II. With the memories of the 1930s and especially of the war still fresh in their minds, the Kremlin leaders regarded Eastern and Central Europe as absolutely indispensable to the national security of the Soviet Union.[1] In addition to strategic considerations, a strong Russian military presence in the heart of the continent could also be expected to help wrest political concessions from the war-weary nations of Western Europe.

The territorial acquisitions on the shores of the Pacific, too, represented an important strategic asset.[2] Coupled with the capitulation of Japan and the general weakness of China, they propelled the USSR into a position of unprecedented strength in the Far East, overshadowed only by the United States. Relatively speaking, the Middle East was less significant to Stalin than were the other two regions.

Nevertheless, it is undeniable that *parts* of the area, such as northern Iran and northeastern Turkey,[3] as well as the Turkish Straits, were of considerable strategic importance to Moscow. At a minimum, they controlled access to Russia's "soft underbelly"—the Ukraine, Transcaucasus, and the predominantly Muslim territories of Central Asia. Conversely, a Soviet military presence in parts of Turkey and Iran would have facilitated possible future expansion into the Mediterranean and toward the Persian Gulf.

The situation that Stalin encountered in the postwar Middle East differed from that in Eastern Europe and the Far East in at least two important respects. First, unlike the other regions, the Middle East had long been a sphere of exclusively Western (mainly British) influence. For this reason, with the exception of northern Iran, the Red Army made no move into the territory of the USSR's southern neighbors. Second, according to the 1941 agreement with Great Britain, Soviet troops were obligated to leave northern Iran no later than six months after the end of World War II. In view of these considerations, the Kremlin was left no choice but to pursue its interests in the Middle East by means of diplomatic negotiations with its wartime allies. As Stalin soon found out, however, neither London nor Washington was prepared to countenance Soviet aggrandizement: the Middle East was viewed vital to Western military, political, and economic interests.[4]

It is conceivable that the Kremlin found Western "intransigence" difficult to understand. Since the USSR had been "permitted" to make important territorial gains in Eastern Europe and in the Far East, why should it be denied the privilege of protecting its national security in the south? On the other hand, given the fact that neither Churchill nor Stalin had viewed their wartime cooperation as anything but an expedient dictated by the necessity to destroy the common enemy, the Soviet leader should not have been overly surprised to find Great Britain and the post-Roosevelt United States determined not to permit Moscow to expand its influence any further than it already had. In any event, while highly successful in Eastern Europe and the Far East, the Kremlin was effectively blocked in the Middle East, a trend that culminated in the forced withdrawal of Soviet troops from northern Iran in 1946.[5]

The Kremlin's stand on the Palestine problem cannot be understood as well without reference to the broader international situation that emerged in the wake of the Allied victory over Germany and Japan. The defeat of these two nations, accompanied by the growing weakness of Great Britain and France, propelled both the United States and the Soviet Union into positions of unprecedented power and, in the case of the former, of worldwide influence; they emerged as the "superpowers" of the postwar era. However, Russia's achievement of such lofty status did not denote equality between Washington and Moscow. Though not widely appreciated in the West, this fact was immediately recognized by Stalin. In formulating and executing Soviet foreign policy he never deviated from the basic premise that under no circumstances should the United States be provoked into a major war against the USSR. This inequality between the two superpowers, which manifested itself in their respective economic and military strength, could not but seriously affect the foreign policy of the Soviet Union.

Needless to say, the permanent reduction of the USSR to the status of a "second-class superpower" was no more acceptable to Stalin than to his successors. After 1945 the Kremlin set out to rebuild the country's shattered economy and undertook a major effort to acquire and improve its atomic and nuclear capability. Concurrently, Stalin was busy in the political arena. Generally speaking, his efforts in this category were conducted along two partially overlapping lines. Initially, in 1944–45, Moscow was hard at work in an attempt to gain Western recognition of the "legitimacy" of the USSR as one of the world's superpowers. To Stalin, this meant, in part, Washington's and London's acquiescence in the proposition that Communist Russia's "legitimate interests" extended beyond the country's 1939–40 borders into the territories of several neighboring states. More specifically, in areas where Moscow's national interests, as defined by the Kremlin, were directly involved, Stalin sought Western recognition of and respect for these Soviet concerns. (This was true of Eastern and Central Europe as well as parts of the Far East and Middle East. In the latter region, as noted, the Turkish Straits, northeastern Turkey, and northern Iran fell into this category.) Elsewhere, including those sections of the Middle East where no *vital* Soviet interests were thought to have been at stake, Western acceptance of the Kremlin's claims to the "legitimacy" of its concerns was demanded on the grounds of the USSR's geographic proximity and general superpower status.

After 1945, when it became obvious that the West had no intention of offering any such blank and far-reaching recognition, Moscow embarked upon a course of political competition with its former allies, concentrating, predictably, on the three major areas contiguous to the Soviet Union and the "People's Democracies": Europe, the Far East, and the Middle East. Stalin's handling of the Palestine problem is then but a single, albeit interesting, example of such a process.

## Attempts at Cooperation

Although the question of Palestine's future had not been included in the official agenda of the Yalta summit, it did come up in informal discussions. The most striking feature of these deliberations seems to have been a tacit agreement by the Allied heads of state "to hand over Palestine to the Jews and to continue Jewish immigration at least for the immediate future."[6] President Roosevelt subsequently reported being struck by the fact that "Stalin had not appeared opposed to Zionism."[7] As correctly argued by Yaacov Roʾi, the Kremlin's conciliatory posture was probably influenced by a desire to demonstrate to the Western Allies its flexibility at a time when it was generally assumed that the question of the Palestine mandate would soon be submitted to the United Nations, whose establishment had been officially agreed upon at Yalta. By virtue of its membership in the new international organization and of its veto power in the Security Council, the USSR fully expected to play a prominent part in deciding the future status of Palestine. Since, as noted earlier, no vital Soviet interests were claimed to be at stake in Palestine, direct Russian involvement in the affairs of the former League of Nations mandate would have meant implicit Western recognition of the legitimacy of Moscow's role in what the Kremlin viewed as a relatively remote sector of the Middle East.[8]

Whatever hopes Stalin may have harbored at Yalta, however, were shattered a short time later: in late February, 1945, Prime Minister Churchill announced his government's decision not to submit the Palestine problem to the United Nations. As subsequently became clear, the move was designed specifically to preclude the possibility of Soviet intervention in the affairs of the strife-torn mandate. Churchill's decision "deprived . . . [Stalin's conciliatory] stand on Palestine, including the support of the Jewish cause there, of its *raison d'être*."[9]

Allied determination to exclude the USSR from efforts to resolve the Palestinian question was once again driven home to the Kremlin in late fall, 1945, when Great Britain and the United States set up the Anglo-American Committee of Inquiry to review the Jewish refugee problem in Europe as well as the situation in Palestine.[10] Stalin's resentment at being circumvented by his wartime allies manifested itself in the highly negative Soviet reaction to the Committee and its recommendations.[11] Convinced that London and Washington had no intention of cooperating with Moscow, the USSR was left no choice but to develop its own approach to the Palestine problem. In addition to predictable propaganda efforts aimed at discrediting the

Western initiative, the Kremlin endeavored to return the issue to the United Nations, where the Soviets could be expected to play a prominent part, and to keep it there until some sort of resolution acceptable to the USSR could be worked out. In short, by 1946, the lines separating the Western powers and the Soviet Union on many major international issues, including Palestine, were clearly drawn. Whatever Stalin's original intentions may have been, it was obvious that thereafter, in Palestine and elsewhere, East-West relations would be marked not by cooperation but by competition.[12]

## Confrontation

With respect to Palestine, the USSR was not entirely powerless. One of the Soviet trump cards, actually played in 1946–47, was the issue of Jewish immigration to Palestine. Though unable to control events directly in the Middle East, Moscow was in a position to afford or deny the East European Jews who had survived the Holocaust an opportunity to emigrate from their respective homelands. Thus, confronted with Western objections to its participation in the resolution of the Palestine problem, the Kremlin, in spite of its public opposition to mass exodus of East European Jews as well as to Zionism,[13] set out to facilitate their emigration to the Western zones of Germany and Austria. The Soviet government did so in full awareness of the fact that most emigrants were determined to proceed to Palestine and to do what they could to ensure the establishment of a Jewish state.[14] As a result, the number of Jewish displaced persons (DPs) in West Germany and Austria swelled from "less than 100,000 in summer 1945 to approximately a quarter of a million early in 1947," making it impossible for the West to disregard "the question of Palestine's political future."[15]

In initiating this policy, the Kremlin appears to have pursued two related objectives. First, since Great Britain was opposed to the mass immigration of Jews to Palestine, while President Truman was in favor of it, large-scale presence of Jewish DPs in the Allied Zones of occupation could have been expected, at a minimum, to exacerbate Anglo-American relations. Second, the influx of a large number of East European Jews into Palestine might well have resulted in a failure of Western efforts to resolve this thorny problem independently of the larger international community. Either way, the chances of the Palestine issue being brought before the United Nations—Moscow's major political objective in 1946–47—would have been greatly improved. It should be noted in passing that Stalin's gambit, followed by the Kremlin's support of the Jewish community's (Yishuv's) political aspirations in Palestine (discussed below), did indeed lead to the desired results. The Soviet moves eventually contributed to the collapse of Anglo-American attempts to settle the Palestine problem outside the UN framework. Once that occurred, forcing Great Britain, in early 1947, to place the issue again on the United Nations agenda, it became difficult to deny the USSR active participation in the search for a resolution of the problem.

With the advent of the cold war in 1946–47, Moscow's quest for Allied recognition of the "legitimacy" of its interests in the Middle East was reinforced by apprehension that the Western powers were determined to establish a regional "position of strength" against the USSR. It should be recalled that, in the context of the deteriorating relations between the two blocs, the Middle East, because of its central location in Great Britain's worldwide defense, transportation, and communications network, its economic value, and its geographic proximity to the Soviet Union, was seen as a particularly important area in London and Washington, as well as in Moscow. For its part, the Kremlin repeatedly voiced concern that the creation of a pro-Western regional military alliance had been under active consideration not only in Great Britain and the United States but also in the Middle Eastern states friendly to the "capitalist" powers.[16]

In any event, once Stalin had decided that cooperation between the USSR and its wartime allies was impossible, the Kremlin began actively searching for means to weaken the Western hold on the Middle East. It required no particularly keen insight to conclude that Palestine represented a "weak link" in Great Britain's regional "Imperial Defense System." It was vulnerable because of the existence in that country of two competing nationalisms—Jewish and Arab—that aspired not only to frustrate each other's ambitions but also to rid themselves of British tutelage. Therefore, in concentrating on Palestine, Moscow could have reasonably hoped to remove the British presence and, in so doing, to initiate a process of imperial withdrawal from the entire Middle East. Stalin must be given credit for recognizing that the eventual attainment of these objectives was more readily facilitated by Soviet backing of Zionist rather than Arab nationalist aspirations in Palestine.

## Emphasis on the UN

Before committing itself openly to the Zionist cause, however, the USSR, as already mentioned, had to overcome Anglo-American maneuvers intended to exclude Moscow from attempts to resolve the

Palestine problem. In 1946–47, the Kremlin did so by insisting that any change in "the status of dependent territories" could be undertaken only in the context of the United Nations.[17] Stalin's persistence paid off in February, 1947, when the British government, despairing of its ability to mediate the Arab-Jewish dispute, referred the Palestine problem to the UN.[18] By that time, Moscow's ability to influence events in the strife-torn country had improved considerably. For one thing, the Jewish population had swelled due to the large-scale immigration of East European Jews. Moreover, as noted, the gradually deteriorating internal situation in Palestine, with the Yishuv and the Arab community pitted against each other as well as against the British, offered the USSR a unique opportunity to exert pressure by supporting Zionist aspirations for an independent Jewish state.

The Kremlin, as might have been expected, welcomed the submission of the Palestine question to the UN. Now that this important step had been taken, Deputy Foreign Minister Andrei Gromyko declared on May 8, 1947, that the USSR was prepared "to take upon itself, together with other permanent members of the Security Council and together with the United Nations as a whole, the responsibility not only for the final decisions that may be taken by our organization on the Palestine problem, but also for the preparation of the decisions."[19] Gromyko was referring to the United Nations Special Committee on Palestine (UNSCOP), whose establishment his government had strongly endorsed. One of the serious bones of contention between Moscow and the majority of the UN members was the problem of great power representation on the Special Committee. While the Soviets, as evidenced by Gromyko's statement, were in favor of including the permanent members, most of the other UN states were not. The issue was resolved on May 15. By a vote of the General Assembly, the great powers were excluded from membership in UNSCOP. However, two of its eleven members—Czechoslovakia and Yugoslavia—belonged to the Soviet bloc.[20]

On May 14, 1947, one day prior to the setting up of UNSCOP, Gromyko delivered an important speech outlining the official Soviet position on the future of Palestine.[21] Moscow's stand rested on two major premises. First, Great Britain had failed in its responsibility as the mandatory power to secure peace in Palestine. Since the Jewish and Arab communities constituted two antagonistic armed camps, united only in their opposition to Great Britain, the mandate had to be terminated without further delay. Second, the Nazi Holocaust had left many survivors homeless and undergoing "great privations" in the DP camps of West Germany and Austria. Because "no Western

European state was able to provide adequate assistance for the Jewish people in defending its rights and its very existence," and because the survivors of the concentration camps had expressed their determination to emigrate to Palestine, the world community had no choice but to honor their wishes.

In reviewing the alternatives open to the United Nations, Gromyko objected to the establishment of an Arab or a Jewish state in all of Palestine on the ground that such a solution would violate the "rights" of the other community and would not "ensure the settlement of relations between the Arabs and the Jews, which constitutes the most important task." These considerations led the deputy foreign minister to conclude that "the legitimate interests of both the Jewish and Arab populations of Palestine can be duly safeguarded only through the establishment of an independent, dual, democratic, homogeneous Arab-Jewish state." However, should "this plan prove impossible to implement, in view of the deterioration in the relations between the Jews and the Arabs, . . . then it would be necessary to consider . . . the partition of Palestine into two independent states, one Arab and one Jewish." Since the Soviet government and media had long been pointing out the deterioration of relations between Palestine's Arab and Jewish communities, usually explained by references to "British intrigues,"[22] Moscow's ultimate vote in favor of partition should not have come as a major surprise.[23]

The USSR officially endorsed a Jewish state in Palestine during the fall, 1947, General Assembly discussion of the UNSCOP report. While the majority of the Committee members recommended partition, some expressed themselves in favor of a unified Arab-Jewish state. In a speech of October 13, Soviet delegate Semen Tsarapkin dismissed the minority report as "impracticable." The Soviet government had reached this conclusion because "relations between Arabs and Jews had reached such a state of tension that it had become impossible to reconcile their points of view." Therefore, since the partition plan "offered more hope of realization," the Kremlin "approved the majority plan in principle."[24] It might be noted in passing that Moscow's attitude was grossly misinterpreted in the West, particularly in Washington. Most U.S. analysts and officials, including Secretary of State George C. Marshall, believed that the USSR was committed to the concept of a unitary Palestinian state (which would favor the Arab side) and would therefore oppose the partition of Palestine.[25]

## Partition

In his General Assembly speech of November 26, 1947, Gromyko formally endorsed UNSCOP's majority report, using this opportunity to offer a lengthy explanation of the Soviet position.[26] Thus he reiterated Moscow's earlier arguments by insisting that the USSR "had no direct material or other interests in Palestine, [except as] a member of the United Nations and . . . a great power that bears, just as do other great powers, a special responsibility for the maintenance of international peace." He went on to say that the partition of Palestine offered "the only workable solution" to this major international problem.

This Soviet stance, Gromyko continued, was in no way directed "against the Arab population in Palestine and against the Arab States in general. . . . On the contrary, the USSR delegation holds that this decision corresponds to the fundamental national interests of . . . the Arabs as well as the Jews." Specifically, Moscow recognized that "the Jewish people has been closely linked with Palestine for a considerable period of history." Nor could the Kremlin "overlook the position in which the Jews found themselves as a result of the recent world war," during which they "suffered more than any other people." In short, Gromyko argued, partition was justified not only because it would "meet the legitimate demands of the Jewish people, hundreds of thousands of whom . . . are still without a country, without homes" but also because it conformed with "the high principles and aims of the United Nations," including "the principle of the national self-determination of peoples."

Gromyko then assured the Arabs that the Soviet government and people "have entertained and still entertain a feeling of sympathy for the national aspirations of the nations of the Arab East," including their "efforts . . . to rid themselves of the last fetters of colonial dependence." For this reason, the USSR delegation distinguished between "the clumsy statements made by some of the representatives of the Arab States . . . obviously . . . under the stress of fleeting emotions, and the basic and permanent interests of the Arab people." The Soviet government, Gromyko concluded, remained "convinced that Arabs and the Arab States will still, on more than one occasion, be looking toward Moscow and expecting the USSR to help them in the struggle for their lawful interests, in their efforts to cast off the last vestiges of foreign dependence."

After the UN General Assembly had voted in favor of the partition resolution, the United States and Great Britain took a number of steps designed to circumvent, if not entirely abort, it. Thus in early

December, 1947, Washington imposed an embargo on arms shipments to the Middle East. Later in the month, the British government announced its decision to withdraw its troops from Palestine
by May 15, 1948. In the meantime, however, London refused to cooperate with the United Nations in implementing the partition resolution. In the light of this development, the United States, in March,
1948, suggested consideration of another alternative—a provisional
UN trusteeship for Palestine.[27] Whatever London's and Washington's
intentions may have been, the above moves affected the Yishuv more
than they did its opponents: the U.S. embargo, in particular, left the
militarily stronger Arab countries free to obtain arms from Great
Britain and other Western sources.

Confronted with these developments, the USSR swung into action. At the UN, the Kremlin had worked successfully to circumvent
the U.S. and British positions.[28] In opposing Washington's trusteeship
proposal, the Soviets charted a course that differed markedly from
the view they had held in 1945. At that time, as noted by Ro'i, Moscow appeared "amenable to the idea of international trusteeship" for
Palestine. Its original attitude was based on the assumption "that
the USSR, as an ally and partner of the two Western powers, would
have been at least a party to the discussion of Palestine's political future and perhaps also to the administration of the trusteeship regime."[29] This was no longer true in 1947–48, however. For one thing,
by mid-1947, the animosity between the "socialist" and "capitalist
camps" had become institutionalized. In addition, in the wake of the
passage of the partition resolution, it was generally expected that
Great Britain would in fact abide by its decision to withdraw from
Palestine by May 15, 1948. For these reasons, it made no sense for
Moscow to settle for anything less than a full implementation of the
UN decision on the future of Palestine.

Outside the United Nations, the USSR supported the Yishuv in
two major ways. In anticipation of its seemingly inevitable showdown with the Arab community and of the likely intervention by
other Arab states, the Kremlin accelerated Jewish emigration from
the satellite countries of Eastern Europe.[30] Of equally crucial importance to the Yishuv's war effort was the transfer to Palestine of arms
and other desperately needed materiel, including aircraft, and the
training of Jewish military personnel in their use. It should be noted
that none of these vital goods and services were provided by the
USSR directly. They were, instead, channeled through Czechoslovakia.[31] While Prague may have been interested mainly in acquiring
hard currency offered by the Zionist agencies responsible for Yishuv's
international arms purchases, it is generally agreed that "such an in-

itiative must have depended on Soviet approval." This conclusion is also supported by "the measure of coordination achieved among the various East European states on the transfer of materiel purchased by the Yishuv in Czechoslovakia to different Mediterranean [as well as to some Rumanian Black Sea] ports."[32] It is difficult to overemphasize the importance of this Soviet military aid. As David Ben-Gurion said on a later occasion, "The arms purchased in Czechoslovakia had 'saved' the young State of Israel."[33]

In summary, the cooperation between the USSR and the Yishuv reached its zenith in the relatively short period between November, 1947, and May 15, 1948, when the state of Israel proclaimed its independence. Soviet assistance was extended for as long as the newly founded country fought for its existence against the invading armies of the neighboring Arab states but declined precipitously in 1949.

## Evaluation

An examination of the Soviet position on Palestine since 1945 suggests that Stalin's perceptions were conditioned by several distinct, though interrelated, considerations. For purposes of analysis, these may be divided into the following categories: military-strategic and political (both short- and long-term as well as regional and international).

As noted earlier, even prior to the advent of the cold war, the Kremlin was voicing concern about "capitalist encirclement" of the USSR. One of the methods chosen to deal with this perceived threat was actual or attempted expansion into areas adjacent to the Soviet Union: Eastern and Central Europe, the Far East, and the Middle East. Of relevance in the context of this discussion were efforts to enhance the national security of the USSR by maintaining a Russian military presence in northern Iran and by extending it into the Turkish Straits area and into Turkey's northeastern provinces.

Politically, Moscow sought Western recognition of the "legitimacy" of its interests in the Middle East by attempting to acquire control over the former Italian colonies and by seeking to participate, on an equal footing with its wartime allies, in efforts to solve some of the region's major political problems. None was more pressing than that of Palestine: the former League of Nations mandate was being torn apart by the seemingly irreconcilable differences between its Arab and Jewish communities, united only in their insistence on the elimination of the British presence from their midst.

As long as the possibility of Soviet-Western cooperation in the Middle East existed, Stalin maintained a low profile and offered no objections to Roosevelt's suggestion to turn Palestine over to the Jews. However, by 1946 it became obvious that the Western powers were resolutely opposed to Soviet military and political expansion in the Middle East; the USSR was denied access to the Turkish Straits as well as to Italy's former colonies. Even more significantly, under strong U.S. pressure, Russian troops were forced to withdraw from northern Iran. In the political arena, the Western nations endeavored to exclude the Kremlin from participation in the resolution of the Palestine problem. These developments left Stalin no choice but to advance Soviet interests by *indirect* means—more precisely, by attempting to weaken the military and political positions of Great Britain, then the leading Western power in the Middle East.

It was not surprising that, in its search for viable opportunities, Moscow centered its attention on Palestine. On the one hand, it occupied an important position in the global defense, transportation, and communications network of the British Empire. On the other hand, internal turmoil made Palestine more susceptible to Soviet manipulation than any other country in the Middle East. For these reasons, in 1946, the Kremlin came out openly in favor of British withdrawal from Palestine.

Nevertheless, Moscow's freedom of maneuver was severely circumscribed by London's and Washington's determination to seek the resolution of the Palestine problem outside the framework of the United Nations, where the USSR, by virtue of its membership and its veto power in the Security Council, could be expected to play a major part. To outmaneuver the Western nations, the Kremlin embarked upon a two-pronged operation. Publicly, it kept insisting that the United Nations was the only legitimate international body empowered to deliberate and settle the future of the former League of Nations mandate. Secretly, and despite official denials, the Soviet government sanctioned emigration of tens of thousands of East European Jews to the Western zones of Germany and Austria. Their determination to proceed to Palestine and their wholehearted commitment to the idea of a Jewish state were correctly judged by Stalin as precluding a peaceful resolution of the Palestine problem. In February, 1947, confounded by its failure to settle the conflict between the Arab and Jewish communities, Great Britain referred the issue to the United Nations. In so doing, London provided the USSR with the long-sought opportunity to project itself into the unfolding dispute.

Once on center stage, the Kremlin was faced with the tactical choice of which of the two local communities it was going to support. It was an easy decision to make. As seen from Moscow in 1946–47, the Soviet Union's chief international rivals seemed to be either dragging their feet (the United States) or hostile to Zionist aspirations (Great Britain). London, in fact, appeared to be backing the Arabs, as evidenced by its refusal to cooperate with the United Nations in the implementation of the November, 1947, partition resolution. In view of these considerations, the only sensible course of action for the USSR to follow was to support the Yishuv. It did so in November, 1947, by voting in favor of UNSCOP's majority proposal and by continuing to insist that partition of Palestine be carried into effect under the supervision of the United Nations. Once the state of Israel was proclaimed, on May 15, 1948, the Soviet Union was the first great power to offer it *de jure* recognition.[34] Moscow continued its moral, political, and military support until Israel's existence was no longer in doubt. (It should be noted in passing that the Zionists, because of the arms embargo imposed by the Western powers, had no choice but to seek Soviet assistance. This coincidence of their respective short-term interests goes a long way in explaining Moscow/Yishuv/Israeli relations between late 1947 and 1949.) This backing, without which Israel might not have survived, consisted of continued encouragement and facilitation of the emigration to Palestine of large numbers of East European Jews (many with military experience).[35] Last but by no means least, the Kremlin, through Czechoslovakia, supplied the Yishuv with the war materiel required to repel the attacks by the neighboring Arab states.

It should be noted that Stalin's short-term objective of eliminating the British presence in Palestine was reinforced by broader, longer-range considerations. To begin with, events in Palestine were probably seen in Moscow as initiating and expediting the British withdrawal from the Middle East. In addition, London's eviction from an important military and political position provided another graphic illustration of the growing weakness of the British Empire.[36] As such, it could only encourage other colonies and dependencies to intensify their efforts aimed at effecting the evacuation of any foreign presence from their territories. In retrospect, these Soviet expectations proved to be well founded.

Moreover, the Kremlin might have anticipated that the establishment of Israel would set in motion two additional processes that, in the long run, were likely to undermine the "capitalist" positions in the Middle East. On the one hand, Arab nationalist resentment would be directed not only against the USSR and the West but also against the traditional governments of the Arab states, which had proved themselves unable to prevent the creation of Israel. On the other hand, the events of 1947−48 would set in motion a drawn-out process of regional strife and turmoil with the young Jewish state pitted against its Arab neighbors. Either way, in the long run, the emergence of Israel could be expected to provide the USSR with new opportunities to play an active role in the politics of the Middle East. It was probably with such possibilities in mind that Gromyko, in his speech of November, 1947, encouraged the Arabs to look to Moscow in their future dealings with the Western powers.

Regional incentives were supplemented by wider international concerns. As noted, Britain's withdrawal from Palestine of necessity affected the future of the entire Empire: indeed, it proved to be a major milestone in its ultimate dissolution. Moreover, Stalin's activism in Palestine also served as an illustration of the extent of the deterioration of Soviet-American relations. It will be recalled that, in the spring of 1947, the United States had replaced Great Britain as the dominant Western power in the Eastern Mediterranean. (This was accomplished by means of the Truman Doctrine, which guaranteed the territorial integrity and security of Greece and Turkey against possible Soviet designs.) Coupled with the Marshall Plan for the economic reconstruction of Europe, President Truman's initiative reflected the growing estrangement between Washington and Moscow. For its part, the Kremlin contributed to the division of the world into two hostile camps by setting up the Communist Information Bureau (Cominform) and by consolidating Soviet control over Eastern Europe.[37]

Yaacov Ro'i has argued convincingly that, in view of the rapidly deteriorating international situation, the handling of the Palestinian problem acquired added importance—Soviet support of the Zionist cause was also designed to win for Moscow the goodwill of the "progressive elements" in the West. Specifically, "the Jews as a traditionally non-conformist element and an influential group in Western and particularly American society and politics were an obvious target for Soviet propaganda." Seen in this context, Stalin's backing of the Yishuv and the endorsement of Israel were probably intended "to prove to . . . [the Jews of the Western world] that . . . [the USSR] represented the force of progress and anti-racialism and to enlist their support in the East-West confrontation."[38]

Whatever the Kremlin's intermediate and long-range expectations might have been, however, it is obvious that, in 1947–48, short-term considerations were of the utmost importance to Stalin and his colleagues. Moscow's primary objective was to force Great Britain to abandon Palestine. That goal, as argued above, was most likely to be achieved by supporting Jewish aspirations for a state in Palestine. Yet, while the Yishuv's and the Kremlin's short-range interests thus converged, accounting for their cooperation and for the eventual success of their respective policies, their long-term interests were *not* complementary.

Once Israel's survival had been secured, it was well understood in Tel Aviv and elsewhere that the country's economic needs as well as long-range security could be guaranteed only through cooperation with the Western powers. The Kremlin, too, was under no illusion that its relations with Israel would remain intimate for any protracted period. In addition to domestic considerations (the creation of Israel had an electrifying effect on the Soviet Union's large Jewish community), Moscow was well aware that its major long-term regional objective—namely, the weakening of Western influence in the Middle East—could be best achieved by supporting the nationalist aspirations of those Arab states that refused to associate themselves closely with Great Britain and the United States and insisted on pursuing an independent course in regional and world politics.

In retrospect, it would appear that Stalin's handling of the Palestine problem was one of his most successful foreign political ventures. On the tactical level, the Kremlin conducted a skillful policy designed to bring that complex issue before the United Nations (particularly the Security Council) and to keep it there until it was resolved to Soviet satisfaction. In the process, Moscow succeeded in neutralizing London's and Washington's efforts to circumvent the international organization with the view to excluding the USSR from active participation in the resolution of the Palestine impasse.[39] The Kremlin thus found itself in a situation, rare in the early annals of the United Nations, of serving as a protagonist of a cause that enjoyed the support of a majority of the UN members but was opposed by Great Britain and, on occasion, by the United States. In the end, as noted earlier, Stalin's efforts were crowned with success.

On a broader, regional plane, Moscow's policy was equally effective. While the Kremlin's strategic goal of weakening Western influence in the Middle East remained constant, Soviet tactics in the Arab East, as outlined above, underwent a major change. Disregarding traditional Communist hostility to Zionism and the early post–World War II backing of Arab nationalist aspirations (Syria, Lebanon, Egypt), Stalin shifted to a position of support for the Yishuv's drive for an independent Jewish state. As a result, the USSR achieved its immediate as well as long-range regional objectives. Great Britain was driven out of Palestine, an important step in the direction of undermining its position in the Middle East. In addition, the establishment of Israel helped stimulate political unrest in most Arab countries and ensured continuing hostility between the Jewish state and its neighbors. The regional turmoil that followed could not but seriously affect the Western presence in the Middle East. It also provided the Soviets with new opportunities to pursue their own objectives. In a major tactical switch, effected in 1955, Moscow once again bestowed its blessings on Arab nationalist aspirations, a stance maintained to the present day.

## Notes

1. Defensively, the territory constituted a vital "buffer zone," separating the USSR proper from the Western powers, above all the United States, entrenched in Western Europe. Offensively, a large-scale Soviet military presence in the satellite states, particularly in East Germany, would be useful in any possible future attempt to conquer Western Europe.

2. Control over Port Arthur and Dairen in southern Manchuria provided the Soviet Pacific fleet with access to the kind of ice-free ports long coveted by the Russian navy. Equally welcome was the annexation of the southern Kuriles and the southern part of Sakhalin.

3. The Red Army had occupied northern Iran in 1941 as a result of a wartime agreement negotiated with Great Britain. The purpose of the accord (and occupation) was to facilitate the delivery of the U.S. lend-lease aid to the beleaguered USSR. For more details, see George Lenczowski, *Russia and the West in Iran, 1918–1948: A Study in Big-Power Rivalry* (Ithaca: Cornell University Press, 1949), chaps. 8–11. For a detailed account of wartime and early postwar Soviet, British, and U.S. interaction in Turkey, Iran, and Greece, see Bruce R. Kuniholm, *The Origins of the Cold War in the Near East: Great Power Conflict and Diplomacy in Iran, Turkey, and Greece* (Princeton: Princeton University Press, 1980). See also André Fontaine, *History of the Cold War from the October Revolution to the Korean War, 1917–1950* (London: Secker and Warburg, 1965), chap. 14.

4. Refusal to permit Russian expansion applied not only to Turkey and Iran but also to the former Italian colonies that Moscow had sought to administer in the early postwar period (see Kuniholm, *Origins of the Cold War*, pp. 269 and 351; see also Fontaine, *History of the Cold War*, pp. 296–97).

5. For more details, see Lenczowski, *Russia and the West in Iran*, chap. 11, and Kuniholm, *Origins of the Cold War*, pp. 383–99.

6. Yaacov Ro'i, *Soviet Decision Making in Practice: The USSR and Israel, 1947–1954* (New Brunswick, N.J.: Transaction Books, 1980), p. 16.

7. "Memorandum of Conversation by Mr. Evan M. Wilson of the Division of Near Eastern Affairs" with Dr. Nahum Goldmann, held in Washington on June 20, 1945, *Foreign Relations of the United States, 1945*, VIII, p. 712.

8. See Ro'i, *Soviet Decision Making*, pp. 15–16.

9. Ibid., p. 17.

10. For details, see J. C. Hurewitz, *The Struggle for Palestine* (New York: W. W. Norton, 1950), chap. 18.

11. See K. Serezhin, "The Problems of the Arab East," *New Times* (February 1, 1946), 23–27. For more details, see Roʾi, *Soviet Decision Making,* pp. 23–25.

12. On February 9, 1946, Stalin, in a major speech, argued that the "world capitalist system" had been responsible for the outbreak of two world wars and was now setting the stage for the third. He also referred to "capitalist encirclement" of the USSR as a threat to the country's security (text in *Pravda,* February 10, 1946).

13. For details, see V. B. Lutskii, *Liga arabskikh gosudarstv* and *Palestinskaia problema* (both published in Moscow by Vsesoiuznoe lektsionnoe biuro, 1946). See also P. V. Milogradov, *Arabskii Vostok v mezhdunarodnykh otnosheniiakh* (same publisher and date).

14. For more details, see Roʾi, *Soviet Decision Making,* pp. 25–33.

15. Ibid., p. 33.

16. For more details, see ibid., pp. 36–38.

17. Ibid., p. 46. For more details, see ibid., pp. 46–50.

18. Hurewitz, *Struggle for Palestine,* p. 273.

19. Text in *Izvestiia* (May 11, 1947).

20. Hurewitz, *Struggle for Palestine,* p. 285.

21. Text in United Nations, General Assembly, *Official Records: First Special Session,* 77th Plenary Meeting, May 14, 1957, I, pp. 127–35.

22. See, for example, *Pravda* (September 30, 1946). For some details, see Arnold Krammer, *The Forgotten Friendship: Israel and the Soviet Bloc, 1947–53* (Urbana: University of Illinois Press, 1974), p. 19.

23. Nevertheless, "the Soviets were careful from May to September 1947 to make no further commitment concerning their ideas on Palestine's political future" (Yaacov Roʾi, "The Soviet Union, Israel and the Arab-Israeli Conflict," in Michael Confino and Shimon Shamir, eds., *The U.S.S.R. and the Middle East* [New York: John Wiley, 1973], p. 126).

24. United Nations, *Official Records: Second Session, Ad Hoc Committee on the Palestine Question,* October 13, 1947, pp. 69–71.

25. See, for example, "Excerpts from the Minutes of the Sixth Meeting of the United States Delegation to the Second Session of the General Assembly," held in New York on September 15, 1947. Asked by Mrs. Roosevelt "whether it was really evident . . . that the U.S.S.R. would be opposed to the majority report . . . [the secretary of state] replied that this was the assumption, since the case offered such a fine opportunity for the Soviets to carry out their ends regarding the Arabs, for the sake of expediency" (*Foreign Relations of the United States, 1947,* V, p. 1148). See also ibid., pp. 1169 and 1183.

26. United Nations, General Assembly, *Official Records: Second Session,* 125th Plenary Meeting, November 26, 1947, pp. 1360–61.

27. For more details, see Hurewitz, *Struggle for Palestine,* chap. 23.

28. For more details, see Avigdor Dagan, *Moscow and Jerusalem* (New York: Abelard-Schuman, 1970), pp. 28–30, and Roʾi, *Soviet Decision Making,* pp. 109–31.

29. Roʾi, *Soviet Decision Making*, p. 132.

30. For more details, see ibid., pp. 141–46.

31. For more details, see ibid., pp. 144–45 and 149–59. See also the study by Krammer, *Forgotten Friendship*.

32. See Krammer, *Forgotten Friendship*, esp. pp. 77–82, and Roʾi, *Soviet Decision Making*, pp. 151–52.

33. As quoted in Roʾi, *Soviet Decision Making*, p. 149.

34. Nadav Safran, "The Soviet Union and Israel, 1947–69," in Ivo J. Lederer and Wayne S. Vucinich, eds., *The Soviet Union and the Middle East: The Post–World War II Era* (Stanford, Calif.: Hoover Institution Press, 1974), p. 161.

35. See Krammer, *Forgotten Friendship*, chap. 5.

36. Before Palestine, Great Britain had withdrawn from India, Pakistan, Ceylon, and Burma. It had also relinquished to the United States the responsibility of supporting Greece and Turkey against Communist subversion and Soviet attack.

37. For some details, see Marshall D. Shulman, *Stalin's Foreign Policy Reappraised* (Cambridge: Harvard University Press, 1963), esp. pp. 14–16. For an opposing, "harder line" evaluation of Stalin's motives, see Adam Ulam, *Expansion and Coexistence* (New York: Praeger, 1969), pp. 423–39.

38. Roʾi, *Soviet Decision Making*, p. 74.

39. One may only wonder about the extent of the contribution that such spies as Maclean, Burgess, and Philby made to the success of Soviet policy in the UN and elsewhere. It does, however, stand to reason that information on major Western moves was available to Moscow, enabling it to calculate its responses in advance. Thus, though basic premises of Soviet policy are not likely to have been affected in any major way, the information secured from foreign sources no doubt facilitated the task of staying on top of the unfolding events. The situation may perhaps be compared with a chess game in which one player is aware of the opponent's next move before it is made.

# The Zionist Perspective

*Michael J. Cohen*

## Postwar Diplomacy

In the Biltmore resolution of May, 1942, the Zionists had demanded, for the first time in their history, the establishment of a Jewish commonwealth in all of western Palestine, as part of the new world order that should arise after the war.[1] The Biltmore program had been affirmed *before* the Jews, or the world at large, had learned of the extent and nature of Hitler's "final solution" to the Jewish problem. This program remained official Zionist policy until August, 1946, when an extraordinary session of the Jewish Agency Executive, meeting in Paris, agreed to compromise, and to partition Palestine into Jewish and Arab states.

At the conclusion of the war in Europe, and once the full scale of the Holocaust was universally understood, following the liberation of the concentration and death camps, the Zionists assumed, *ipso facto*, that enlightened world opinion would recognize the legitimacy of their demand for a Jewish state in Palestine. They influenced the official American investigation of the refugee situation in Europe by Earl Harrison. Harrison's recommendation that 100,000 Jewish refugees be admitted immediately into Palestine was adopted by President Truman.

Many Zionists at the time, and since, did not appreciate (or chose not to) that Truman's efforts were directed more to relieving a humanitarian problem in Europe (and thereby giving gratification to an important ethnic minority in the United States) than to transforming the political disposition of Palestine. The Zionists failed to see that the gentile world had not drawn the same conclusions they had from the decimation of the Jewish people during the war. In London, Foreign Secretary Ernest Bevin argued, with a certain logic, that the war against fascism had been fought precisely in order to make Europe a place where all minorities, including the Jews, might henceforth live in peace. If Bevin's personal disposition toward the Jews was suspect, then what were the Zionists to make of the views of one of their ostensibly strongest supporters, Winston Churchill? In August, 1946, as leader of His Majesty's Opposition, Churchill told the House of Commons: "No one can imagine that there is room in Palestine for the great masses of Jews who wish to leave Europe, or that they could be absorbed in any period which it is now useful to contemplate."[2]

The Zionist campaign for a Jewish state was fought after the war along two complementary axes. First, there was the diplomatic activity, designed to bring universal political support for Zionist demands, which focused on London and Washington. Second, there was a campaign of nationwide, including urban, violence conducted against the mandatory in Palestine itself, designed to wring political concessions from the British, at a minimum, or to precipitate their complete withdrawal, at a maximum.

In the English capital, where supreme executive control over Palestine was exercised, Dr. Chaim Weizmann, the Zionist elder statesman, now a semi-invalid, was deeply disillusioned. Since the issue of the Balfour Declaration in 1917, which many Jews regarded as his own personal diplomatic triumph, Weizmann had aligned Zionist fortunes with the British. But the Churchill government had offered little more than encouragement, and glittering promises for the future, which remained unfulfilled after the war. Churchill's administration had done little or nothing to rescue European Jewry during the war, and after it Churchill himself had procrastinated when Weizmann reminded him of his promise to grant the Jews a "generous partition" once the Nazis were defeated.

When, in July, 1945, the Labour party defeated the Conservatives, the former soon demonstrated that their preelection manifesto, promising to set up a Jewish state in all of western Palestine (and, to the embarrassment of the Zionists, even to arrange for the migration of Palestine's Arabs to neighboring countries), had been just so much election propaganda. The novel, blunt style of Ernest Bevin was soon put down to crass anti-Semitism, and the Zionists felt even more the need to cultivate those they still regarded as their friends. Thus, notwithstanding severe criticism of Churchill leveled at private meetings, the Zionists determined not to attack him in public.

The Zionist attitude toward Bevin himself was ambivalent. On the one hand, like Bevin's own officials at the Foreign Office, the Zionists, too, developed a healthy respect for the foreign secretary's natural intelligence and his obvious power within the British Cabinet. On the other, they were dismayed and disgusted by his insensitivity to Jewish suffering in Europe. They adopted a smear campaign designed to discredit the government's Palestine policy as deriving primarily from Bevin's own personal animus toward the Jews. It was a smear that Bevin himself obligingly lived up to, with undiplomatic asides about the Jews "pushing to the head of the queue" (of refugees in Europe), and about New York's Jews pressing for Palestine as the central refuge for the Jewish refugees, since they did not want to take in their brethren in the United States.

One example, perhaps the most outstanding and the most successful, of a Zionist campaign in which a humanitarian cause was freely mixed with politics and a preconceived publicity campaign was the *Exodus* affair. In July, 1947, the Zionists dispatched from France some 4,500 Jewish refugees to Palestine, on board a Chesapeake Bay steamer, aptly renamed *Exodus 1947*. The steamer was tracked by the British navy and, when still outside Palestine's territorial waters, boarded by British marines. In the bloody fight that ensued, which was reported live to the world by Haganah transmitters, many injuries and some fatalities occurred. The Jewish captain of the ship believed that he could still make it to the Palestine beaches and land his complement. In contrast, as recent research has revealed, the British commander was at the point of giving up. At this point, the Jewish Agency authorities in Tel Aviv ordered the captain to surrender and to allow himself to be towed into Haifa harbor.

The Jewish Agency was undoubtedly concerned with averting further casualties, securing quick medical treatment for the wounded, and perhaps preventing the *Exodus* from capsizing. However, it also wished to extract the maximum publicity from the spectacle bound to ensue at Haifa, where Agency representatives treated members of the United Nations Special Committee on Palestine to a firsthand view, blow by blow, of British immigration policy. The whole affair, from the first engagement on board ship to the final manhandling of the refugees by British soldiers at Hamburg and their transfer to camps in the British-occupied zone of Germany, was conveyed to the world by a well-oiled publicity machine. The British, and Bevin in particular, were outmaneuvered at every step, and the inhumanity of Britain's Palestine policy, in its refugee aspect, was indelibly inscribed on world public opinion.[3]

During the war there had existed a certain parallel between the Weizmann/Churchill nexus in London and the Stephen Wise/Roosevelt relationship in Washington. For over a decade, American Jewry had adhered faithfully, predictably, almost automatically to the Democratic party, and to President Roosevelt personally. The latter's untimely death, in April, 1945, perhaps saved him from an inquest similar to that performed on Churchill by the Zionists in London. (Roosevelt's policies toward the Jews have since come under the censure of historians.)[4] His successor, Harry S Truman, was granted a period of grace, which he seized upon only too eagerly, going out of his way to publicize his concern for the Jewish survivors of the Holocaust.

However, the great difference in the United States was the rise to prominence in the Zionist movement of Rabbi Abba Hillel Silver, a Republican in his domestic politics. Silver revolutionized American Jewish politics when he made Zionism into a vote-catching issue. Silver had not pressed Roosevelt over the rescue of Jews during the war, but—whether by sure instinct or sheer coincidence—he perceived quite early that Truman, an unelected, insecure president, was highly anxious and apprehensive about the Jewish vote. Silver's public protests against American collusion in Bevin's anti-Zionist policies eventually made him *persona non grata* at the White House. Truman suspected, not entirely without grounds, that Silver's direction of the Zionist lobby was also motivated by his domestic political inclinations.

Fascinating corroboration of the reputed power of the Zionist lobby at that time has been provided recently by the memoirs of Eliahu Elath (then called Eliahu Epstein), at the time head of the Zionist office in Washington and destined to become Israel's first ambassador to the United States. Elath has revealed how the Russians, too, tried to secure the services of the Zionist lobby. During the early months of 1948 the Russians became concerned that the American retreat from partition, and their trusteeship proposal, might delay the British exit from Palestine. Therefore, Russian diplomats in the American capital, including Andrei Gromyko himself, approached the Zionists and urged them repeatedly to activate their lobby at the White House in order to block the State Department's initiatives.[5]

## Revolt in Palestine

The Yishuv (the Jewish community in Palestine) emerged from the war traumatized. It experienced an overwhelming sense of helplessness and vulnerability in regard to the fate of the Jewish people during the war. Hitler had carried out his extermination of the Jewish people relatively undisturbed, and the Yishuv itself watched, helpless, as Rommel twice almost conquered Egypt and threatened Palestine itself. Both in Europe and in Palestine, the Jews' fate had been determined for them by other nations, who possessed one attribute the Jews had yet to secure—sovereignty. The lesson was quite clear, and, as noted above, the conclusion was already drawn by May, 1942, in the Biltmore program.

In July, 1943, Churchill had appointed a Cabinet committee to formulate a plan for Palestine's future after the war. He had stipulated that the solution be based on the principle of partition. But in November, 1944, following the assassination of the minister of state, Lord Moyne, in Cairo, Churchill had halted all further consideration of the issue (the committee's partition plan was already drafted and tabled for the Cabinet agenda). Weizmann and Jewish Agency leaders in Palestine determined to root out the terrorists from their midst. In what became known as the *saison* (literally, the hunting season), Haganah forces tracked down the dissident forces, imprisoned some, and handed others over to the British. However, Zionist hopes that this campaign would reconcile Churchill's administration proved misplaced. The *saison* ground to a halt in May, 1945, as the Jewish Agency failed to produce any tangible political reward for its collaboration.[6]

After the war, Churchill's indifference, and Bevin's blatantly anti-Zionist policies, provoked a radical change of policy in Palestine.[7] Unknown to Weizmann, in October, 1945, Ben-Gurion authorized the start of a coordinated *meri ivri* (Hebrew revolt) against the British in Palestine. The Haganah joined in uneasy alliance with Menachem Begin's Irgun in a concerted effort to coerce the British back into a pro-Zionist line. With the British base along the Suez Canal in doubt, the Haganah tried to demonstrate by nationwide operations that the Jews were capable of sabotaging or neutralizing any strategic assets that Palestine might offer. In contrast, the Irgun, in classical terrorist tradition, planned punitive operations aimed at forcing the British to evacuate, by raising the price of holding on to Palestine beyond that which the government would be able or willing to pay.

The revolt began on the last night of October, 1945, with a meticulously planned operation that at one stroke sabotaged the British railway system in Palestine in 153 different places. The Irgun, and the more radical splinter group, Lehi (headed by later prime minister Yitschak Shamir), destroyed rolling stock and locomotives. Two police launches (used for tracking down the ships that brought in "illegal" Jewish immigrants) and the Haifa oil refineries also sustained damage. The *Times* of London recognized that the entire operation, which dislocated British logistics in Palestine but resulted in very little loss of life, was an elegantly executed demonstration of Jewish power.

There is some irony in the fact that Ben-Gurion launched this revolt at the very time when, unknown to him, the British were negotiating with the Americans the appointment of a joint committee of inquiry into the Jewish refugee problem and the option of resettling some of them in Palestine. One may speculate that, had the Zionist leadership known that the Americans were about to become involved, the first operation of their revolt might have been delayed. Their second, and last large-scale, operation in June, 1946, destroyed at one blow all the land bridges connecting Palestine with its neighbors. The "night of the bridges" reflected the Zionists' disappointment with the Anglo-American Committee report and was intended to serve as a further warning to Britain, which had just made a unilateral offer to the Egyptians to evacuate the Canal base.

Nevertheless, in early 1946 the Zionist leadership was already moving inexorably, if as yet unofficially, from Biltmore to partition. Its hands were being forced by two complementary developments. First, the Anglo-American Committee recommended against the establishment of either a Jewish or an Arab state in Palestine; and second, President Truman, who was either unable or unwilling to secure the entry of the 100,000 from the British (except within the frame of a comprehensive political settlement), was tiring of the whole problem and about to throw in his hand.

Zionist historiography has blamed the British, and Bevin personally, for sabotaging the Anglo-American report, with its allegedly favorable proposals. However, as admitted within Zionist councils at the time, the report would indefinitely have denied the Zionists the sovereignty they so desperately sought. In return, they might have secured the immigration of the 100,000 refugees, but what then? By the summer of 1946 the number of Jewish refugees in Allied DP camps had risen to over 250,000. Could the Zionists have simply abandoned the others, and could the Yishuv have survived with the addition of just 100,000 more immigrants?

The revolt in Palestine, far from yielding the desired political rewards, very nearly brought disaster upon the Yishuv. The Haganah's attack on Palestine's land bridges precipitated a British counterattack. Early on the Sabbath morning, June 29, 1946, some 17,000 British troops swooped down in a nationwide search-and-arrest operation. Some 2,700 Jews were detained, including most of the Jewish Agency Executive and a large part of the Haganah command. The Yishuv was stunned, believing that the British operation had paralyzed its defense forces and removed its leaders with a view to replacing them with British stooges. Although he refused to become a Zionist Pétain, Weizmann warned his colleagues that their revolt, instead of wringing political concessions from the British, was now threatening them with a premature, full-scale military conflict with the wrong enemy, the far superior military forces of the British army. Under the pressure of Weizmann's ultimatum and resignation threat, the Jewish Agency called off its revolt. The Haganah never again attacked British forces during the course of the mandate.

The Irgun carried out one further operation, intended as a reprisal for the British attack of June 29. On July 22, 1946, Irgun forces penetrated the King David Hotel in Jerusalem, the nerve center of the British civil and military administration in Palestine. They planted explosive charges that destroyed an entire wing of the hotel. Despite telephone warnings to evacuate (historical controversy surrounds the arrival time and reaction to these warnings), over ninety men and women in the hotel at the time lost their lives. The King David explosion caused grave political harm to the Zionist cause, just when the Americans and the British were about to agree on a plan for granting provincial autonomy to Palestine (the so-called Morrison-Grady plan). In Palestine itself, the tragedy produced a universal reaction and revulsion and provided the opportunity, even necessity, for the Jewish Agency to break off and dissociate itself from its joint revolt with the Irgun.

## The Return to Partition

In August, 1946, the Jewish Agency Executive met in Paris in order to determine future policy. Ben-Gurion was undoubtedly shocked by the turn of events in Palestine, which—during his own absence abroad—had quite evidently drifted out of control, far beyond anything he himself had contemplated. He agreed to terminate operations against the British, if only to avert further counterblows, which might uncover additional arms caches of the Haganah and even disclose the large-scale arms-smuggling operation it was conducting. All this would have had a disastrous effect on the Yishuv's capacity to withstand the assault that, in his opinion, would inevitably be launched by the Arabs.

Although Ben-Gurion had long ago arrived at the practical conclusion that the Zionists would have to make political compromises, he himself, due to internal party politics, was unwilling to initiate— or even associate himself publicly with—the retreat from Biltmore. One of the most interesting features of Zionist diplomacy during this period was the emergence of Dr. Nahum Goldmann from the second to the first ranks of Zionist diplomacy. In the vacuum left by Ben-Gurion, Goldmann was afforded the opportunity to make his diplomatic debut, one he exploited to the maximum.

In Washington, Truman had tended, initially, to accept the Morrison-Grady plan. But he was forced by the Zionist lobby to hold up his assent. Their pressures left him bitter and frustrated, in despair of ever finding a way out of the Palestine impasse. He told a visiting delegation that he was sick of the way the Jews were trying to "run this country." In Paris, Goldmann told his colleagues on the Agency Executive that he had just received a transatlantic telephone call from David Niles, Truman's aide on Zionist affairs. Niles cautioned that unless the Zionists could produce a reasonable compromise soon, the president would "wash his hands" of the whole business. Goldmann warned: "Unless we are ready to tell the President that we are ready to accept the Jewish State in an adequate part of Palestine, it is no use going to Washington and trying to obtain these improvements. I felt for years that partition of Palestine is the only way out. Biltmore is no realistic policy at the moment, because we have no Jewish majority and we cannot wait until we have a majority to get the State."[8]

American pressure on the British, if it could be secured, was regarded by the Zionists as their strongest—if not their only remaining—trump card. Goldmann proposed that he fly to Washington, in mid-session of the Executive, in order to secure presidential support for partition.

Many members of the Executive who in 1937 had opposed the partition plan proposed by the Peel Commission now confessed to "a harrowing sense of guilt," for, had they secured their own state before the war, it could have provided a refuge for many of those Jews who instead had perished in Hitler's death camps. For many, the fate of the Jewish DPs, now about to spend a second postwar winter in makeshift camps in Europe, was their prime concern. Any plan, even the provincial autonomy proposed by the Morrison-Grady scheme, would expedite the migration of 100,000 refugees and was therefore preferable to chimeras about sovereignty over all of western Palestine.

Ben-Gurion himself apparently did not vote for Goldmann's mission. But he abstained, knowing only too well that the mission would be approved by a comfortable majority. He also appreciated that Goldmann's own proposals were tantamount to an acceptance of provincial autonomy as an interim formula leading, hopefully, to partition.[9]

Some Zionist leaders, notably Moshe Sneh (until recently head of the Haganah National Command) and Abba Hillel Silver, regarded the Executive's agreement to negotiate partition as a colossal blunder, which amounted to bartering away their bargaining position in advance. They feared, with good reason, that the "moderates"—men like Goldmann, Eliezer Kaplan (Jewish Agency treasurer), and Moshe Shertok (later Sharett, Israel's first foreign secretary)—were willing to compromise still further and settle for provincial autonomy.

Dr. Goldmann stayed in Washington from August 6 to 11, 1946. His most important talks were held with Under Secretary of State Dean Acheson. Goldmann later reported to his colleagues that he had secured American, indeed presidential, support for partition. But he proved unable ever to translate this claim into the hard currency of political pressure on the British. On the contrary, Acheson's own record of their meetings shows quite clearly that Goldmann had stated that the Morrison-Grady plan was preferable to the Anglo-American report, "because it at least looked towards partition." It was Acheson's impression that Goldmann's new proposals boiled down to the demand for improvements on the provincial autonomy plan.[10]

Upon his return to Paris, where the Jewish Agency Executive was still convened, Goldmann led his colleagues to believe that he had made a significant breakthrough in Washington, and that they might now look forward to American pressure on the British to agree to partition. But Goldmann's diplomatic style presumed a divine monopoly of political wisdom and a mission to guide less-endowed protagonists to a reasonable compromise. His tactics of disinformation and subterfuge would result in further confusion.

**The Yom Kippur Statement**

The Americans did *not* publicly support partition prior to October, 1947, nor did they ever attempt to coerce the British into doing so. On October 4, 1946, President Truman made his celebrated Yom Kippur statement, on the eve of the mid-term congressional elections. It was widely believed at the time, and is said in many history books, to have registered presidential support for the partition of Palestine. The moderates in the Zionist camp chose to regard the statement as a vindication of Goldmann's diplomacy.

Truman's motives do not fall within the range of this chapter, but quite clearly the desire to poll the Jewish vote in the imminent elections took a high priority. What is important to note here, from the Zionist perspective, is that President Truman did *not* in fact endorse the Zionists' partition plan. While suggesting that public opinion in the United States might favor partition, the president himself expressed a preference for a compromise between the British proposal (provincial autonomy) and that of the Zionists: "I cannot believe that the gap between the proposals which have been put forward is too great to be bridged by men of reason and goodwill. To such a solution our Government could give its support."[11]

It was in Truman's own political interest to foster the popular belief that he had declared in favor of partition. Equally, it was in the Zionists' interest not to confute such beliefs. The statement certainly left an indelible impression on the British, although it still failed to generate the results hoped for by the Zionists.

Zionist executives in Washington appreciated only too well the real significance of the Yom Kippur statement, since they themselves had supplied the original draft to the White House. Truman had passed on the Zionist draft to the State Department, where, quite predictably, it had been watered down by the insertion of the phrase "bridging the gap" between the British and the Zionist proposals. On the morrow of the statement, Eliahu Epstein had registered his disappointment to David Niles. Niles retorted that the main thing was that most people had *understood* the president's statement as being in support of partition. Epstein agreed that most of the press had headlined their reports "Truman's Support of a Jewish State."[12] (A further pertinent point, rarely observed, is that in the Yom Kippur statement Truman failed to urge the migration of the 100,000 but spoke instead, vaguely, of "substantial immigration.")

Rabbi Silver, who all along had objected to Goldmann's diplomatic lead, handed in his resignation as head of the American Zionist movement. He termed the Yom Kippur statement bluntly "a smart pre-election move" that had been extracted prematurely from the White House. Silver predicted that the president would cash in at the elections on whatever goodwill the statement had generated, and then would be content to let the matter drop, as he "has done time and again in the past after similar maneuvers on the eve of elections."[13]

The Yom Kippur statement was Truman's last declaration on Palestine for more than a year. When in January, 1947, Moshe Shertok asked the State Department to take part in the last Arab/Zionist/British conference to be convened on Palestine, his request was flatly rejected. Likewise, Truman maintained his absolute refusal to receive any Zionist lobbyists at the White House.

### The Zionist Perspective on the British Evacuation

At the first Zionist Congress to be convened after the war, in Basel in December, 1946, Dr. Chaim Weizmann was deposed as head of the World Zionist Organization. In deference to the elder statesman, no president was elected in his place. An "unholy coalition" of Ben-Gurion and Silver now ruled the Zionist movement—a social democrat and a right-wing conservative, controlling a powerful constituency in Palestine and in the United States, respectively. Weizmann was deposed on a vote against his appeal to attend the London conference without prior conditions (i.e., an advance British commitment to partition). However, the Zionist leaders informed the British that, whereas they were bound by the Congress decision not to attend the conference "officially," they would be willing to attend "unofficial" private talks.

Despite their public image of self-assurance and outward calm, neither Ben-Gurion nor Silver took any comfort in the prospect of an early British withdrawal from Palestine. The prospect of anarchy and civil war, following a premature, precipitate British exit, was not one that any responsible leader could have wished for. When Bevin attended the United Nations General Assembly in New York, in November, 1946, Silver had approached him with a view to extracting some assurance, even if confidential, that the British would be willing to discuss partition. Bevin had retorted that he doubted if the Arabs would ever agree to partition. Undoubtedly still laboring under the impression of the Yom Kippur statement, Bevin stated that he now believed that the best thing would be to offer the mandate to the Americans and, if they did not want it, to let the United Nations decide what was best for Palestine. Silver winced at the latter remark.[14] Similarly, two months later, in February, 1947, when the London conference stood on the brink of failure, Ben-Gurion sought a private meeting with Bevin and implored him to continue with the mandate.[15]

The prospect of British withdrawal was apparently so awful to contemplate that some Zionist leaders, Ben-Gurion especially, simply refused to believe that it would happen, notwithstanding repeated British declarations to that effect. They believed, as many Zionist historians have reiterated since, that the British referral to the United Nations in February, 1947, was simply a machiavellian maneuver calculated to cause the international body to prick its fingers badly on this thorny, intractable problem, so much so that it would ultimately, with great relief, hand Palestine back to the British, to do with as they pleased.

This thesis was given an aura of orthodoxy and credibility by one of the Zionist diplomats of the time, David Horowitz (later an influential governor of the Bank of Israel), who later recorded being told by Harold Beeley that, due to the inevitable East-West fissure at the United Nations, the Zionists would never secure the required majority for partition.[16] A later version of this same thesis maintained that the British, during the course of their evacuation, colluded with the Arabs in order to cause maximum Jewish casualties, designed to evoke frantic appeals from the Yishuv for a British rescue effort, again on the latter's own terms.

As late as February, 1948, a Jewish Agency official was dispatched to London with the specific mission of unearthing Britain's real intentions. His first report, dated February 15, referred to a Foreign Office plot to permit considerable Arab penetration into Palestine and to sabotage military preparations by the Jews. However, his final report, of March 7, reassured his colleagues in Palestine that the British would not condone any action against the United Nations partition plan; nor would the British help the Arabs against the Jews.[17]

Ben-Gurion either did not receive or did not believe this last report. On March 8, 1948, he confronted the British high commissioner and told him that he believed it to be the British intention to sabotage the United Nations decision by political means. Three days later, Ben-Gurion wired his personal assessment of the situation to Moshe Shertok, then in New York:

> It is becoming clear that the termination of the Mandate [May 15] means merely giving up any formal obligation and responsibility under national or international law, leaving free arbitrary [hand] for British troops for indefinite period in indefinite areas of the country. Further sabotaging UN policy, helping Arab League in carrying out its designs against [Jews] British troops retaining not only port in Haifa, but . . . possibly also port of Tel Aviv and any other place, crippling thereby independence Jewish State [while] leaving full scope invading [armies] to exterminate Yishuv. These dangers must be brought immediately to the attention UN authorities and US Government.[18]

## The UN Partition Resolution

The UN partition resolution of November 19, 1947, was a critically important achievement for Zionist diplomacy. It gave the Jews international sanction for the establishment of the state of Israel, even if they needed to resort to arms to realize the resolution. The UN resolution was ultimately also responsible for the aborting of the State Department's trusteeship proposal, advanced publicly for the first time in March, 1948. Given the hostility of the parties concerned to trusteeship, even State Department officials came to appreciate that external armed opposition to Jewish statehood was tantamount to aggression against a United Nations plan.

The November resolution was not entirely the product of Western humanitarianism, nor was its passage exclusively the result of freely expressed concern for a decimated people. Its origin lay in the UNSCOP report, which at the end of August, 1947, had recommended, unanimously, that the British should evacuate Palestine forthwith and that the mandate should be terminated. The campaign of Jewish terror had reached its peak during the summer, with the reprisal hanging of two British sergeants. The *Exodus* affair, already noted, gave the Zionists a major publicity success, which not only helped to offset the revulsion at Jewish terrorist actions, but demonstrated to the world quite clearly to what extent the British had lost control over Palestine.

When the General Assembly opened on September 17, 1947, the American delegation, on instructions, equivocated. The Zionists soon appreciated that, without forthright American support, the solution recommended by the UNSCOP majority report—partition—would not secure the required majority. The Zionists mounted an intensive lobby, via Democratic party channels and their supporters in Congress. During September alone Truman received some forty to fifty appeals from members of Congress pressing him to instruct the American delegation to support partition. When that endorsement was finally announced, on October 11, 1947, Leo Sack, a public relations expert hired by the Zionists in Washington, presented the following sobering assessment of events so far: "We had won a great victory, but under no circumstances should any of us believe or think we had won because of the devotion of the American Government to our cause. We had won because of the sheer pressure of political logistics that was applied by the Jewish leadership in the United States."[19]

But America's public endorsement did not generate American pressure at the United Nations, on its allies and clients. At the end of October, Shertok told Loy Henderson, head of the Office of Near Eastern Affairs at the State Department, that, unless the Americans made their own intentions clear, it was doubtful if the Latin American states would vote for partition. Henderson replied that his government was anxious that the solution be a UN plan and not come to be regarded as "an American solution"; any attempt by the American delegation to "corral" votes for the majority plan by arm-twisting tactics would inevitably leave that impression.[20]

Even with the declared support of both the American and the Soviet delegations, the amended partition plan was adopted only narrowly on November 25, 1947, by the United Nations' Ad Hoc Committee on Palestine with twenty-five votes in favor, thirteen against, with seventeen abstentions. This was just a single vote short of the two-thirds majority required by the United Nations constitution for adoption by the General Assembly. The fact that the required majority was secured at the decisive vote just four days later was due to an unprecedentedly intensive Zionist lobby that finally mobilized, at the eleventh hour, the support of the White House.

Truman denied later that he had taken any hand in the propartition lobby. Indeed, the State Department documents record his instructions to Under Secretary of State Robert Lovett, on November 24, warning against the use of "threats of improper pressure of any kind on other Delegations." Lovett duly instructed the United Nations delegation that, whereas they were voting for the partition plan because it was a majority report, they were not to coerce other delegates to follow their lead.[21]

Witnesses on both the American and the Zionist side have nevertheless established that the White House, with or without the president's personal sanction, *was* involved in a pressure campaign to change the votes of those smaller countries that had either opposed or abstained from the vote on November 25. Three days after the decisive passage of the partition resolution, Michael Comay, in charge of the Jewish Agency's New York office (later an Israeli ambassador to the United Nations), wrote to a friend: "The President became very upset and threw his personal weight behind the effort to get a decision. It was only in the last 48 hours on Friday and Saturday that we got the full backing of the United States."[22]

At the White House, David Niles, who had worked both for Roosevelt and for Truman, was particularly active. Smaller countries, such as the Philippines and Liberia, came in for close attention. Liberia was especially vulnerable, since its economy was dependent upon the export of its rubber to a single company, Firestone. Mobilized by former Under Secretary of State Welles, Harvey Firestone warned President Tubman of Liberia that, unless his country changed its vote to support partition, the company might have to reconsider its plans for extending its holdings there. Liberia duly changed its vote. Several Central American countries were apparently offered heavy money bribes to change their vote.

It should not be assumed that the Zionists and their supporters held any monopoly on "strong-arm" tactics. Since the beginning of the General Assembly, the Arab delegates had warned the Americans frequently that they would defect to the Soviet camp if the United

States voted for partition. The Arab threat fell flat when the Soviets themselves declared in favor of partition in October, 1947. It would seem also that the domestic political influence of the Jewish community outweighed any geo-strategic-economic incentive or leverage that the Arabs could proffer at that time. It should be remembered that the United States was then importing a mere 6 percent of its domestic oil requirements, and just 8.3 percent of that amount originated from the recently developed Saudi oilfields. Ibn Saud himself made it perfectly clear to American diplomats that, quite contrary to what the oil lobby in Washington was telling the State Department, he would *not* impose oil sanctions against the West (thereby depriving himself of sorely needed dollars) due to any differences over Palestine.[23]

## From Trusteeship to Independence

Following the November, 1947, resolution on Palestine, the British ceased to be a determining factor in the solution of the Palestine problem. Zionist leaders may have suspected British motives, or even their intention to leave, but the British government was quite set on extricating its forces with a minimum of political and military loss. Zionist efforts were concentrated in two spheres: on the diplomatic front, in Washington and New York, to prevent the American retreat from partition that had begun on the morrow of the UN resolution; and in Palestine itself, where in the civil war that erupted the infant Jewish army had to demonstrate the Zionists' ability to seize the sovereignty held out, though not guaranteed, by the United Nations.

On March 19, 1948, the American delegate to the United Nations proposed to the Security Council that the partition resolution be suspended, indefinitely, and that Palestine be placed instead under a UN trusteeship until suitable conditions permitted agreement on a permanent solution. Given the efficiency with which the Zionist lobby had worked since 1945—and in particular its crowning achievement, the securing of a two-thirds majority for the partition resolution itself—it may seem at first sight to be incredible that the lobby failed to anticipate or head off the State Department initiative.

The State Department's motives were clear enough, and need not be detailed here. During the early months of 1948 events both in Europe and in Palestine conspired against the Zionist interest. The prospect of a third world war, this time against the Soviets, seemed ever more likely. In Palestine, the first stages of the civil war went badly for the Jews, and many of their sympathizers began to fear a second Holocaust. The State Department maintained that it had not been the intention of the United Nations to provoke an unmanageable conflict in Palestine, which was likely to spread and turn the Middle East as a whole into another theater of East-West confrontation.

All this was perfectly clear to the Zionists, who mobilized all their forces to counter the State Department campaign against partition. Dr. Weizmann was intercepted in London, on the day before his departure for Palestine, and rushed to New York. He was unable to secure an audience with the president until March 18, on the very eve of the State Department's announcement of its trusteeship plan. However, Truman's reassurance to Weizmann that the United States was still committed to partition proved to be of vital importance over the next two months. Coming as it did just before the State Department's initiative, Truman's private assurance left him looking, in the words of his own diary entry, like "a liar and a double-crosser." This private reassurance, given in ignorance of the imminent change in his administration's policy, established a commitment that became even stronger once the trusteeship proposal proved to be a lame duck.

However, for all the abundant evidence on the direction of American policy, the Zionists failed to foresee the trusteeship proposal. Perhaps they could not conceive of an American retreat in the face of Arab violence and threats, with all the consequent damage that would result to the prestige of the infant and still-revered international forum, the United Nations. An early cue was given in February, 1948, when Warren Austin stated before the Security Council that, whereas the body was empowered to act against breaches of the international peace in Palestine, it was *not* authorized to enforce specific political solutions (i.e., partition). Nahum Goldmann missed the key significance of Austin's statement, and in his report back to Tel Aviv he dwelt upon the latter's proposal to set up yet another committee, comprised of Security Council members, to consult with Jews and Arabs on partition. Goldmann feared that this new committee would propose border modifications to the UN plan and try to cut back Jewish immigration.[24] No warnings were received from Eliahu Epstein, the Zionist representative in Washington; to the contrary, he later expressed total surprise in regard to the State Department proposal, notwithstanding intimations from several of his contacts in the American capital.[25]

The question of just how powerful the Zionist lobby was during this period has evoked considerable historical debate. Those who have put forward the thesis of "Jewish powerlessness" have read into the trusteeship episode demonstrable proof of the Jews' weakness. In the view of Dr. Zvi Ganin, the State Department's trusteeship scheme was a coup that amounted to "the greatest defeat of Jewish diplomacy since the issuance of the White Paper in 1939."[26] Yet, at the same time, Ganin agreed that the Jews' setback was due also, if not primarily, to their own failure to utilize the intelligence available to them. In addition it was conceded that *force majeure*, in the form of the Soviet threat in Europe, and the deterioration in the Yishuv's military position were both extraneous factors working against Jewish sovereignty at that juncture.

The first months of the civil war in Palestine, from December, 1947, to March, 1948, were in fact difficult ones for the Jews. Many Jewish settlements were isolated, as main arteries were rendered vulnerable to Arab ambush. Jerusalem was cut off from the coast. At the end of March, 1948, the Haganah high command proposed a new strategy, Plan Dalet (D). Its objects were to "gain control of the area allotted to the Jewish state, and defend its borders and those blocs of Jewish settlements and such of the Jewish population as were outside the partition borders."[27] The plan was the result of a political decision: to consolidate the area allotted the Jews by the UN decision before initiatives such as the trusteeship proposal were used to abort it. The plan also reflected the life-and-death necessity of securing lines of interior communication between Jewish settlements in outlying Galilee, the Negev, and Jerusalem.

No meaningful negotiations between Jews and Palestinian Arabs had taken place since the mid-1930s. In 1937 the Zionists and those Arabs associated with the Nashashibi family had tended to agree on the Peel partition plan. But the Husseinis, under the leadership of the Mufti, Hajj Amin al-Husseini, had begun a reign of terror that effectively stifled any tendency to compromise with the Jews. This seemed to foreclose any negotiating option. During the war the Jews' alienation was completed when the Mufti collaborated with Hitler and endorsed the latter's "solution" to the "Jewish problem."

For the Zionists, their natural negotiating partner seemed to be King Abdullah of Jordan, who had cast his eyes on the West Bank of Palestine since 1937. The annexation of Arab Palestine was to be the first stage in the realization of his ambition to rule over a reconstituted "Greater Syria." Abdullah's rule was also preferable to many Palestinians, notably the Nashashibis. The British, too, ruled out the intransigent Mufti, yet feared that the Arab League would not permit Abdullah to enjoy a monopoly in Palestine.

During the period of 1947–48, Abdullah met twice with Golda Myerson (Meir), a senior member of the Jewish Agency Executive. At their first meeting, early in November, 1947, prior to the passage of the UN resolution, they soon agreed that the Mufti was their common enemy and that Palestine should be partitioned between Israel and Jordan, along the lines of the UN plan. During that winter contacts were maintained through intermediaries. But, with hostilities spreading in Palestine and the Arab League increasingly committed to intervention as the stream of Palestinian refugees began, Abdullah felt constrained to join in the fighting. At the end of April, 1948, that is, *before* the end of the British mandate, Jordan's Arab Legion crossed the border and was involved in fighting near the Sea of Galilee.

At their second meeting, May 10, 1948, Myerson and Abdullah tried to reach an agreement that would avert a full-scale clash. Abdullah attempted to persuade the Jews to put off their declaration of independence for a year, after which Palestine would unite with Jordan under his kingship in a "Judeo-Arab" kingdom, whose parliament and cabinet might have a 50 percent Jewish membership. Myerson rejected this proposal outright and proposed instead a peace treaty binding Abdullah not to invade any areas allotted to the Jews by the UN plan. In return, Israel would recognize Abdullah's annexation of Arab Palestine, and he might send a governor to rule there. It was Myerson's impression that Abdullah was then more afraid of his Arab rivals than of the Jews and that he did not really want to fight. But he had become involved in the Arab League's plans for invading Palestine and could not disentangle himself. On the eve of their independence, the Jews, having overcome initial reverses, were riding on a wave of military success and not inclined, much less able, to help Abdullah out of his difficulties.[28]

One of the more unsavory features of the civil war was the campaign of urban terror by both sides. One of the most-publicized examples was the massacre of over 200 Arab civilians at the village of Deir Yasin on April 9, 1948. But this was by no means the first outrage. If one is historically minded, one might go back to the very first year of the mandate, when Arabs, in protest of British immigration policy, burned down an immigrant hostel in Jaffa. Those Jews who tried to escape the inferno were shot. Or, to return to the civil war in 1948, just two weeks before Deir Yasin, on March 22, three British army trucks, loaded with high explosives and parked in Jerusalem's main street, blew up. Fifty Jews were killed, and dozens more mutilated. In apparent "revenge" for Deir Yasin, just three days later a convoy of Jewish doctors, students, and nurses, traveling under the aegis of the Red Cross to Mount Scopus in East Jerusalem, was attacked by Arabs. The assault occurred in broad daylight and lasted for seven hours, in full view of a British guard contingent, which refused to intervene. There were seventy-seven Jewish casualties, many of them burned alive inside ambulances.

Each side was guilty of its own outrages, and each side had its martyrs. In the words of Christopher Sykes, "Both sides inclined to indulge in atrocity propaganda for which both sides had ample material."[29] But there was one significant difference between Jews and Arabs, which had far-reaching repercussions. Whereas the Jews appreciated the countereffect of such propaganda on the morale of their own community, the Arabs did not and, in their exaggerations, contributed to the mass flight of Palestinian Arabs.[30]

It should also be emphasized that the mass flight of the Arabs from Palestine had begun long before Deir Yasin. For instance, the Arabs of Haifa—especially the Christians, who comprised half of the town's Arabs—began to flee in December, 1947, on the morrow of the UN resolution. By the end of March, 1948, while the tide of the war still favored the Arabs, some 25,000 Arabs had already left Haifa. This was in spite of Jewish pleas for them to stay, since the Jewish authorities felt they would not be able to run the harbor without the Arab workers. The most obvious reason for the Arabs' flight was the collapse of their communal institutions and the fact that their leaders were the first to leave. Jewish victories during the last weeks of the mandate, of course, intensified Arab fear and accelerated their departure. Many Arabs believed quite naturally, yet wrongly, that once the Jews took over they would wreak vengeance for pogroms carried out by the Arabs during the mandate (e.g., at Hebron in 1929).

In great contrast, the Jewish Agency instructed its civil servants to prepare to take over the administration of the new Jewish state. In April, 1947, a Zionist General Council had appointed a National Administration of thirteen members and a National Council of thirty-seven; these were destined to become Israel's Provisional Government and Provisional Council of State, respectively. The National Administration was given "powers to deal with all matters pertaining to security, transport, supply, trade and industry, labor, manpower, agriculture, immigration, police, etc."[31] All Jewish government officials were instructed to stay at their posts and informed that they would continue to receive their salaries on the same scale as before. A "Key Chart" was drawn up by Agency experts "showing the transfer of departmental functions from the Palestine Administration to the projected Ministries."[32] The establishment of a Jewish civil administration proceeded apace with the Haganah military campaign: "Just as the 'Hagana' forces netted every army camp, police station, and strong-point relinquished by the British forces, so did the newly-established departments aim at taking over the services, property, and functions which the departing government was abdicating."[33]

## Israel Established and Recognized

Following the domestic outcry that had ensued after the trusteeship proposal, Truman had confused matters still further by convening a press conference on March 25, at which he tried to explain that the United States had not in fact reversed its position on partition and that the new plan was merely a temporary measure designed to avert further bloodshed in Palestine, but not intended to prejudice the ultimate political disposition of the country. The Zionists, on the other hand, did not view the trusteeship plan as a purely temporary measure, but as an indefinite, potentially fatal deferment of their sovereignty already sanctioned by the United Nations. That the trusteeship plan failed even to get off the ground was due not so much to any opposition from President Truman as to the opposition of both Arabs and Zionists and the incredulity of other delegations at the United Nations. As discussion dragged on at Flushing Meadow, it all assumed a surrealistic air, since from the beginning of April, 1948, the Haganah took the offensive and by force of arms established the state proffered by the UN resolution.

The Jews' military victories in Palestine affected events at the United Nations in two senses. First, they turned the UN plan into hard geopolitical fact and, concurrently, rendered the State Department's initiative an academic pipe-dream. By May, 1948, any attempt to impose trusteeship on Palestine would have necessitated the dismantling, probably by force, of the Jewish state. Second, the establishment of Israel seemed to solve, at long last, the serious dilemma with which Truman had been laboring since August, 1945. By mid-May, 1948, with all other State Department initiatives stymied, the simplest course of action, as seen from the White House, seemed to be an immediate recognition of the political and military *fait accompli* in Palestine.

It is well known that Truman's sudden recognition of Israel took his own delegation to the United Nations completely by surprise. It was deemed necessary to dispatch Dean Rusk to New York to prevent the resignation of the entire delegation, *en masse*.[34] The *de facto* recognition was masterminded by Clark Clifford, who did not even leave the Zionist representative in Washington time to consult his superiors in Tel Aviv. The very fact that the Zionists themselves had not even applied for recognition is perhaps in itself measure of the White House's desire to appease the Jewish constituency and to make amends for the events of the previous March.

By his own later testimony, Clifford indicated that the instant recognition was designed to anticipate "a similar move by the Soviet Union, which hardly deserved a monopoly on Israeli gratitude."[35] However, a close study of the all-important confrontation at the White House between top officials of the State Department and Truman's aides, which preceded the final decision to grant recognition, reveals other, no less important motives. In a memorandum of May 9 Clifford had argued that immediate recognition of the Jewish state would retrieve for the United Nations the prestige lost during the previous months, when all kinds of unrealistic solutions had been advanced. Fortunately, continued Clifford, the "realistic" approach was also the one that would bring the most domestic political benefit.[36]

Clifford presented his ideas at the White House meeting on May 12. Putting aside all previous reticence, he now argued frankly that a pro-Zionist statement on Palestine would help Truman to secure the Democratic nomination for the presidency (then under challenge by a group trying to draft General Eisenhower). Clifford maintained that prompt American recognition would restore the president's standing with the Jews to where it had been prior to the State Department's trusteeship proposal of March 19. According to one record of that tension-laden meeting, Clifford argued that "with a national election less than six months away, the President should move towards redeeming himself with Jewish voters by immediately recognizing the existence of the Jewish State."[37] The heads of the State Department, who must have been embarrassed by the failure of their own various initiatives, concentrated on rebutting Clifford's "domestic" argument. Secretary of State George Marshall delivered his well-known tirade against the injection of "straight politics" into foreign policy and threatened to vote against Truman. Under Secretary of State Robert Lovett described Clifford's proposal as "a very transparent attempt to win the Jewish vote, but . . . it would lose more votes than it would gain." Truman bowed to Marshall's protests, or at least that was the impression of most of the participants at the meeting. But Clifford pressed on regardless and stage-managed the early recognition of Israel. On the afternoon of May 14 he informed Lovett that the president had been submitted to "unbearable pressure" to recognize the Jewish state.

Undoubtedly, by the middle of May, 1948, there was much to be said for the pragmatic recognition of Israel. In addition to the fact that the Zionists had overcome Palestinian Arab opposition, there was also the existence of an unofficial, open-secret pact between the Jewish Agency and Abdullah to partition Palestine along the lines of the UN resolution. Even before the passage of the resolution, a member of the Eastern Department at the Foreign Office had predicted that the only alternative to the annexation of Arab Palestine by Abdullah "would be a puny Arab Palestine dominated by the unreliable Mufti, incapable of maintaining its independence and a sure source of unrest and even war."[38]

However, there can also be no doubt that the weight of the American Jewish electorate, as evaluated by the staff of a beleaguered president, also played a decisive role. The Zionist cause sustained a severe political setback in March, 1948. But the Zionists rose to the occasion. On the one hand, in Palestine itself the Haganah went on the offensive, and the Jewish Agency took all necessary steps to ensure a smooth transfer of government to themselves. On the other, in Washington, the White House was so impressed by the course of events in Palestine, and the sterility of State Department initiatives, that it decided on the immediate recognition of Israel (as Truman had in fact promised Weizmann, via an intermediary). This was a step also calculated to regain the political ground the president had lost in March. In this sense, Truman's recognition of Israel anticipated not only the Soviet Union, but also the Zionist lobby.

## Conclusion

From the Zionists' perspective, the Holocaust had "vindicated" their ideological platform in a manner that surpassed even their most morbid nightmares. The Holocaust served the Zionists as a moral imperative requiring the establishment of a Jewish state in Palestine, long after Zionist diplomats came to appreciate that Western statesmen were moved by more mundane, material considerations. Indeed, how could the establishment of a Jewish state have served to salve Western consciences, when Western leaders did not in fact suffer the pangs of remorse that the Zionists believed they should have?

The sense of debt to the Jewish people felt by Christianity has been a recurrent theme of modern history. Since the demise of the Ottoman Empire during the nineteenth century, it has been accompanied by various schemes to return the Jews, "the people of the Bible," to their ancient biblical homeland. After World War II such plans assumed immediacy, and the myth was propagated that the establishment of the state of Israel was in some form a recompense for the sufferings of the Jews under the Nazis.

But much of the mythology surrounding the establishment of the state of Israel (frequently disguised as serious history) has underestimated or dismissed two basic facts. First, it was the Zionist lobby in the United States, with its unremitting pressure, that repeatedly mobilized the support of a wavering president. Second, it was the Jews' own military efforts and administrative skills that earned them their state, during the crucial last weeks of the Palestine mandate.

Against a backcloth of great power rivalry and Arab dissension, the Zionists were able to seize a unique historical opportunity, one that was legitimized by the majority of the international community as represented at the United Nations.

## Notes

1. For the text of the Biltmore program, see J. C. Hurewitz, *Diplomacy in the Near and Middle East, 1914–1956*, 2 vols. (Princeton, N.J.: Princeton University Press, 1956), II, pp. 234–35.

2. *Parliamentary Debates* (Commons), Fifth Series, vol. 426, col. 1253.

3. On the *Exodus* affair, see Nicholas Bethell, *The Palestine Triangle: The Struggle between the British, the Jews and the Arabs, 1935–48* (London: André Deutsch, 1979).

4. See Henry L. Feingold, *The Politics of Rescue: The Roosevelt Administration and the Holocaust, 1938–1945* (New Brunswick, N.J.: Rutgers University Press, 1970), and Haim Genizi, *American Apathy: The Plight of Christian Refugees from Nazism* (Ramat-Gan: Bar-Ilan University Press, 1983).

5. Eliahu Elath, *The Struggle for Statehood, 1945–1948*, 2 vols. (Tel Aviv: Am Oved, 1979, 1982; in Hebrew), vol. II.

6. On the war period, see my book *Palestine: Retreat from the Mandate, 1936–1945* (New York: Holmes and Meier, 1978).

7. See my book *Churchill and the Jews* (London: Frank Cass, 1985).

8. Goldmann speech to Jewish Agency Executive on August 3, 1946, Z6/21, Central Zionist Archives, Jerusalem (CZA). The "improvements" Goldmann referred to were in the Morrison-Grady plan. The Zionists wanted a more rapid rate of immigration and more extensive powers of autonomy over a larger territory.

9. On the Paris Executive, see my book *Palestine and the Great Powers 1945–1948* (Princeton: Princeton University Press, 1982), pp. 141–47, and Joseph Heller, "From Black Saturday to Partition," *Zion*, 43/c–d (1979), 314–61 (in Hebrew).

10. Acheson note of meeting on August 8, 1946, 867N. 01/8746, National Archives (NA), Washington; and Acheson to Averell Harriman (London), August 12, 1946, *Foreign Relations of the United States (FRUS) 1946*, VII, pp. 679–82.

11. Ibid., p. 703.

12. Elath, *The Struggle for Statehood*, pp. 424–25.

13. Silver to Ben-Gurion, October 9, 1946, Ben-Gurion Archives (BGA), Sde Boker.

14. Bevin and Silver meetings of November, 1946, FO 371/52565/E11549, Public Record Office (PRO), London.

15. Ben-Gurion note of meeting with the lord chancellor, Sir William Jowitt, February 13, 1947, Weizmann Archives (WA), Rehovot; and British note of Bevin and Ben-Gurion meeting, February 12, 1947, CO 537/2333, PRO.

16. David Horowitz, *State in the Making* (New York: Alfred A. Knopf, 1953), pp. 142–43.

17. *Israel Documents, December 1947–May 1948* (Jerusalem: Israel State Archives [ISA], 1980; in Hebrew), nos. 205, 258.

18. Ibid., no. 270, quoted in my article "The Birth of Israel—Diplomatic Failure, Military Success," *Jerusalem Quarterly*, 17 (Fall, 1980), 29–39.

19. Meeting of American Zionist Emergency Committee, October 13, 1947, 2266/10, ISA.

20. Shertok and Henderson meeting, October 22, 1947, 501 BB. Pal/10-2247, Box 2182, NA.

21. Telephone conversation of Lovett, Johnson, and Hilldring, November 24, 1947, *FRUS 1947*, V, pp. 1283–84.

22. Comay to Gering (chairman, South African Zionist Federation—Comay himself was South African in origin), December 3, 1947, ISA 2266/15.

23. On the oil lobby and the role of salaried ex–State Department officials, see Aaron D. Miller, *The Search for Security* (Chapel Hill: University of North Carolina Press, 1980), and Henrietta M. Larsen, Evelyn H. Knowlton, and Charles S. Popple, *New Horizons: The History of the Standard Oil Company* (New York: Harper and Row, 1971), esp. p. 634.

24. *Israel Documents*, no. 225, N. Goldmann to E. Kaplan, February 25, 1948.

25. Cohen, "The Birth of Israel," p. 37.

26. Zvi Ganin, *Truman, American Jewry, and Israel, 1945–1948* (New York: Holmes & Mier, 1979), p. 169.

27. See Netanel Lorch, *Israel's War of Independence* (Jerusalem, 1968), pp. 89ff.

28. On Abdullah's contacts with the Zionists, see Sir Alec Kirkbride, *From the Wings* (London: Frank Cass, 1976), pp. 21ff.; Joseph Nevo, *Abdullah and Palestine* (Tel Aviv: Tel Aviv University Press, 1975; in Hebrew), pp. 79ff.; and Zeev Sharef, *Three Days: An Account of the Last Days of the British Mandate and the Birth of Israel* (London: W. H. Allen, 1962; translated from Hebrew), pp. 73–76.

29. Christopher Sykes, *Crossroads to Israel* (London: Collins, 1965), pp. 364–65.

30. Ibid.

31. For this and following, see Sharef, *Three Days*, pp. 46ff.

32. Ibid., pp. 55–57.

33. Ibid., p. 63.

34. Rusk memorandum, June 13, 1948, *FRUS 1948*, V, p. 993.

35. Clark Clifford, "Factors Influencing Truman's Decision to Support Partition and Recognize the State of Israel," in *The Palestine Question in American History* (New York, 1978), p. 42. This is a reprint of a paper presented to the American Historical Association in December, 1976.

36. Clifford Papers, Box 13, Harry S Truman Library, Independence, Mo. (HSTL).

37. John Snetsinger, *Truman, the Jewish Vote and the Creation of Israel* (Stanford, Cal.: Hoover Institution Press, 1974), p. 139. See also the contemporary record of the meeting, written by George Elsey, a White House aide, editorial note, *FRUS 1948*, V, p. 876.

38. Minute by J. E. Cable, November 4, 1947, FO 371/62226/E10711. On Abdullah's negotiations with the Zionists and British and American opinions thereof, see my book *Palestine and the Great Powers*, pp. 325–34.

# The Arab Perspective

*Walid Khalidi*

Even before the First Zionist Congress in Basel (1897), Sultan Abdul Hamid had expressed in 1891 the fear that granting Ottoman nationality to Jewish immigrants in Palestine "may result in the future in the creation of a Jewish government in Jerusalem."[1] The pressures of the European powers on Constantinople in the period from the 1880s to 1914 to facilitate Zionist immigration and settlement in Palestine only emphasized the foreign provenance of the Zionist movement in Palestinian eyes. In 1899 the Palestinian mayor of Jerusalem pleaded in a letter to Zadok Kahn, the chief rabbi of France, "In the name of God, leave Palestine alone";[2] after the restoration of the Ottoman Constitution in 1907, deputies from Jerusalem and other Palestinian cities actively lobbied in Constantinople against Zionist immigration.[3] The Palestinians and other Arabs did not see the emerging conflict as one between two rights. They could not accept that after a hiatus of two millennia contemporary Jews had a political title to Palestine that overrode the rights of the contemporary Palestinians. The Palestinians saw themselves as the descendants of the aboriginal inhabitants of the land, including the pre-Hebraic and post-Hebraic ethnic strands.

With the Balfour Declaration, the Zionist movement was identified outright with British imperialism. The Declaration and its subsequent incorporation in the League of Nations' mandate system were regarded as lacking in moral or legal validity, since they had not derived from Palestinian consent. They were seen as violations both of the principles enunciated by President Wilson and of the promises made by Britain during the war. By the end of World War I the Palestinians seemed in their own eyes to have changed in status from partners in the Ottoman Empire to subjects of a colonial empire and potential subjects of a protégé—the Zionist movement—of this empire. Ironically, Palestinian deputies from Jerusalem had sat in the

Ottoman Parliament of 1876 twenty years before the Zionists held their own first congress.

From the beginning the Zionists were seen as determined to revolutionize the status quo in Palestine in the demographic and landholding balances as well as in the overall power equation between the Zionist immigrant and the Palestinian resident. But if Zionist colonization had taken place under the Ottomans in spite of Constantinople, it was now the express purpose of the British mandatory. The White Paper of 1922 established the "economic absorptive capacity" of the country as the sole criterion of Zionist immigration. This paved the way for the steady change in the demographic balance at Palestinian expense.

As this balance shifted in favor of the Zionists and more land was acquired by the central Zionist institutions, the threat of dispossession assumed an increasingly concrete and imminent character. In the words of the Shaw Commission of Inquiry (1929), "The Arabs have come to see in the Jewish immigrant not only a menace to their livelihood but a possible overlord of the future."[4] Meanwhile, there seemed to be little possibility of legal redress, since neither the mandatory nor the Zionists would accept the principle of one-man-one-vote for fear that an elected Palestinian majority in the legislature would undermine the Jewish national home policy.

Between 1919 and the end of World War II the ratio of the Jewish population to the total rose through mass immigration from 9.7 percent (1919) to 16.8 percent (1925) to 17.8 percent (1930) to 28.6 percent (1935) to 31.4 percent (1940) to 35.1 percent (1946). Meanwhile, the area acquired by the Jews increased from 2.04 percent of the total area of the country (1919) to 7.0 percent (1946).[5]

It was against this background that successive "disturbances" broke out, culminating in the "great rebellion" of 1936–39. Discussing this Palestinian rebellion, the Royal Commission under the chairmanship of Lord Peel had this to say (June, 1937):

> We have no doubt as to what were the "underlying causes of the disturbances" of last year. They were
> (i) The desire of the Arabs for national independence
> (ii) Their hatred and fear of the establishment of the Jewish National Home. . . . They were the only "underlying causes."
> All the other factors were complementary or subsidiary.[6]

To be sure, the Royal Commission proceeded to suggest the partition of the country. The Palestinians were as shocked by this proposal then as they were to be ten years later when the UN partition recommendation was passed, and for almost identical reasons. They could not accept this explicit legitimization of the Zionist political title at their own expense. Hundreds of thousands of Palestinians would become a subject minority. The Zionist state would acquire about 33 percent of the total area of the country (including the most fertile regions of Galilee and the coastal plain between Acre and Jaffa) at a time (1937) when Jewish land ownership did not exceed 5.6 percent of the area of Palestine. The Palestinians feared the confiscation of their land. They were horrified by the Royal Commission proposal of their "forcible transfer," if necessary, from the Zionist state, and deeply angered by the envisaged incorporation of the Palestinian rump state into Transjordan. Even the Royal Commission sounded somewhat sheepish in its summation: "Considering what the possibility of finding a refuge in Palestine means to many thousands of suffering Jews, is the loss occasioned by partition, great as it would be, more than Arab generosity can bear?"[7] The immediate effect of the partition proposal was to add fuel to the flames of the rebellion and to prolong it until 1939, with consequences disastrous to the Palestinians.

The key to understanding the increasing Zionist relative weight in the power equation does not lie only in the quantitative change in favor of the Zionists in the demographic and landholding balances already noted. Writing in 1937, Hancock observed: "The Jews in the main represent a cross-section of western society at its highest point of efficiency. As a result there is a de facto inequality which at every point of contact between the two societies expresses itself in visible material forms."[8] In 1944 Loftus remarked, "The Jewish economy of Palestine is radically different from the Arab economy and is in fact not very dissimilar from that of the U.K."[9]

At the same time, the Palestinians never really recovered from the results of their confrontation with Britain. In addition to the considerable losses incurred in human life and economic dislocation; the dissolution of all political organizations; the arrest, exile, or disarming of the Palestinian peasantry (even while the Yishuv was being systematically armed and trained); the death, detention, and scattering of thousands of the most active members of the rebellion—all these factors further reduced the weight of the Palestinian side in the bilateral balance with the Yishuv.[10]

With the issuance of the White Paper of 1939, the British for the first time since 1917 seemed ready to play the role of the holder of the balance in Palestine—hence Zionist anger. The Palestinian and Arab leaders had rejected the White Paper principally because the promised independence in a unitary state ten years later was in effect contingent upon prior (and unlikely) Zionist approval. Nevertheless, the White Paper did contribute to keeping the Palestinians quiescent throughout the war years, as did the new economic war boom and Eden's support for the idea of Arab unity. Meanwhile, two significant wartime developments added considerably to the Zionist weight in the balance of power with the Palestinians: some 30,000 members of the Yishuv enrolled in the British forces, and a war industry developed in Palestine (answering the needs of the British military) based on Jewish talent and installations available to the Yishuv.[11]

If the Palestinians were preponderant vis-à-vis the Zionists in 1917, the reverse was true by 1945. And if the presence of Britain had been indispensable to the Zionists in the twenties and thirties, this was no longer necessarily the case. The shift in Zionist strategy from British to American sponsorship had already become evident by 1942 (the Biltmore program). This brought two formidable new actors to the scene: the United States administration and the American Jewish establishment. The tripartite coalition between the Yishuv and these two was to set the pace for developments in Palestine in the remaining years of the Palestine mandate.

The one hope for the Palestinians, then, lay in British adherence to the 1939 White Paper in conjunction with active support from the newly created Arab League.

## From the Labour Government to the Anglo-American Committee

Musa Alami, the moderate Palestinian leader, was chosen by the Palestinian parties to represent them in the preparatory committee of the Arab Congress that met in Alexandria from September 25 to October 7, 1944, before the formation of the Arab League. The analysis and policies expounded by Alami at the Congress became the basis for Arab League actions until the autumn of 1947. Alami warned that the British and the Zionists were working on four options: partition; cantonization; "political parity" with a Jewish majority; and a unitary state with "numerical parity"—all of which involved repudiation of the White Paper of 1939. The reason the British were retreating from the White Paper was "without any shadow of doubt their feeling that the Arabs are pusillanimous . . . and that therefore there is no danger in incurring their anger."

Alami urged the following policies: (1) negotiations with Britain on the basis of the White Paper of 1939, which Britain had "pledged its honour to implement"; (2) the dispatch of a high-level delegation to London, Moscow, and Washington; (3) the establishment of a National Fund for Palestine with an annual expenditure of £1 million for the next five years, to be used for agricultural development and the amelioration of the social and economic conditions of the Palestinian farmer to forestall Zionist land acquisition; (4) effective legislation in the Arab countries to bar the importation of Jewish industrial goods from Palestine; (5) effective measures to curb illegal Jewish immigration via the Arab countries into Palestine; and (6) amnesty to the Palestine leaders in exile or detention since 1937. In an earlier session, another of his ideas—setting up information offices in the Western capitals—had also been proposed.[12]

It will be noted that Alami's strategy was three-pronged: diplomacy; reform in Palestine; and sanctions against the Zionists. What is lacking is any reference to military preparedness. This omission is an index of Alami's moderation and fundamental faith in Britain, in spite of his warnings about British hesitations. The feeling that, in the last analysis, Britain would not abandon the Palestinians was widely shared among Arab leaders, with the outstanding exception of Palestinian leader Hajj Amin al-Husseini. It derived partly from the Western liberal upbringing of many Arab leaders and partly from their calculation of where British interests lay. But the total neglect of military preparedness may also have reflected a sense of unadmitted impotence and clienthood vis-à-vis Britain—the perceived *real* decision maker in the Arab world. Arab neglect of military preparedness—which persisted beyond the UN partition decision—stands in stark contrast with contemporaneous Zionist conduct.

A year later, in October, 1945, Azzam, the secretary-general of the Arab League (founded in March, 1945) visited London, where he met Attlee, Bevin, and George Hall, British colonial secretary. His reactions to this visit exemplify official Arab attitudes of the time. He found Attlee "modest . . . attentive . . . convinced of our cause." Bevin was "enormously self-confident . . . a man of high values and principles but open to argument on the basis of his principles . . . convinced of his ability to solve the problem of the Jews. . . ." Bevin hinted that he wanted to arrange for a peace conference between Arabs and Jews; when Azzam said this had been tried and had failed, Bevin replied that nothing had been decided yet. Azzam offered to admit Jewish refugees into the Arab countries if Britain and the United States did the same. To George Hall, Azzam emphasized that the 1939 White Paper "was not an *ad hoc* or *ad interim* measure but the studied outcome of twenty turbulent years . . . a compromise solution between the Palestinians and the Jews." Azzam added that "the biggest mistake of the Zionists is that they despised us and depended on the forces of the West instead of coming to see us as *Jews* rather than as Germans, Poles and Russians." Referring to the meeting between FDR and King Ibn Saud and the subsequent letters about it from Washington, Azzam made much of "this promise on behalf of America made by both Presidents Roosevelt and Truman that nothing would take place affecting Arab interests in Palestine without our prior consultation and that the United States would not intervene forcefully." Azzam informed Hall that in addition to the written assurance from FDR to Ibn Saud, there had also been at their meeting "a verbal promise that FDR made when he put his hand in Ibn Saud's and swore on his honor not to support the Zionists against the Arabs."[13]

Early in November, 1945, the Arab League Council met, and it was to this Council that Azzam reported on his trip to London the previous month. Azzam said that he had set out on this trip with some foreboding but had returned feeling optimistic. He had been very impressed by the Arab (Information) Office already set up by Alami in London. The deliberations focused on propaganda and its efficacy, on which there was agreement. But Pachachi (prime minister of Iraq) felt that not enough was being spent on it, and Nokrashi (prime minister of Egypt) protested, "Propaganda is a whole new field for us." Azzam wanted Arab League propaganda to concern itself with a wide range of issues, but Pachachi insisted that it should be restricted to the Palestine problem because of its urgency. Pachachi castigated the League for not moving fast enough in the establishment of the National Fund proposed by Alami, but Nokrashi advised thorough preliminary investigation. Only Pachachi seemed imbued with a sense of urgency, warning about Jewish strength: "once the Jews establish their state they will build up an army . . . that could invade Syria, Lebanon, and even Iraq." Azzam protested this "exaggeration" and believed that once Egypt achieved its independence "there can be no fear of a Jewish army." But Pachachi retorted that the Zionists had "culturally qualitative power" and tactlessly pointed to the fact that a country of 18 million like Egypt was ruled by 40,000 British troops.[14] Underlying the divergent perceptions of the urgency of the Palestine problem were different priorities and preoccupations: Egypt was fully engaged in the revision of its treaty with Britain. But underlying these priorities and preoccupations also was the struggle between the major Arab capitals to lead and mold the newly created Arab League.

On November 13, 1945, President Truman made public his letter written in August urging the British prime minister to admit 100,000 Jewish immigrants into Palestine. This was immediately seen by Palestinians and other Arabs as a frontal assault on the 1939 White

Paper—the cornerstone of Arab diplomacy. On the same day Bevin announced the formation of the Anglo-American Committee and the continuation of Jewish immigration at a monthly rate of 1,500 in spite of the 1939 White Paper. In December both houses of the U.S. Congress adopted resolutions for "unrestricted" Jewish immigration into Palestine. Such confidence as existed in the American "undertakings" to Ibn Saud was severely shaken, and the involvement of the United States in the solution of the Palestine problem was increasingly seen as a sign of ill omen. A joint declaration on Palestine made on January 16, 1946, by King Ibn Saud and King Farouk was meant partly as a warning to Washington and London, partly as an attempt to reassure Arab public opinion, and partly to preempt the Hashemite capitals in the championship of the Palestinians. The declaration said that the two monarchs "associated themselves with all Moslem Arabs in their belief that Palestine is an Arab country and that it is the right of its people and the right of the Moslem Arabs everywhere to preserve it as an Arab country. . . ."[15]

## From the Anglo-American Committee to the UN (February, 1947)

The Anglo-American Committee's report completely ignored the joint declaration by Ibn Saud and Farouk, inasmuch as it was tantamount to the dismantlement of the 1939 White Paper policy on immigration and land transfers. Its publication caused the calling of the first summit of Arab heads of state (May 28–29, 1946) at Anshass, Egypt, in order to demonstrate that Ibn Saud and Farouk were not speaking only for their own countries.

The summit unanimously called for completely stopping Zionist immigration; preventing Arab land from passing into Zionist hands; and the independence of Palestine. Any policy adopted by the United States and Britain in contradiction to these demands would be considered "a hostile policy directed against Arab Palestine and therefore against the Arab countries themselves. Therefore any adoption of the resolutions of the Anglo-American Committee in a manner prejudicial to the Arabs of Palestine would be considered as a hostile act directed at the Arab countries themselves." The summit agreed on the need for financial aid to the Palestinians for purposes of "propaganda and the preservation of their land" and pledged its support "with every means possible . . . should the Palestinians have to defend themselves."[16]

Within a week of the Anshass summit, President Truman had reiterated on June 6 his request for the admission of 100,000 Jews into Palestine. Thus began the dialogue of the deaf on the Palestine problem between Washington on the one hand and the Palestinians and other Arabs on the other, which continues to this day.

On June 8, 1946, an extraordinary session of the Arab League Council was called in Bludan, Syria, to follow up on the Anshass summit. The Iraqi delegation set the pace, and Pachachi, the prime minister, said that it all boiled down to "what measures we are prepared to take to compel the United States and Britain to observe their limits . . . in the implementation of the AAC's Report." Jamali, the Iraqi foreign minister, observed, ". . . the Zionists have made Palestine an issue of domestic American politics and seize the occasion of every election to elicit the support of American officials. . . . The United States and Britain . . . pay no attention to what we say or write unless we also act. . . ."

The counterweight to the Iraqis were the Saudis. Yasin, the Saudi delegate, urged that prudence and reality define the limits of the possible. The Palestinians must not be given unrealizable promises, and a delegation of the Arab League and the Palestinians should proceed to London and Washington.

The Egyptians and, surprisingly, the Syrians backed the Saudis. Eventually Azzam suggested a compromise. Negotiations with Britain would be started, but "secret resolutions" would be taken that would go into effect in the event of the implementation of the AAC report. The secret resolutions were (1) to withhold from Britain and the United States "any new economic concessions"; (2) to refrain from supporting their special interests in international bodies; (3) "moral boycott"; and (4) "to consider cancellation of such concessions as they have in the Arab countries." Azzam was authorized to tell Britain and the United States that the League Council had decided for the time being to keep certain secret resolutions to itself but that "when the time came for their implementation, relations with the Arab countries would be grievously affected."[17]

The Iraqi delegation expressed its dissatisfaction with this outcome and served notice that it reserved its right to freedom of action. At this Syrian Premier Jabiri flew into a rage, accusing Iraq of wanting to break up the League, but cooler tempers eventually prevailed.[18] Azzam's compromise is a good example of the politics of clienthood: Washington and London were to be deterred, but they were not to be told what would deter them.

The Council also took measures to strengthen the Palestinians internally. These included tightening the boycott of Zionist goods, legislation against the sale of land by citizens of the Arab countries to the Zionists or the facilitation of Jewish illegal immigration via the Arab countries, and the allocation of funds for propaganda and

land preservation. There still was no action relating to military preparedness, in spite of the rapidly deteriorating security situation in
Palestine.

Perhaps the most important measure affecting the Palestinians
internally was the formation of a new Arab Higher Committee,
whose chairmanship was left open to Hajj Amin al-Husseini, the
Mufti of Jerusalem. Hajj Amin had spent most of the war years in the
Axis countries and arrived in Cairo from France on June 20, 1946.
Upon his arrival in Egypt, Hajj Amin had been ostentatiously received by King Farouk, partly to bolster his own image in Arab eyes
and partly to embarrass both Britain and the Hashemites, who had
little love for Hajj Amin.

This enmity between Hajj Amin on the one hand and London,
Amman, and Baghdad on the other is crucial to the understanding of
this period. The British never forgave Hajj Amin his leadership of the
great rebellion in 1936–39. They had refused to invite him to the
1939 London Conference and had plotted to assassinate him in exile
in Iraq in 1941. After his wartime sojourn in the Axis countries, they
were more determined than ever to thwart him. Their closest Arab
allies in this venture were Amir Abdullah of Transjordan and Amir
Abdulilah, the regent of Iraq.

Abdullah's territorial ambitions in Palestine and Syria were well
known. The Peel (1937 Royal) Commission had whetted his appetite
by proposing the incorporation into Transjordan of the Arab rump
state of a partitioned Palestine. The Palestinian struggle against partition, led by Hajj Amin, had caused Britain to set the partition plan
aside.

At the same time, Abdullah's relations with the Zionists had
been cordial since 1922 and had been consolidated by the mid-
thirties. Abdullah felt fewer constraints than other Arab leaders in
maintaining these relations, partly because of the politically un-
sophisticated nature of Transjordanian society.

The Iraqi regent's anger at Hajj Amin stemmed from the latter's
leading role in the anti-Hashemite *coup d'état* in Baghdad in 1941.
The regent's postwar Palestine policy was based on maintaining the
initiative inside the Arab League, denying Hajj Amin Arab League
help, and supporting "moderate" elements among Palestinians (e.g.,
Musa Alami). While Iraq coordinated policy with Amman along
these lines, it is unlikely that it was privy to all Abdullah's dealings
with the Zionists.

Within Palestine itself (which the British prevented Hajj Amin
from entering until the end of the mandate), Hajj Amin was unques-

tionably the paramount Palestinian leader. Even the moderates were on his side against partition.

Representing the Palestinians at the Arab League Council meeting in Bludan was Jamal Husseini, the second most important Palestinian leader after Hajj Amin. Jamal had just been released from detention by the British, partly in the hope that he would become a counterweight to Hajj Amin, particularly as he was Alami's brother-in-law. But Jamal's only intervention during the Council's deliberations was to the effect that the Palestinians recognized that the Arab League was made up of sovereign states, each with its own political relations. The Palestinians did not want to embarrass anybody, and all they asked for was "help from the Arab *peoples* with the encouragement of the Arab governments." Jamal was convinced that with adequate financial help and materiel the Palestinians could "overcome the Jewish forces."[19] This was very much the line of Hajj Amin, though Jamal did not always see eye to eye with him. It reflected Palestinian concern for autonomy, particularly in the face of Abdullah's ambitions, but it also reflected Hajj Amin's concern for the maintenance of his leadership with the least interference from the Arab governments. It is revealing that Jamal did not ask for direct military help from the Arab countries.

Within about a fortnight of the conclusion of the Bludan Conference, on July 2, President Truman announced U.S. readiness to give technical and financial aid for the transportation of 100,000 Jews to Palestine.

The British, on the other hand, responded to the Arab request for negotiations by opening the London Conference on September 9. The Conference was held against the background not only of President Truman's July statement on the transportation of Jewish immigrants, but also of a subsequent more momentous announcement, on August 14, that he had transmitted a partition scheme to London with the observation that the proposal seemed to merit serious consideration. The plan had earlier been submitted to the American government by the Zionist leader Nahum Goldmann, and it envisaged the Peel (1937 Royal Commission) frontiers as well as the Negev as the area of the proposed Jewish state. Meanwhile, on August 12 and 19 Abdullah had held secret meetings with a Zionist emissary, in which he discussed his plans for partition, "Greater Syria," and the assassination of Hajj Amin.[20]

The London Conference adjourned on October 2, 1946. The Arab delegates had construed the "Morrison Plan" as partition, and therefore turned it down. On October 5 came President Truman's Yom

Kippur statement, which was seen by the Arabs as a formal endorse-ment of Goldmann's partition plan and the *coup de grâce* to what was left of the 1939 White Paper.

Before the London Conference reconvened on January 26, 1947, inter-Arab controversy over the "Greater Syria" project, hitherto dor-mant for some time, suddenly flared up. A new Anglo-Transjordanian Treaty had been signed on March 22, 1946, on the basis of Trans-jordanian independence, and Abdullah had been proclaimed king on May 25, 1946. On November 11, 1946, Abdullah reaffirmed Trans-jordanian commitment to "Greater Syria." This triggered bitter ex-changes with both Syria and Lebanon that lasted some two weeks.[21] It was difficult for many Arabs to believe that Abdullah was acting entirely on his own and that the timing of his moves was unrelated to the London talks or to President Truman's pro-partition declara-tion—even though Abdullah's meetings with the Zionist emissary the previous August were not known at the time.

The "provincial autonomy" plan presented by Bevin after the re-sumption of the London Conference was also construed by the Arab delegates as partition. Its rejection by both the Arabs and the Zion-ists (who saw it as a move *away* from partition) led to Britain's deci-sion to refer the matter to the United Nations.

### From the UN (February, 1947) to the Abandonment of the Mandate (September, 1947)

Anglo-Egyptian talks on the revision of the Anglo-Egyptian Treaty had broken down in December, 1946, and relations between Cairo and London were greatly strained by July, 1947, when Egypt com-plained against Britain to the Security Council. Meanwhile, the United Nations Special Committee on Palestine (UNSCOP), formed on May 15, 1947, produced its report on September 3, 1947. Much of UNSCOP's life span coincided with Egypt's preoccupation with its dispute with Britain. The Anglo-Egyptian dispute also spilled over into Anglo-Syrian relations, inasmuch as the Syrian delegate at the Security Council, to the great chagrin of Britain, strongly backed Egypt. In early July London warned Damascus "that all future moral aid from Britain will depend on Syria's stand on the dispute between Great Britain and Egypt."[22] On July 18 a sharp message from Bevin requested that Syria regard a compromise between Britain and Egypt "in the light of the Arab world's need for a practical arrangement that would permit Great Britain to contribute to the defense of the region . . . not on the basis of a compromise that responds to the personal opinion" of Syria's representative at the UN.[23]

It was against this background that King Abdullah on August 4 once again reactivated the issue of "Greater Syria," this time by calling specifically for the formation of a Constituent Assembly to establish "Greater Syria" and unite it with Iraq. On August 17 he went a step further and sent a special envoy to President Shukri Kuwatli of Syria inviting him to attend the Constituent Assembly! Abdullah's moves acquired greater regional significance in the light of the fact that on April 15, 1947, he had concluded a treaty with Iraq and on January 11, 1947, a treaty with Turkey.[24]

Simultaneously Syria was negotiating with the Tapline company the passage of the oil pipeline from Saudi Arabia through its territory. Negotiations had begun on July 27, 1946 (two weeks after the adoption of the secret Bludan resolutions), but had reached a stalemate by March 6, 1947, partly because of disagreement on certain terms of the convention and partly because of rising anti-American public opinion.[25] The two other transit countries, Lebanon and Jordan, had already signed agreements with Tapline. On August 21, impatient with Syria, William Lenahan of Tapline sent an ultimatum to Mardam, the Syrian prime minister, giving him nine days to sign; otherwise "Tapline will proceed immediately with construction along a route which does not traverse any portion of the Syrian domain."[26]

Shaken by these developments, Kuwatli sent a personal envoy, Muḥsin Barāzī, to King Ibn Saud and King Farouk. Barāzī arrived in Riyad on August 21, 1947, and from there went to Cairo on August 24. Barāzī's account of his mission is most revealing of the priorities and perceptions of the three anti-Hashemite capitals of Damascus, Cairo, and Riyad on the eve of the publication of the UNSCOP report.[27]

Kuwatli told Ibn Saud that every time Abdullah had raised the "Greater Syria" issue, Kuwatli had asked the British what they thought, only to be told that they themselves were not involved. Two months earlier, however, London had told Damascus that it had a "special status . . . of guidance and advice" in Transjordan. Upon receipt of Abdullah's letter concerning the Constituent Assembly for Greater Syria, Kuwatli had asked the British whether this step came under their "guidance and advice." Meanwhile, Damascus and Riyad should coordinate with one another. Kuwatli wanted to call on Transjordan to join Syria on the basis of "a republican plebiscite"; should this come about, the Transjordanian towns of Ma'an and Aqaba would be "returned" to Saudi Arabia. At the same time Kuwatli wanted to conclude a treaty with Saudi Arabia with defense clauses to counter the Transjordanian-Iraqi Treaty.

Ibn Saud told Barāzī that he did "not sleep at night" from worry over Syria: ". . . if the Sharif [Abdullah] enters Syria this will be a blow aimed at me . . . a threat to me." Ibn Saud thought the British wanted "the Sharifians in Syria for their own purposes and may want to avenge themselves because of Syria's support of Egypt" in the Security Council. He was against a bilateral treaty with Syria, because Egypt might be angered at its exclusion; if Egypt were included, the British would assume this was aimed against them, and Abdullah would be in Damascus "within two days." He had told the British that if Abdullah entered Damascus and they did not reach agreement with Egypt over the treaty, then Syria and Egypt would go Communist. He also told them he could not keep quiet about Abdullah's latest move (the Constituent Assembly for Greater Syria and union with Iraq) and wanted a written assurance from London that Abdullah's army would not be used against Syria. Ibn Saud intended to discuss the matter with Washington and believed that Washington would help if London did not. He wholeheartedly endorsed Kuwatli's idea of a call to Transjordan to join Syria on the basis of a republican plebiscite, but did not wish any reference to be made to the return of Ma'an and Aqaba to Saudi Arabia.[28]

On the Tapline issue Ibn Saud wanted Syria to sign the convention and ordered that a telegram be sent immediately to Kuwatli to that effect. Barāzī tried to mollify him by assuring him that the delay was due to "procedural" issues and that Kuwatli himself was strongly in favor of signature. But to Ibn Saud's advisors Barāzī confided, "Public opinion is angry at U.S. policy on Palestine and the majority of deputies are against ratification by Parliament." Barāzī urged that Tapline withdraw its ultimatum to Mardam (a copy of which was given to Ibn Saud by company representatives during Barāzī's visit); at Ibn Saud's request the letter was withdrawn.[29]

In Cairo, Farouk warned that Syria should not trust British assurances about Abdullah and complained that Ibn Saud was "too considerate" toward Britain. He was in favor of Syria's exposing the "Zionist character" of Abdullah's schemes: "Abdullah collaborates with the Zionists, who are a . . . greater danger to the Arabs than the British because the danger from Britain is bound to come to an end."[30]

No sooner had the UNSCOP report appeared than Saleh Jabr, the prime minister of Iraq, asked for a meeting of the Arab League Political Committee, which was scheduled for September 16–19 in Lebanon. Meanwhile, Jabr visited Damascus, Beirut, and Amman to arrange for a truce on the "Greater Syria" issue and to secure agreement that the Political Committee's meeting would be exclusively devoted to the Palestine problem.[31] Jabr came to the meeting armed with a joint resolution of both houses of the Iraqi Parliament adopted on March 24, 1947. The resolution stated that, considering Britain's referral of the Palestine problem to the UN and "the excessive Zionist pressure on the American government that has compelled it . . . to pressure Britain to adopt a pro-Zionist policy," the least that could be done "to preserve that small portion of justice" contained in the 1939 White Paper was to inform Britain and the United States of their responsibility for the deteriorating situation in Palestine; to declare the independence of Palestine as an Arab state at the UN; and to inform Britain and the United States that, in the event of Arab failure at the UN, the secret resolutions of Bludan would be implemented. The Iraqi Parliament's joint resolution interpreted the Bludan resolutions as "a collective reconsideration by the Arab League states of their economic and political relations with Britain and the United States."[32]

Jabr set the framework and the tone of the meeting of the Political Committee (held at Sofar, Lebanon) by insisting from the beginning on two measures: to notify Britain and the United States promptly that the secret Bludan resolutions would be implemented in the event that the UN General Assembly recommended a solution "not in favor of the Palestine Arabs" and to allocate funds to enable Palestinians and "other Arabs" to undertake "swift and decisive action" in the same event.[33]

As at Bludan, the counterweight to the Iraqis was the Saudi delegate, Yasin. He questioned the competence of the Political Committee to take such resolutions, believed the Bludan resolutions were "too fluid," warned that no resolutions that the Arabs were not prepared to implement should be communicated to Britain and the United States, and advised deferment of the issue to the next League Council meeting.[34]

Yasin did not get much support from the other delegates in criticism of the Bludan resolutions. The discussion shifted rather to whether these resolutions should be "confirmed" and whether a decision should be taken on "notifying" Britain and the United States of them. It was eventually decided to confirm the resolutions but to defer the decision on notification to the next Council meeting. Jabr declared his dissatisfaction with this timorous outcome and insisted that the record should contain the reservation by Iraq that "Iraq will without hesitation cancel its oil concessions in the event of the implementation of a decision against the interests of the Arabs of Palestine."[35]

On the issue of funds for the Palestinians, Jabr argued for the need to agree on a specific sum, but it was resolved "to provide the utmost in funds, materiel, and manpower" and to set up a Technical Committee to get into specifics and to submit its first report within three weeks.[36] This was the closest approach to date to the problem of military preparedness.

Another skirmish that took place between Iraq and the others involved the issue of the Arab Higher Committee's representation in the League Council. Jabr insisted that the Council nominate the AHC representative (to enable Baghdad to veto Hajj Amin's membership) but was overruled by the Committee.[37]

On September 26, a week after the conclusion of the Sofar Conference, Britain announced its decision to abandon the mandate.

### From September, 1947 to the UN Partition Recommendation (November, 1947)

The Arab League Council met at Aley, Lebanon, on October 7–15, 1947, under the shadow of Britain's decision to withdraw from Palestine. The Technical Committee's impressive report appeared, on time, on October 9 and acquired greater grimness in view of Britain's decision. The key figure on the Technical Committee turned out to be General Ismail Safwat, a former Iraqi chief of staff whose professional credentials and integrity made him politically acceptable to the anti-Hashemite capitals. He presented the report to the Council.

Safwat warned that Britain's decision to withdraw from Palestine threatened the country with "very grave developments that were bound to develop to the advantage of the Zionists unless the Arab states promptly mobilized their utmost force and efforts to counter Zionist intentions." The Zionists had at their disposal "political, military, and administrative institutions and organizations characterized by a very high degree of efficiency . . . and capable of transforming themselves into a Zionist government enjoying all the means of control." The Zionists could immediately field a force of 20,000 well-armed and well-trained troops that could rely on twice that number of trained reserves. They enjoyed the advantage of good inner lines of communication and well-defended settlements. They had a special mobile force trained in commando tactics and a small arms industry and had accumulated machinery for advanced arms production. Volunteers from Europe and the United States were being recruited. The members of the Irgun and Stern Gang were specialists in terrorism. The Palestinians had nothing remotely comparable to this in "manpower, organization, armaments, or ammunition." The 350,000 Palestinians who lived in areas of Jewish demographic preponderance were in dire danger.

Safwat recommended immediate recruitment, training, and arming of volunteers, either by the governments or through popular organizations, depending on the political decisions of the governments; deployment of the largest possible numbers of Arab regular troops close to the Palestinian frontiers, the units in each contiguous country to have their special command; establishment of an overall general command to which these special commands and all other forces in Palestine should be subordinated; dispatch of 10,000 rifles to the Palestinians as a "first installment"; allocation of £1 million to the Technical Committee; and deployment of military planes to monitor the Palestinian coast.[38]

Britain's decision to withdraw and Safwat's report brought the Council for the first time face to face with the issue of military preparedness and the possibility of intervention by the regular Arab armies. Nokrashi, the Egyptian prime minister, bluntly informed his colleagues that, because of problems with Britain, Egypt could not entertain such intervention but would help in every other way possible.[39]

The Council fell back on some of Safwat's recommendations: the allocation of £1 million and the deployment of troops on the border, to which even Egypt agreed. Instead of Safwat's general command, the Council confirmed the Technical Committee as the *de facto* general command, but this was a specious move, since the committee did not have and could not have the powers of a general command. In the event, only Lebanon, Syria, Iraq, and Palestine were represented on it. Conspicuously absent were Egypt and Saudi Arabia, while the Transjordanians put in an appearance or two.

The issue of the notification of the secret Bludan resolutions, which the Council was supposed to resolve, was also dodged. In spite of Jabr's prodding, the Council merely decided that "the implementation of [these resolutions] was mandatory in the event of a solution that affected the right of Palestine to be an independent Arab state."[40] Again, those deterred were not to know what they were to be deterred by or indeed that they were being deterred.

During the meeting of the Council, Hajj Amin had turned up in Aley from Egypt. He vigorously lobbied for the establishment of a Palestinian government under the aegis of the Arab Higher Committee. The move was vintage Hajj Amin, and it underlines the implausibility of subsequent assertions in explanation of the 1948 Palestinian exodus that the Arab Higher Committee had "ordered" the Palestinians to vacate their country. The idea of a Palestinian government was quashed by Jabr, who refused to meet with Hajj Amin in spite of the latter's attempt to see him.[41]

With Egypt unwilling to commit its regular forces, Jabr tried at the conclusion of the Aley conference to line up Lebanon, Syria, and Transjordan behind Iraq. With Azzam's help he secured an invitation from King Abdullah to the heads of the delegations to meet in Amman. But King Abdullah's "Greater Syria" initiatives of the previous August still rankled with Kuwatli, who—after initially agreeing to the meeting—sent to Amman only a member of the Syrian delegation, not Prime Minister Mardam.[42]

It was against this background that the United Nations General Assembly passed its partition recommendation on November 29, 1947.

### From Partition (November, 1947) to Trusteeship (March, 1948)

The Arab countries were stunned by the partition resolution and infuriated by American susceptibility to the Zionists. Typical of these reactions was the note on October 10, 1947, from the Syrian minister in Washington to Damascus: "We in the United States could easily be in Tel Aviv—the only difference is in the skies, the terrain, and the language . . . everything around us is Zionist . . . I cannot understand how a friendly government [the United States] could permit its own citizens . . . to attack friendly states [the Arab governments] in their vital interests . . . via contributions exempt from taxation on the grounds that their purpose is charitable."[43]

In the same vein, Faris Khoury, the Syrian delegate at the UN, wrote on October 25, 1947: "American partisanship toward the Zionists under intensive Zionist pressure is flagrant . . . the United States has even threatened China with the withholding of a loan to it . . . as well as Chile, Paraguay, Costa Rica, and Brazil." In the same note Khoury forwarded an interesting proposal. He argued that in order to forestall partition, the Arab states, directly or indirectly, should sponsor an alternative plan based on the model of Swiss cantonization.[44] The plan was in fact put forward at the UN General Assembly by Lebanese delegate Chamoun just before the passage of the partition recommendation.

In spite of the Soviet Union's support of partition, the thrust of Arab anger was against the United States, which was seen as the architect of the plan. The Arab countries, ironically, were staunchly "pro-Western" in the sense of being "anti-Bolshevik"; halfhearted attempts to contact the Soviets were made only by some members of the Syrian delegation, though Hajj Amin also may have been in contact with them.[45]

The reasons for Palestinian opposition to the UN partition recommendation were the same as in 1937, except that the UN proposal allotted 50 percent more territory to the Jewish state. It was against partition that the Palestinians had rebelled in 1937–39. In Palestinian eyes, partition did not involve a compromise but was Zionist in conception and tailored to meet Zionist needs and demands. Partition was seen as imposing unilateral and intolerable sacrifices on the Palestinians. Some 500,000 Palestinians (40 percent of all Palestinians) would suddenly lose their majority status in a Jewish state, whereas only some 10,000 Jews would be in the Palestinian state. Within the proposed Jewish state, Jewish land ownership did not exceed 1.67 million dunums (1 dunum = 1,000 square meters) out of a total area of 15 million dunums.

The morality of the UN partition resolution was compromised in Palestinian and Arab eyes by the UN General Assembly's rejection of relevant draft resolutions proposed by the Palestinian and Arab delegates. One such resolution requesting that the International Court of Justice be consulted on whether the UN General Assembly was "competent to enforce or recommend the enforcement" of partition was defeated in the Ad Hoc Committee by a twenty-one to twenty vote. Another, proposing that all UN member states should participate in alleviating the plight of Jewish refugees in Europe "in proportion to their area, economic resources . . . and other relevant factors," failed to pass in a sixteen to sixteen vote (with twenty-five abstentions) in the Ad Hoc Committee. In the circumstances, the Palestinians and Arabs felt that they were not bound by the partition resolution, which in any case was a nonmandatory recommendation of the General Assembly.

Immediately after the UN partition vote, riots broke out in most Arab capitals against the United States. The U.S. Legation in Damascus was stormed, prompting the chargé to send a curt note to the Syrian Foreign Ministry: "The displeasure which the Syrian Government and people may feel towards any policy . . . of the American Government is no ground for violence of the type which occurred yesterday."[46]

Just before the UN recommendation, and in obvious anticipation of it, Safwat had submitted his second report on November 27. His warnings were more categorical: "It is well nigh impossible to overcome the [Zionist] forces with irregulars. . . . the Arab countries . . . cannot afford a long war . . . since time is in favor of the enemy." His main conclusion was that the Arab countries "should ensure superiority in numbers and materiel and act with maximal speed."

Meanwhile, Safwat urged that priority should be given to training, arming, and organizing the Palestinians "to enable them to defend themselves."

Safwat confessed that he had no detailed information about the armed forces of the Arab states and urged that a meeting of the Arab Chiefs of Staff should be held immediately. He argued that it was self-evident that no military action was feasible without a general military command, which itself should be subordinate to a Higher Political Command, and he called for these two commands to be constituted. He spelled out the contributions of each Arab country to these commands. Egypt and Iraq should each contribute a division, Syria two brigades, and Lebanon a battalion. Volunteers from the Arab countries should be trained and armed and held as a reserve force for the regular armies.[47]

Meanwhile, Syria was daily becoming more deeply involved in the operations of the Technical Committee, whose base was near Damascus; and Kuwatli was personally, if informally, chairing its meetings. Early in December, 1947, he appointed General Taha Hāshimī as inspector-general in charge of recruiting a volunteer force to be designated the Arab Liberation Army (ALA). Hāshimī had been a chief of staff as well as prime minister of Iraq and, although not altogether a *persona grata* to the Iraqi regent, was on cordial terms with Safwat.

Hāshimī was skeptical of Hajj Amin's efforts to organize Palestinian resistance—a view shared by Kuwatli—and urged the subordination of Hajj Amin's irregulars to the Technical Committee, to which Hajj Amin strenuously objected. On December 6 Kuwatli appointed Fawzi Kawukji as commander of ALA forces in the field. Kawukji was a popular Garibaldian officer of Lebanese origin, who had fought in the Palestinian rebellion in 1936 but had less than perfect relations with Hajj Amin.[48]

The British became increasingly wary of the activities of Damascus; on December 10, 1947, Broadmead of the British Legation in Syria warned that "until the end of the Mandate the Palestine Government will remain administratively responsible throughout Palestine, irrespective of whether or not military forces have been withdrawn from any particular area." He confirmed an earlier communication to the effect that "the evacuation of British military forces would be through the port of Haifa. I now wish to make it clear that the military evacuation of the country will be from South to North."[49] It was probably these warnings that caused Mardam about this time to say that "it is not permissible that Syria, alone, should bear the burden of providing volunteers; Lebanon, Iraq, and Jordan should do their part."[50]

Between December 8 and 17, 1947, the Political Committee met in Cairo to face up to the situation created by the UN partition recommendation and to consider Safwat's second report. As in earlier meetings, Iraqi Prime Minister Jabr held the initiative. Partition had been the result of American efforts, but if the secret Bludan resolutions had been conveyed in time, the United States would have had "to think twice before continuing its support of Zionism." He called for "the cessation of the activities of all oil companies in Iraq and Saudi Arabia and the cancellation of current concessions in conformity with the Bludan resolutions." He declared that Iraq "was prepared to stop all concessions *provided Saudi Arabia and the other states do likewise.*"[51] The proviso, though not altogether unreasonable, raises some doubts about the seriousness of the Iraqi posture.

Jabr then addressed himself to Safwat's conclusion that only regular armies could overcome the Zionist forces. "Each country should make explicit the degree of its preparedness to use its regular forces in an expedition to save Palestine and prevent the establishment of a Zionist state. . . . Should the Arab states make clear such an intention, Britain and the United States would realize the gravity of the matter and act to thwart partition."[52]

The meeting was particularly stormy, with the Syrians, feeling cornered, finally retorting—much to the disgust of the Iraqis—that the Bludan resolutions did not involve oil concessions only but military and political treaties with the Western powers as well (i.e., the Anglo-Transjordanian and Anglo-Iraqi treaties).[53]

Nevertheless, some action had to be taken, particularly in view of Safwat's second report. The Council eventually adopted resolutions based on Safwat's subsidiary recommendations, again dodging his principal ones. (1) The Technical Committee would be provided with 10,000 rifles (2,000 each from Syria, Iraq, Saudi Arabia, and Egypt; 1,000 each from Lebanon and Jordan); (2) light arms would be rushed to the more threatened Palestinian areas; (3) 3,000 fully equipped volunteers would be dispatched before the middle of January (500 each from Palestine, Egypt, Iraq, Saudi Arabia, and Syria; 300 from Lebanon; and 200 from Transjordan); (4) a second £1 million would be put at the disposal of the Technical Committee.[54]

At the final meeting of the Committee, Jabr warned that "Iraq saw no way out but for itself to seek all means necessary to prevent partition and the creation of a Zionist state."[55] These Iraqi reservations on Arab League resolutions had by now become a pattern that, together with the explicitness of this latest sample, suggests that the Iraqis may for some time have been contemplating action on their own in the military-diplomatic field, if not in relation to oil concessions.

On his way back from the United Nations, the Iraqi statesman and *éminence grise* Nuri Said had joined the Iraqi delegation at this Cairo meeting of the Political Committee, where he read Safwat's second report and was deeply impressed by it. He related that, like Jabr, the main conclusion he drew from the Cairo meeting was that the Arab League was not "serious" about Palestine. Nuri said that he and Jabr made up their minds to implement Safwat's second report. To that end they stopped in Amman on their way back to Baghdad. They conveyed their "doubts" concerning the League to King Abdullah, who assured them that "if Iraq supported Transjordan with all its forces and resources, the two kingdoms alone could implement Safwat's report."[56]

On December 12 Safwat was surprised to be offered the chief command by Azzam. He turned down the offer, on the grounds that he did not know what the League's objective was. This could only be one of three: to overcome the Zionist forces; to exert pressure on them to compel them to accept Arab demands; or "to foment a rebellion and support it . . . as an armed demonstration against partition in order to achieve political ends, since no rebellion could produce a significant military outcome." Azzam argued that the objective was one of the first two, but that meanwhile there was need to gain time until the issue of the participation of the regular forces was resolved. Safwat provisionally agreed to go along.[57]

Meanwhile, Anglo-Iraqi talks on the revision of the Anglo-Iraqi Treaty had been going on since May, 1947. On January 1, 1948, a high-level Iraqi delegation, led by Jabr and including Nuri Said, left for London. By January 11, the so-called Portsmouth Treaty had been signed because of the forthcoming attitude of British Foreign Secretary Bevin, according to Nuri.

At the conclusion of the treaty talks, the Iraqis asked for a special meeting with the British on the Palestine problem, on the ground that "the revision of the Treaty was insufficient by itself to consolidate Anglo-Iraqi relations, which would remain susceptible to disturbance so long as the Palestine problem was unresolved." Nuri said somewhat diffusely that there was "complete accord" with the British on Palestine "to proceed in the direction that would satisfy Palestinian aspirations in particular and Arab aspirations in general."[58]

Against this background as well as the spiraling civil war in Palestine, Kuwatli sent Barāzī on his second mission to Riyad and Cairo on January 21, 1948. A major topic of discussion with Ibn Saud was the recent Anglo-Iraqi Treaty. Ibn Saud "was visibly anxious." He suspected the Iraqi regent and Nuri, the more so because the British had already pressed Ibn Saud to send his son Prince Feisal to London to discuss an Anglo-Saudi treaty: "We are not Iraq. . . . A treaty with us would be . . . one between equals." Ibn Saud was in complete agreement with Barāzī's analysis that King Abdullah "was determined to exploit partition to annex the Arab section of Palestine as a prelude to the realization of his dream of Greater Syria." King Farouk had warned Ibn Saud that Britain intended to establish a network of treaties with all the Arab countries.[59]

Barāzī was present with Ibn Saud when the news was received on January 22, 1948, that the Iraqi regent had suddenly repudiated the Portsmouth Treaty in the face of violent anti-British demonstrations caused largely by popular anger against Britain's Palestine policy. Ibn Saud marveled at this turn of events and was "greatly relieved" by it.[60]

Barāzī had sensed a certain "aloofness" in Ibn Saud's attitude. Discreet inquiry revealed that the cause was Kuwatli's rejection of Ibn Saud's earlier request that Syria sign the convention with Tapline. Kuwatli had written to Ibn Saud that "national interest should be put above economic interest," which had thrown Ibn Saud into a royal tantrum. He complained to Barāzī: "What does Shukri take me for? . . . Am I his cook that he should give me lessons in patriotism?" Barāzī tried to soothe him: "Shukri is the same old Shukri . . . the symbol of opposition to the Hashemites. . . . We do have a public opinion. . . . We cannot appear to approve of the United States . . . otherwise what happened in Iraq would happen to us."[61] In Cairo King Farouk warned Barāzī that Britain would try to impose a treaty on Syria, which should resist the attempt. He argued that "it would be beneficial to Palestine not to comply with Britain's request."[62]

Between February 7 and 22, 1948, the Political Committee met to discuss the deteriorating situation in Palestine. Since its previous meeting in December, the Iraqi Cabinet headed by Jabr had fallen in the wake of the repudiation of the Portsmouth Treaty. The Iraqi delegation to the February meeting was led by Foreign Minister Pachachi (a former premier). Unlike Jabr and Nuri, Pachachi was seen as representing the "nationalist trend" (*al-tayyār al-waṭanī*) in Iraq, with which the other Arab capitals were more comfortable. One indication of the different Iraqi mood was that Pachachi agreed to Hajj Amin's representing Palestine on the Committee.[63]

In addressing the Committee Safwat stoically stuck to his leitmotifs, ending with the same exhortation—that is, only regular forces could produce results and therefore the Chiefs of Staff should meet forthwith to plan joint action and make up, while there still was time, the many deficiencies in the regular Arab armies.[64]

The Political Committee endorsed Safwat's requests that the Arab governments hasten the dispatch of the balances in their allotted quotas of men, money, and arms for the Arab Liberation Army. It still avoided the issue of a general military command, but did establish a Palestine Committee (as a subcommittee of the Political Committee) to direct "high policy"—except that there was no general military command to direct.

Hajj Amin once again called for the establishment of a Palestinian Administration under the aegis of the Arab Higher Committee at the end of the mandate. Decision on the matter was deferred, most probably in order not to embarrass Pachachi further vis-à-vis the regent in Iraq.[65]

Since the UN partition vote in November, fighting had been escalating viciously in Palestine. Early on, the Irgun and Stern groups had introduced the use of car bombs (used still earlier against the British), and by March Hajj Amin's irregulars were retaliating in kind. Attacks on settlements were answered by the Haganah blowing up Arab suburbs and villages. Jewish convoys were ambushed by Arabs, and vice versa. By January 10, 1948, 1,974 had been killed and wounded. Hajj Amin's irregulars were particularly effective in ambush warfare, and by the end of March the situation in Palestine appeared to the unprofessional eye to be one of military stalemate.

It is not too fanciful to speculate that this appearance of a military stalemate may have contributed to the movement in the United States and the UN away from partition and in favor of trusteeship, and that this in turn (in addition to inter-Arab tensions) may have contributed to Arab hesitance to act on Safwat's main demands. There is evidence, for example, that by the end of March the signal to their capitals from the Arab diplomats in London and New York was that the political battle against partition had already been won. Indeed, these diplomats were now advising their governments to show moderation and restraint in order to consolidate Arab political victory.[66]

### From Plan Dalet (Early April) to the Fall of Tiberias and Haifa (April 18–23)

No such euphoria was felt by Safwat. On March 23 he warned: "One must place no trust in the charlatanism of the Arab press. . . . The operational initiative in most of Palestine is in Zionist hands. . . .

Our relatively stronger garrisons in Jaffa, Jerusalem, and Haifa are strictly on the defensive, and I doubt their ability to stand up to the Zionists, who are being held back only by their fear of the British."[67]

Perhaps the single most important development on the Arab side since the partition vote was the conversation in London in March, 1948, between Tawfiq Abul-Huda, the Transjordanian prime minister, and Bevin to the effect that at the end of the mandate the Arab Legion would enter Palestine, but confine itself to the Arab sector under the partition plan.[68] Abdullah had already indicated as much in another secret meeting with the Zionists—this time with Golda Meir on November 17, 1947.[69] Nor was he too reticent about the matter even with Arab Palestinians. On March 21, for example, he received the mayor of Jaffa, Yusif Haikal, in Amman. The mayor reported that Jaffa was surrounded and under constant bombardment. The Zionist objective was to cause the inhabitants to panic and flee. The Arab regular armies should enter the country to put an end to Zionist aggression. Abdullah's answer was that he did not know how militarily strong the other Arab countries were, nor how much of their strength they were willing to use in the fight against Zionism. What he did know was that "his army alone could not fight or overcome the Zionists."[70]

Although Zionist military planning in this period does not fall within the scope of this chapter, it is worth noting that few Western sources have adequately covered it. This is partly because there has been little direct resort even to the published Hebrew sources (e.g., *Sefer Toldot Ha-Haganah* and *Sefer Ha-Palmach*).[71] Of special relevance for the study of Zionist military preparedness in the period 1945–48 are the successive plans drawn up by the Haganah Command, that is, Plan B (September, 1945), the "May, 1946, Plan" and its two appendices of October and December, 1946, respectively, the "Yehoshua (Joshua Glauberman) Plan" (early 1948), and "Plan Dalet" (D Plan), finalized on March 13, 1948. It is not easy to visualize, after reading the last two, how the Palestinian state under the partition plan could have survived their implementation.[72]

Plan Dalet went into effect in the first week of April. It is not implausible to assume that among the important political factors that influenced its timing were the trend away from partition in the United States and the United Nations and the now famous Truman-Weizmann secret meeting of March 18. The temptation to consider this meeting insignificant is unwarranted. The impact of this event was probably no less than that of the Tawfiq Abul-Huda and Bevin meeting of the same month.

On the military side, the advanced phase reached in British

withdrawal and in Haganah mobilization, the arrival of the first large consignment of arms for the Haganah from Czechoslovakia, and the fact that the Palestinians had until then held their ground and given as much as they had taken—all these factors must have been particularly relevant in timing the launching of Plan Dalet.[73] The many subsidiary operations of the plan were designed to dovetail with one another, and it was their cumulative impact that had shattered the Palestinian community before the end of April.[74] The dynamics of the politico-military competition between the Labor-dominated Haganah and the Revisionist Irgun added an important dimension to the Zionist offensive.[75]

By April 10 it became clear that a major objective of Plan Dalet was to carve out a corridor linking Tel Aviv with the Jewish quarters of West Jerusalem, with the double objective of cutting the Palestinian state (in the partition plan) in two and incorporating the *whole* of Jerusalem and its environs in the Jewish state.[76] Several Palestinian villages in the suburbs of both Tel Aviv and Jerusalem, as well as those on the plain between, came under simultaneous attack. The strategic Palestinian village of Castel, some five miles west of Jerusalem, was captured by the Haganah, only to be recaptured by the charismatic Palestinian guerrilla commander Abdul Qadir Husseini. Abdul Qadir himself was killed in the counterattack; while the battle for Castel was raging, the Irgun and the Stern groups perpetrated the massacre at Deir Yasin, about two miles as the crow flies from Castel. Arab Liberation Army Commander Kawukji simultaneously carried out his first personally led attack against a Zionist colony (Mishmar Haemek southwest of Haifa) and was repulsed.

On April 10 the Palestine Committee met in Cairo to consider this configuration of three disasters. Tempers were high, and the usually suave Azzam accused Transjordan of being subservient to Britain. The Syrian and Lebanese premiers declared their countries' readiness to intervene and asked the Transjordanian and Iraqi delegates to seek clarification of their countries' intentions with regard to the new developments.[77] The anti-Hashemite mood was due partly to the persistent suspicions of Hashemite intentions and partly to exasperation at the "low profile" adopted by Iraq in contrast to its earlier blustering stance. At any rate, this is the first instance of a serious discussion of regular army intervention in the light of the catastrophic turn of events in Palestine. On April 11 the Palestine Committee, largely influenced by Syria, decided to exert every effort to seek Egyptian regular army intervention in spite of Nokrashi's well-known opposition. They argued that if Egypt could be persuaded to intervene, the other countries would follow suit.[78]

By April 12 King Farouk seemed to have been won over. Before all the members of the Political Committee he had a statement read out in his name to the effect that "should Arab armies enter Palestine, he wanted it clearly understood that this measure should be looked upon as a temporary one, unrelated to any attempt at permanent occupation or fragmentation" (i.e., partition).[79] This was at once a message of warning to the Hashemites and of assurance to the others. Nevertheless, it would be some time before Nokrashi himself followed in the royal steps.

Between April 12 and 17 Haganah forces attacked villages in the neighborhood of Tiberias, and on April 18 Tiberias itself fell. The same day Safwat cabled Abdullah in uncharacteristic language: "I have no reserves left . . . Tiberias implores your majesty . . . I appeal to your sense of pity to intervene." On the same day Abdullah had cabled Kuwatli: "We have no more room for the refugees from Tiberias and other parts of the country. . . . Our army is transporting the women. . . . We urge your help"; Kuwatli replied: "We will do our duty by the refugees . . . but transporting women is not enough. If you will order your forces to advance on Tiberias we shall do the same."[80] Later the Political Committee asked Abdullah to use units of the Arab Legion (stationed in Palestine under British command) "to stop the massacres and return the inhabitants of Tiberias to their homes." On April 21 he replied that "Tiberias fell in the presence of the British army, which is still there . . . God willing, the liberation of Galilee will occur after May 15."[81] But Abdullah was already committed to both the British and the Zionists not to enter Galilee.

If the shock of the fall of Tiberias was great, it was overshadowed by the fall of Haifa on April 22–23. The suddenness of the British withdrawal from the residential quarters of Haifa on April 21, and the speed with which Zionist forces occupied the vacated areas, constituted for Palestinians proof positive of collusion between the British and the Zionists. Earlier statements repeated by the British that their final withdrawal from the country would be through Haifa had assured the Palestinians and Arabs that Haifa would remain intact at least until the end of the mandate. The fall of Haifa removed the vestiges of Arab faith in Britain that still remained and plunged the Arab capitals into a period of unprecedentedly frenzied activity. But traumatic as the fall of Haifa was, it, too, was overshadowed by the impending fate of Jaffa and Jerusalem.

On April 25 the Damascus Military Committee cabled Azzam in Cairo: "Jaffa has been under heavy bombardment for the last 24 hours. Morale is low. We fear its fate will be similar to that of Haifa."[82] On April 26 the Haganah launched Operation Jevussi for the conquest of East Jerusalem. It was also the Haganah that had captured Tiberias and Haifa, but the offensive against Jaffa was started by the Irgun.[83]

A key role in the next few days was played by Premier Solh of Lebanon. His strategy was to bring the senior Hashemite country (Iraq) together with Egypt. To that end he convinced Iraqi Regent Abdulilah to visit King Farouk, which he did on April 25. Within hours the Political Committee was for the first time addressing itself to the appointment of a supreme commander. Egypt nominated King Abdullah, and by April 26 the regent had prevailed upon even the Syrian premier, Mardam, to agree.[84] By April 30 the first meeting of the Arab Chiefs of Staff was being held in Amman.

The military chiefs were briefed by Safwat. They unanimously recommended to the Political Committee, then also in session and awaiting the result of their deliberations, that the minimum force required to overcome the Zionists was six divisions and six squadrons of aircraft.[85]

The Political Committee was taken aback and considered the military chiefs "too cautious." They insisted on the beginning of operations "with such forces as were available." Commenting on this decision of the Political Committee, Safwat observed: "It was clear they believed . . . the mere deployment of regular forces and their commencement or pretense at commencement of operations would cause the major powers to intervene . . . and politically compel the Zionists to accept Arab demands. . . . Hence when operations started the Arab force was much less than half the minimum required."[86]

On May 10, with five days to go before the end of the mandate, the Chiefs of Staff met again to draw up the final plan. On May 12, with three days to go, Nokrashi obtained from the Egyptian Parliament its approval of intervention in Palestine by the regular Egyptian forces.[87]

On May 14 Hazzāᶜ Majāli, a senior aide of King Abdullah, was standing beside Azzam as both watched the Arab Legion pass through the streets of Amman on its way to Palestine. Majāli was rather buoyed by the martial sight, but Azzam "poured out his fears of the strength of the enemy . . . and the support the enemy enjoyed at the UN and from the major powers of both East and West."[88]

The terrain is strewn with myths and semimyths, but the following can be established:

  • Between 1945 and 1947 the Arab Palestinians and the Zionists were heading on a collision course more rapidly than at any previous time, since the irreducible minimum the Zionists adamantly insisted on (partition with a Jewish state in the greater part of Palestine) was anathema to the Palestinians.

- The only chance, however remote, of preventing the collision lay in Anglo-American endorsement of the 1939 White Paper, coupled with the liberalization by the United States and the British Dominions of their own immigration laws to allow the immediate mass admission of the Jewish survivors from the refugee camps.

- There was not the slightest chance that partition could be implemented peaceably. The very mechanics of taking over the vast new Palestinian areas that were to constitute the Jewish state inevitably involved wide-scale fighting and destruction, both inside and outside the borders of this state.

- Britain's evacuation strategy compounded its original irresponsibility in abandoning the mandate in the circumstances prevailing. It claimed *de jure* jurisdiction over the whole country even though it was not in *de facto* control, thus deterring intervention by the Arab states before the end of the mandate. At the same time, the preponderance of military criteria in its evacuation of key localities (e.g., Haifa) had additional disastrous consequences for the Palestinians.

- In spite of its evacuation strategy and its historic role as the architect of the Jewish national home, Britain nevertheless succeeded somewhat in deflecting Arab anger from itself toward the United States. This was made possible in part by the salience of U.S. intervention (the public presidential role), its gratuitousness (there had been no historic legacy of Arab-American enmity), and its perceived motivation (the domestic electoral considerations of both the White House and the Congress).

- The Arab countries were torn between centrifugal and centripetal tendencies. In the last analysis the latter prevailed, even though Arab military intervention came too little and too late.

- We have an early instance in 1947−48 of the impingement of the Palestine problem on Western oil supplies. Like the military intervention, the suspension of talks with Tapline by Syria came not as an act of deliberate choice but under the weight of events and the pressure of public opinion.

- Trusteeship in March, 1948, was a mirage without the firm support of Truman. This is why the Weizmann-Truman meeting in March, 1948, is so important. But even with Truman's support, it could have had a chance of success only within a concerted Anglo-American plan such as was outlined above.

- There was nothing mysterious, much less miraculous, in the exodus of the Palestinians. There is categorically no truth in the claim that they were ordered to leave by Hajj Amin or the Arab capitals. Hajj Amin was not in the business of liquidating his own constituency, nor were the Arab capitals in the business of flooding themselves with Palestinian refugees to demonstrate their failure against the Zionists. The explanation lies in the military unpreparedness of the Palestinians and Arabs and the thoroughness of Zionist military planning and operations. Deir Yasin was not a unique event—only the single most revolting one.
- There were two wars in 1948: the "regular war" *after* May 15, 1948, and the civil war from November, 1947, to May 15, 1948. In many ways the civil war was the more crucial and certainly the more devastating to the Palestinians. The civil war ended with the establishment of the state of Israel but also with the virtual destruction of the Palestinian community.
- The plight of the Palestinians generated immense pressures of Arab and (in Egypt) Muslim public opinion, which finally compelled the Arab countries to intervene militarily. Belated and inadequate as it was, but for the intervention of the Arab armies after May 15, 1948, the whole of Palestine would have been conquered by the Zionists in that year.
- If the history of the *regular* war needs to be *re*written, the history of the *civil* war has still to be written.

There remains the question of the key to the British Secretariat in Jerusalem that was left under the doormat. That is myth. The truth (from the diary of Sir Henry Gurney, British chief secretary) is as follows: "May 14: The Police locked up their stores (worth £1 million) and brought the keys to the UN, who refused to receive them. I had to point out that the UN would be responsible for the administration of Palestine in a few hours' time (in accordance with the November Resolution) and that we should leave the keys on their doorstep whether they accepted them or not; which we did."[89]

## Notes

1. Neville J. Mandel, *The Arabs and Zionism before World War I* (Berkeley: University of California Press, 1976), p. 10.

2. See W. Khalidi, ed., *From Haven to Conquest* (Beirut: Institute of Palestine Studies [IPS], 1971), pp. 91ff.

3. Mandel, *Arabs and Zionism*, pp. 32ff.

4. *The Political History of Palestine under British Administration* (Memorandum by His Britannic Majesty's Government presented to UNSCOP, Jerusalem, 1947), p. 10.

5. Khalidi, *Haven to Conquest*, appendix I.

6. *Political History of Palestine*, p. 21.

7. Quoted in Khalidi, *Haven to Conquest*, p. lxx.

8. Sir Keith Hancock, *Survey of British Commonwealth Affairs* (London: RIIA, 1937), I, p. 447.

9. P. J. Loftus, *National Income of Palestine, 1944* ([Jerusalem]: Government Printer, 1946), p. 48.

10. For Palestinian casualties at the hands of the British military, as well as numbers of Palestinians executed and held in detention camps, see Khalidi, *Haven to Conquest*, appendix IV; for arms confiscated from Palestinians and Jews in the period 1936–45, see *A Survey of Palestine* (Jerusalem: Government Printer, 1946), II, pp. 594ff.

11. See ibid., p. 1011, for war production in Jewish factories.

12. *Al-Mashrūᶜ al-inshāʾ ī al-ᶜArabī* (Arab Development Project) (Jerusalem: Maṭbaᶜat Bayt al-Maqdis, 1946).

13. "Maḍbaṭat al-jalsa al-thāniya min dawr al-ijtimāᶜ al-ᶜādī al-thānī li-Majlis al-Jāmiᶜa" (Minutes of the Second Meeting of the Second Ordinary Session of the Arab League Council), November 5, 1945.

14. Ibid.

15. Quoted in *Supplementary Memorandum by the Government of Palestine* (Jerusalem: Government Printer, 1947), p. 5.

16. "Muqarrarāt Muʾ tamar Anshāss" (Resolutions of the Anshass Conference), IPS Archives, Geneva.

17. "Maḍābiṭ jalsāt Majlis al-Jāmiᶜa: Al-dawra ghair al-ᶜādiyya, Blūdān, June 8–12, 1946" (Minutes of Meetings of Arab League Council, Extraordinary Session, Bludan, June 8–12, 1946).

18. "Aᶜmāl al-wafd al-ᶜIrāqī fī Majlis al-Jāmiᶜa al-munᶜaqid fī Blūdān" (Report on Activities of the Iraqi Delegation to the Bludan Conference).

19. "Minutes of Extraordinary Session, Bludan."

20. E. Sasson, "Reports of Meetings with the Amir Abdallah at Shuneh, 12 and 19 August, 1946," Central Zionist Archives, S25/9036.

21. Majid Khadduri, "The Scheme of Fertile Crescent Unity: A Study in Inter-Arab Relations," in Richard N. Frye, ed., *The Near East and the Great Powers* (Cambridge: Harvard University Press, 1951), pp. 141ff.

22. Handwritten note from President Kuwatli to Prime Minister Mardam, July, 1947, Mardam Papers.

23. Patrick Scrivener (British Legation, Damascus) to Prime Minister Mardam, July 18, 1947 (in French), Mardam Papers.

24. Muḥsin Barāzī, "Mudhakkirāt" (Memoirs), *al-Ḥayāt*, January 16, 1953.

25. William Lenahan (Tapline, Beirut) to Prime Minister Mardam, August 21, 1947, Mardam Papers.

26. Ibid.

27. Barāzī, "Mudhakkirāt."

28. Ibid.

29. Ibid.

30. Ibid.

31. "Taqrīr Fakhāmat al-sayyid Ṣāleḥ Jabr, December 26, 1947" (Report by His Excellency Saleh Jabr, December 26, 1947), unpublished document, IPS Archives.

32. "Mulakhkhas aʿmāl al lajna al-siyāsiyya fī Lubnān, 16–19 September, 1947" (Summary of Deliberations of the Political Committee in Lebanon, September 16–19, 1947), unpublished document, IPS Archives.

33. Ibid.

34. Ibid.

35. Ibid.

36. "Qarārāt Sirriyya, Ṣofar" (Secret Resolutions [of Political Committee, September 16–19], Sofar), unpublished document, IPS Archives.

37. "Report by Saleh Jabr," and "Summary of Deliberations."

38. "Al-taqrīr al-awwal alladhī rafaʿahu amīr al-liwāʾ al-rukn Ismaʿīl Ṣafwat, October 8, 1947" (First Report Submitted by Brigadier General Ismail Safwat, October 8, 1947), unpublished document, IPS Archives.

39. Muhammad H. Heikal, "Ḥarb Filasṭīn li-awwal marra bilā raqāba" (The Uncensored Story of the Palestine War), *Akhir Sāʿa*, May 13, 1953.

40. "Qarār sirrī, Aley, October 9, 1947" (Secret Resolution [of Arab League Council], Aley, October 9, 1947), unpublished document, IPS Archives.

41. "Report by Saleh Jabr."

42. Ibid.

43. Syrian Minister (Washington) to Prime Minister Mardam, October 10, 1947, Mardam Papers.

44. Faris Khoury to Kuwatli, October 25, 1947, Mardam Papers.

45. "Difāʿ al-wafd al-ʿIrāqī ʿan Filasṭīn fil-dawra al-thāniya li-ijtimāʿ al-umam al-muttaḥida" (Defense of the Palestine Cause at the Second Session of the UN by the Iraqi Delegation), unpublished document, IPS Archives; also Barāzī, "Mudhakkirāt."

46. Robert B. Memminger (U.S. Legation) to Mardam, December 1, 1947, Mardam Papers.

47. "Al-taqrīr al-thānī alladhī rafaʿahu al-liwāʾ al-rukn Ismāʿīl Ṣafwat" (The Second Report Submitted by Brigadier General Ismail Safwat), November 27, 1947, unpublished document, IPS Archives.

48. Ṭaha Hāshimī, "Mudhakkirāt ʿan Ḥarb Filasṭīn" (Memoirs of the Palestine War), *al-Ḥāris*, March 1, 1953.

49. From Broadmead (British Legation) to Acting Minister of Foreign Affairs, Damascus, December 10, 1947, Mardam Papers.

50. Hāshimī, Manuscript Memoirs, IPS Archives.

51. Memorandum from Saleh Jabr to Political Committee, December 15, 1947, unpublished document, IPS Archives.

52. Ibid.

53. Memorandum prepared by Mardam in reply to Jabr memorandum, Mardam Papers, IPS Archives.

54. ''Qarārāt sirriyya bi sha'n Filasṭīn'' (Secret Resolutions concerning Palestine), December 17, 1947, unpublished document, IPS Archives.

55. Memorandum from Saleh Jabr to Political Committee.

56. Nuri Said, *Ba'd haqā'iq 'an qaḍāyā al-'Irāq al-akhīra wa Filasṭīn* (Certain Facts about Recent Issues in Iraq and Palestine) (Baghdad: Maṭba'at al-sha'b, n.d.).

57. Report prepared by Committee headed by General Ismail Safwat, Baghdad, July 25, 1949, unpublished document, IPS Archives.

58. Said, *Certain Facts.*

59. Barāzī, ''Mudhakkirāt.''

60. Ibid.

61. Ibid.

62. Ibid.

63. *Taqrīr fakhāmat al-sayyid Ḥamdi al-Pāchāchī wa muqarrarāt al-lajna al-siyāsaiyya fīl-ijtimā' al-sābi' al-'ādī, al-Qahira, February 7, 1948* (Report by His Excellency Hamdi Pachachi and the Resolutions of the Political Committee during the [Arab League Council's] Seventh Ordinary Session) (Cairo: n.p., February 7, 1948).

64. Report prepared by Committee headed by General Ismail Safwat.

65. *Report by Hamdi Pachachi.*

66. Armanāzi (minister in London) to Mardam, March 30, 1948, and Faris Khoury (UN) to Mardam, April 4, 1948, Mardam Papers.

67. ''Taqrir mūjaz 'an al-ḥāla fī Filasṭīn'' (Brief Report on General Situation in Palestine), March 23, 1948, report prepared by Safwat for the Palestine Committee, IPS Archives.

68. Sir John Bagot Glubb, *A Soldier with the Arabs* (London: Hodder and Stoughton, 1957), p. 63.

69. Central Zionist Archives, S25/4004.

70. Yusif Heikal, ''Jalsāt fī Raghdān'' (Meetings at Raghdan [Palace]), unpublished manuscript, IPS Archives, pp. 11–12.

71. Benzion Dinur, ed., *Sefer Toldot Ha-Haganah* (History Book of the Haganah), 8 vols. (Tel Aviv: Marakhot, 1954–72), esp. chaps. 61–62, 65, and 74–76; and Zrubebel Gilad, ed., *Sefer Ha-Palmach* (The Palmach Book), 2 vols. (Tel Aviv: Hakkibutz Hameuchad, 1953).

72. Dinur, *Sefer Toldot*, III, pp. 239–41, 1472–75, 1897–901, 1939–43, 1955–60.

73. Ibid., chap. 76, pp. 1526–29. For the latest version of the Weizmann-Truman meeting of March 18, 1948, see Peter Grose, *Israel in the Mind of America* (New York: Alfred A. Knopf, 1983), pp. 271ff.

74. Dinur, *Sefer Toldot*, chap. 78, pp. 1561ff.; and Khalidi, *Haven to Conquest*, pp. 759 and 856–57.

75. Dinur, *Sefer Toldot*, esp. chap. 77, pp. 1540ff.

76. Ibid., pp. 1395ff.

77. Minutes of a Meeting of the Political Committee, Cairo, April 10, 1948, Mardam Papers.

78. Minutes of a Meeting taken by Mardam, Cairo, April 11, 1948, Mardam Papers.

79. Memorandum on Meeting between Political Committee and King Farouk, Cairo, April 12, 1948, Mardam Papers.

80. Mardam Papers, IPS Archives.

81. Ibid.

82. Ibid.

83. Dinur, *Sefer Toldot*, chap. 77 *passim* and pp. 1551ff.

84. Draft of memoirs by Mardam, Mardam Papers.

85. Report prepared by Committee headed by General Ismail Safwat.

86. Ibid.

87. Heikal, "Uncensored Story."

88. Hazzāʿ Majāli, *Mudhakkirātī* (My Memoirs) (Beirut: Dār al-ʿilm lil-malāyīn, 1960).

89. Sir Henry Gurney, "15 March–14 May, 1948," unpublished diary on Palestine, p. 108.

# Historical Overview

*J. C. Hurewitz*

The foreign policy of any government, if not disclosed on adoption, becomes patent on execution. What is not always clear is the authorship and the diplomatic strategy that the policy was designed to uphold and to promote. Such strategies are almost always the product of collegial input, even in authoritarian political systems. For precise confirmation of the plural origins, the researcher has to gain access to the classified archives of the concerned government. Without privileged access, the researcher has to await declassification of the official records.

I enjoyed privileged access to such American records in my assignment to Washington from 1943 to 1946, when it was my duty, in part, to ascertain the diplomatic and political strategies toward wartime and postwar Palestine of Britain and the Soviet Union and of the Zionists, the Palestine Arabs, and the Arab governments. The details that revealed the framing of these strategies and the identity of their authors did not often become known to government researchers in Washington. On sensitive issues such as the future of Palestine, intergovernmental communication—even between intimate allies such as Britain and the United States—rarely led to the sharing of these national secrets.

As the officer responsible for intelligence coverage on Palestine in the Research and Analysis (R&A) branch of the Office of Strategic Services in World War II, I saw copies of much of the general flow of pertinent classified materials, including exchanges between Washington and London at the top diplomatic—and at times executive—levels. Only seldom were there texts of classified British policy guidelines on Palestine. During the war, for example, the Near East Section of R&A did not receive copies from England of the partition proposal of the (British) Cabinet Committee on Palestine, to say nothing of the Cabinet discussion of that item or the interministerial exchanges on the subject. I did not see these documents or, for that matter, any of the minutes and proposals of the related discussion in the Middle East War Council in Cairo; or the briefing materials that in April, 1944, formed the basis of the British-American talks on the Middle East in London, including the agreed record at their close; or the proposal in April, 1945, by the minister of state resident in Cairo for a unitary state in Palestine; or the case against the proposed partition of Palestine by Foreign Secretary Anthony Eden in the same month; or the joint evaluation in June of Palestine policy by the Colonial and Foreign offices. I saw none of these records until 1976–77, when I was preparing the manuscript for volume 2 of *The Middle East and North Africa in World Politics*. Without original documentation, my colleagues and I had to speculate on the contents and intent of evolving strategies and policies in Whitehall on almost all issues of British imperial responsibility but of mutual Allied concern, as our British counterparts had to do in reverse.

British materials that came our way were classified documents on such subjects as gun-running, illegal immigration, or political violence and were sometimes followed by requests for our cooperation in apprehending political terrorists, on whom we had even less information than our ally. Much more plentiful, of course, were unclassified materials supplied by the Palestine administration and the ministries in London; and the British Information Services in New York always responded to our requests for *Parliamentary Debates* and *Parliamentary Papers* or for press reactions to issues relating to Palestine, on which their clippings—or cuttings, as they call them— were more substantial than our own.

On the other hand, OSS (Cairo), which directed the agency's Middle East operations, sent us three sets of every newspaper and many periodicals appearing in Palestine in Arabic, Hebrew, and English; we were permitted to clip two copies of each issue and saved the third for deposit in the Library of Congress. These papers reached our office twice each week in clusters of three days' output, usually within forty-eight to seventy-two hours of publication of the latest issue. Action on our requests for specific ephemera, such as the posters or internal notices and brochures of the Jewish terrorist groups and of the reactivated Arab political parties or biographies of individual Arab and Jewish politicians and underground leaders, was often slow; rarely were our needs unfulfilled.

The Soviet Union evinced only marginal interest in Palestine during the war. The parallel communications traffic with Moscow was thus virtually nonexistent.

It should also be noted that Britain, even as the mandatory power in Palestine and the predominant power in the Arab East, was not always able to learn by direct or indirect means the policies of the Jewish and Arab leaders in Palestine and their supporters abroad. Early in 1945, for example, the British Residence in Cairo, the seat of the privileged ambassador—who, in any wartime crisis, exercised greater authority in Egypt than the government—was unable to procure a reprographic copy of the court records of the secret trial in the Egyptian capital of the Jewish assassins of Britain's Middle East resident minister, Lord Moyne. Within two weeks of the trial's end a microfilm of the proceedings appeared on my desk in Washington—unsolicited by me and, I might add, unknown to Whitehall. A couple of months later, once again without explicit request, a trunk full of the personal papers of Hajj Amin al-Husseini, the Mufti of Jerusalem, including his passport, came to R&A's Near East Section in Washington with the compliments of the American forces in Germany.

In the context of this wartime experience, my primary impression of the papers in this book is the deepening of our knowledge of the perspectives that informed the policy-making processes among the contending parties in Palestine and its involved Arab neighbors as also among the concerned extraregional powers. The authors have derived fresh insights from the study of official records of the period in Britain, the United States, Israel, and Lebanon, where the Institute for Palestine Studies began assembling the widely scattered documents that make up the archives of the Palestine Arab national movement, and Switzerland, to which the retrieved Institute archives were removed after Israel's 1982 invasion of Lebanon. Such insights have begun to clarify our appreciation of the stages leading to the untidy end of Britain's rule in Palestine.

In Moscow there must also be a comparable classified record of the changing Soviet policies toward the dying mandate. In the absence of its release to scholars, speculation on its probable nature remains the order of the day. But, on Soviet policies and intentions, the speculation acquires growing credibility, as interested researchers are able progressively to confirm the policies and the motivations of the other major regional and international actors with which the USSR interplayed.

Continuing Soviet secrecy contrasts sharply with Britain's liberal policy ever since January, 1968, when under the Public Records Act of 1967 Her Majesty's Government shaved twenty years off the old fifty-year rule, thus opening for research enough classified materials at one time to keep droves of doctoral candidates, mostly from the United States, well stocked with unpublished documents. By 1979 all except still sensitive files on the windup of the Palestine mandate, as on all other diplomatic and political issues of the first three postwar years, were thrown open to scholars, even those from the Soviet Union, some of whom I encountered in London. These materials Roger Louis has plumbed with enviable thoroughness for *The British Empire in the Middle East 1945–1951*. He eked out the British evidence by exploring related documents in the National Archives (Washington) and the Israel State Archives (Jerusalem) and an impressive array of private papers on both sides of the Atlantic. We are the beneficiaries of his definitive analysis of the Labour government's Middle East policies, of which Britain's reluctant withdrawal from Palestine formed a large part.

Louis prudently builds his assessment of Labour's developing Palestine strategy around the role of Ernest Bevin—starting with the initial effort to cling to Palestine that gave way to internationalizing the dispute and, when the gamble to hold onto the contested land through a United Nations trusteeship failed, to cutting the losses. The key decisions along the way were undeniably those of the indomitable foreign minister, a heavyweight not only physically but intellectually, despite his less than sure grasp of literary expression. I was told that early in the foreign minister's career his office staff, among them his personal secretaries, who were charged, among other duties, with drafting Bevin's speeches for the House of Commons, began betting with one another on whether and at what point in the delivery he would depart from the formal text. He is reported, on one such occasion, to have ad-libbed, "If you open that Pandora's box you never know what Trojan 'orses will jump out."

Roger Louis—and Alan Bullock in the third volume of his majestic biography of Bevin—lay to rest a widely held contemporary belief that Labour's foreign minister was anti-Semitic or, more precisely, anti-Jewish. I would nonetheless suggest that Louis probably underestimates the influence on Bevin's judgments of old Foreign Office hands, many of whose careers reached back to the 1930s, when the propriety of Britain's pervasive imperial presence in the Middle East under many guises was generally acknowledged, even if also challenged by Italy, Germany, and nationalist movements in the region. That mindset must have contributed to the decision to send the ship *Exodus 1947* back to the British-occupied sector of Germany. This act may have gratified many Britons angered by the exploits of the Jewish terrorists in Palestine at the time; but the blow to Britain's image in West Europe and North America was severe.

In assessing Bevin's management of Middle East issues, one must bear in mind that his public career grew out of the general recognition of his established authority as a labor leader. In Churchill's War Cabinet Bevin had fulfilled with distinction his duties as minister of labor and national service. On the substance of foreign affairs, in the Middle East as elsewhere, he needed instruction. That was why he assembled in Whitehall a conference of the chiefs of the Middle East missions hardly more than six weeks after taking office. In a word, it was the career diplomats who framed the strategic guidelines for Britain's Middle East policies, and on Palestine in particular they endorsed the principles that had evolved over the preceding eight years, ever since the fall of 1938, when the Chamberlain government discarded the partition proposal. The main thrust of Britain's postwar effort in the Arab East—the retention of Britain's supremacy through the promotion of Arab unity and the transformation of the Office of the Middle East Resident Minister into the British Middle East Office—bore all the marks of their Foreign Office origins. The emphasis on changing from Britain's preferential status to a cosmetic stance of equal partnership was unmistakably attributable to Bevin's authorship. It is instructive, moreover, that Bevin's second conference of chiefs of Middle East diplomatic missions occurred in July, 1949, at the very time that Dr. Ralph J. Bunche finally put in place the Arab-Israel armistice regime. Once again, the influence of the career diplomats on the foreign minister's understanding of the unfolding Middle East condition was unmistakable. It was then that Bevin finally acquiesced in the reality of Israel within its armistice lines, an Israel 45 percent larger than the UN General Assembly's resolution had recommended.

What shines through the Louis evaluation is the seeming incomprehension, among British statesmen and diplomats, of the working of the American political system, especially the part of the American president in the making of foreign policy. The American political system, after all, is a presidential executive system. The departments of State and Defense are not merely federal agencies. They are the president's advisory agencies. He can take or leave their advice as he sees fit. The appointed bureaucrats develop expertise on developments in foreign countries they are assigned to monitor; they understandably become sensitized to the attitudes of the peoples and governments of those countries. The president, however, is an elected official who is accordingly sensitive to the ever-shifting mood of the electorate. In theory, the president finds the point of accommodation between the foreign and the domestic imperatives. In practice, he inclines to favor the domestic. If British officials—not least the foreign secretary and his prime minister, Clement Attlee—were not as finely tuned to the idiosyncrasies of American politics, it was an understandable, though at times also a costly, oversight.

Less excusable was the occasional comparable disregard of the process by some American foreign service officers who cultivated an exaggerated notion of their own importance in foreign policy making, alongside the president and his immediate White House aides. In Foggy Bottom this seemed to be a hangover among the tight-knit group of foreign service alumni of America's interwar isolationism when—at least before 1937—the president only intermittently took an interest in foreign policy. By the opening postwar years many of these officers filled top positions in the department and did not always appreciate or accept gracefully the enlarging role of the White House staff in foreign policy determination, foreshadowing the later rivalry between the State Department and the National Security Council.

The tension between the State Department and the personal aides of President Truman is a primary theme of Peter Grose's analysis of the American perspective on the final years of the Palestine mandate. Much of the American documentary evidence appears in the then annual *Foreign Relations of the United States*, prepared by the historical division of the Department of State; the volumes of 1945 through 1948 appeared between twenty-three and twenty-eight years after the actual drafting of the documents. Once the selected diplomatic materials were published, the National Archives in Washington opened the remaining records of that year to scholars. Thus, in that period, the National Archives ran a few years ahead of the Public Record Office in London in gratifying researchers.

Grose's paper, like that of Louis, is distilled from a book, in this case titled *Israel in the Mind of America*, for which a good deal of the investigation was done in the same public archives, giving greater attention, however, to the collections in Washington and Jerusalem and less to those in London than Louis had. Grose also drew upon the private papers in the Roosevelt, Truman, and Ben-Gurion libraries. By spreading his net so widely, Grose demonstrates how unfamiliar American presidents were with the realities in the Middle East. The fantasies of President Roosevelt on peaceably resolving the Arab-Zionist dispute after the war are otherwise of antiquarian interest only.

Far more significant were Truman's decisions and how he reached them. Grose has put into clear context the erratic shifts in United States policies on Palestine, particularly after the question was placed on the agenda of the United Nations General Assembly. The State Department and the White House were both writing the policies, each with a different constituency in mind. State was responding chiefly to pressures of the cold war as it bore upon the Middle East, and the White House, chiefly to domestic pressures. So long as the president did not personally intervene, State went its own way. Thus the American position before the General Assembly's Ad Hoc Committee on Palestine in the fall of 1947 was developed essentially by State, and the pressures on friendly delegations before the final vote in the plenary assembly, by the White House. Less than four months later, State bypassed the White House staff in seeking the suspension of the partition process, and the president—without taking State into his confidence, as was his prerogative—reciprocated by granting Israel *de facto* recognition less than eight hours after its proclamation of independence.

The Department of State and the White House staff were manifestly working at cross purposes in managing the Palestine problem at the United Nations. The phenomenon of an executive agency trying to undercut the president it was supposed to serve confused all observers, American as well as non-American. Yet despite the contradictory positions on Palestine, State and the White House staff were equally determined to contain the Soviet Union, and each seemed persuaded that its policy guidelines would best safeguard that purpose. This simply compounded the confusion. In the meantime, on no other major international issue in any permanent organ of the United Nations in 1947–48—the disposition of the former Italian colonies excepted—were the United States and the Soviet Union voting on the same side. Disharmony in Washington within the executive branch of the federal government, seeming harmony at the United Nations between the cold warriors—was anything better calculated to bewilder the uninitiated?

As the paper by Oles Smolansky explains, the Kremlin viewed its policy on Palestine as productive. It contributed to the early end of the mandate and, accordingly, also of the British presence in the strategic heart of the Middle East. Coming in the wake of the withdrawal from India, Burma, and Ceylon, the departure from Palestine could hardly fail to quicken the unraveling of Britain's Middle East empire, so central to Britain's survival as a world power. By emphasizing that the victims of the Holocaust merited the right of national self-determination, the Soviet government was appealing to the humanitarianism of those in Western Europe who had outlived the bestiality of Nazi rule. By invoking the principle of national self-determination not for the Jews alone but for the Palestine Arabs too, the USSR must have calculated that it would win plaudits among liberation movements in Africa, the Middle East, and Southeast Asia and thus help extend the range of potential Soviet influence throughout the Eastern Hemisphere.

This is all conjecture, as indeed it must be, in view of the secrecy of the inner workings of the Soviet system, especially its foreign-policy-making mechanism. Use of the Soviet archives may be denied. But a battery of dedicated scholars in the non-Soviet industrial world in the past thirty-five years have been interpreting the tea leaves in the brew of Moscow's rhetoric and infrequent public policy statements, matching these against verifiable Soviet behavior and trustworthy reports by third-country officials who have dealt with the USSR. This is the stuff of Smolansky's analysis, which he shores up with reference also to such visible actions of the Soviet government as its permitting thousands of Jewish refugees uprooted by the Holocaust to migrate from Eastern to Western Europe for movement to Jewish Palestine and later to Israel and permitting Czechoslovakia to transfer arms to the Yishuv early in 1948 and later also to the nascent Jewish state, for throughout this period the United States did not lift its embargo on such traffic. In the absence of the actual documentation that must be presumed to exist, such speculation, drawing upon the available cumulative wisdom of the professional Kremlin watchers, carries persuasive plausibility.

Each of the concerned extraregional powers, in turn, appeared to act on the assumption that, for the protection of its perceived interests, it could bend Middle East contestants to its will. Each, over time, has learned to its sorrow that Middle East actors have minds of their own and can remain unyielding even under high pressure. Britain was already feeling the brunt of the Arab League's refusal to cooperate on any but the League's own terms. How ungrateful, many old Middle East hands in Whitehall must have reasoned. After all, without British sponsorship in the second half of World War II, there would have been no Arab League, at least not that soon. The comparable experiences of the United States and the Soviet Union, with both Arab and Israeli governments, were yet to come. But, as Michael J. Cohen implies in his provocative essay, the Zionist leaders in the final years of the mandate already knew where they wanted to go, even though they differed in their notions on how to get there, and they enjoyed the backing of a powerful consensus in the Yishuv and among Jews across Western Europe and North America, notably the United States.

A cursory reading of Cohen may sound repetitive, for he has consulted the same archives as Louis and Grose. On reflection, it becomes clear that the distribution of emphasis differs. Cohen gives closer consideration to the documents in the Israel State Archives than do the others. Also like Louis and Grose, Cohen had earlier immersed himself in detailed documentary study, so that his chapter derives from two books in sequel, *Palestine: Retreat from the Man-*

date, *1936–1945* and *Palestine and the Great Powers, 1945–1948.* In the search for an explanation of postwar developments leading to the establishment of Israel, he offers an Israeli perspective. Demonstrating the author's manifest familiarity with Zionist diplomacy, the analysis ranges over personal rivalries and ideological differences among the Jewish leaders in their struggle for statehood. Cohen's treatment of the interplay of diplomacy and domestic American politics and the working of global diplomacy at the United Nations at times seems to lack the depth that informs his exploration of the British and Zionist components.

His preoccupation with the ever-changing diplomatic environment, as it conditioned the dispute over Palestine, may perhaps account for his casual handling of the interplay of diplomacy and domestic politics and military and political planning, organization, and action in the Yishuv in the final months of the mandate, after the adoption of the UN General Assembly's partition resolution in November, 1947. With the progressive dismantling of the Palestine government's administrative apparatus and the stoppage of its services, the Zionist leaders picked up the pieces. They created the provisional government and its administrative machinery in cooperation with the UN Palestine Commission for which the Assembly resolution had provided. They took the requisite military measures to defend the Yishuv, pending the departure of the British. They proclaimed the birth of the state of Israel. Over these themes, Cohen passes only lightly.

The collapse of the mandate also generated parallel political, military, and administrative challenges and opportunities for the realization of Palestine Arab sovereignty. But Walid Khalidi, in an otherwise elegant chapter, never explicitly states why the Palestine Arabs failed to move into the breach. He points out, it is true, that, at a meeting of the Arab League Council in Aley (Lebanon) in October, 1947, Amin al-Husseini, the Mufti of Jerusalem, made a vigorous bid for the creation of a Palestinian government. The Mufti's proposal, at the insistence of Prime Minister Saleh Jabr of Iraq, was rejected. The Mufti repeated the request in February, 1948, at a meeting of the Council's Political Committee in Cairo; once again, it was turned down. Yet, overall, the Palestine Arabs appear only dimly in the shadows of the Arab League Council's deliberations from November, 1945, through May, 1948.

Khalidi's reconstruction of the Arab perspective implies that the Palestine Arabs had become the wards of the Arab League from its birth in March, 1945. He attributes the passivity of the Palestinians to their nonrecovery from the confrontation with Britain in the revolt of 1936–39. It was then that the Palestine government deported the principal Palestine Arab leaders and dissolved their political directorate (the Arab Higher Committee) and their political parties. That is only part of the explanation. A full inquiry into the subject, including the League Council's reconstitution of the Palestine Arab Higher Committee in November, 1945, is still awaiting an author.

This omission apart, Khalidi has produced an invaluable analysis based on largely unpublished and hitherto unused sources—the minutes, reports, and resolutions of the pertinent meetings of the Arab League Council and other documents that the Institute on Palestine Studies has assembled as well as related private papers, memoirs, and articles, mostly in Arabic. For the first time we are led step by step through successive semiannual and extraordinary meetings of the Arab League Council as it girded itself for a custodial role in the mounting Palestine crisis. A week or so before the formation of the Anglo-American Committee of Inquiry in November, 1945, the Council began to develop a coordinated strategy for its members, including information offices in London and Washington, for defending the interests of the Palestine Arabs. By the fall of 1947 the Council's Political Committee had become the policy maker and crisis manager, and its Technical Committee, stationed in Syria, was placed in charge of operations to frustrate the implementation of the General Assembly's partition resolution. Khalidi's essay, which has opened up a subject long neglected, confirms the need for a comprehensive study of the unfolding Palestine Arab and Arab League positions on the end of the mandate.

Missing from the discussion in this book is a systematic analysis of the role of the United Nations in the termination of the mandate. In accepting with enthusiasm the General Assembly's proposal, the Jewish Agency (as the spokesman for the Jewish national home and its worldwide supporters, particularly the World Zionist Organization) and the elected administrators of the Yishuv (representing the Palestine Jews) put into action their vibrant composite political system and, jointly with the UN Palestine Commission (UNPAC), took the necessary steps to create a provisional council of government, which on May 14, 1948, became the provisional government of Israel. These steps, executed in accordance with the General Assembly's guidelines, endowed the action with international legitimacy. Meanwhile, the Palestine Arabs, the concerned Arab governments, and the Arab League flatly rejected the General Assembly's recommendations and refused to cooperate with UNPAC, thereby abdicating the field in Palestine to the Yishuv. The Palestine Arabs and their regional supporters thus, in effect, took a high-risk gamble and lost.

The UN dimension, in the light of the unfolding official evidence made available to scholars in London, Washington, Jerusalem, and Geneva as well as at UN headquarters in New York, awaits integrated study. Despite this omission, the essays in the present book enrich our appreciation of the climax of the mandatory phase of the dispute over Palestine. Written to explain divergent points of view, the essays present contrasting—and, at times, conflicting—interpretations. It is in the nature of the exercise that it should be so. What distinguishes the volume is the vigorous exchange of ideas in the quest for a consensual understanding of why the mandate ended the way it did. The contributors, representing a younger generation of historians, have produced fresh evaluations that rest on new sources. Each chapter is itself a historical statement, including the bibliographical essay by Robert Stookey. Together they contribute to a sound appreciation of a critical phase of a dispute that four decades later still seems to defy peaceable accommodation.

# Historiographical Essay

*Robert W. Stookey*

The following discussion is limited to documents and publications that appear to me to have direct relevance to the series of events with which the foregoing chapters are concerned. It is not intended as a comprehensive bibliography on Palestine. Necessarily, it is selective, as the literature even on this restricted aspect of the territory is extensive and heterogeneous. Some items of interest may well have gone unmentioned. Following a listing of some useful background works, the discussion addresses materials pertinent to the perspectives of the principal actors in the extinction of the Palestine mandate. Some works overlap two or more of the five viewpoints. In order to avoid excessive repetition, most of these have been cited in a single context, which has involved an arbitrary, if unavoidable, choice.

The history of Palestine under the mandate is essentially that of Britain's ultimately thwarted effort to find common ground between two nationalisms, Zionist and Arab, each claiming the right to exclusive possession of the same territory. The rationale and goals of the Zionist movement were expounded by its founder, Theodor Herzl, in *Der Judenstaat*, published in 1896 and later in various English translations—for example, *The Jewish State: An Attempt at a Modern Solution of the Jewish Question*, 3rd ed. (London: Zionist Organization Central Office, 1936). Two senior executives of the World Zionist Organization working in London during World War I published significant works: *Trial and Error* (New York: Harper, 1949), the autobiography of Chaim Weizmann, who became Israel's first president; and Nahum Sokolow, *History of Zionism*, 2 vols. (London: Longmans, Green, 1919). Representative of the extensive literature on Zionism are Ben Halpern, *The Idea of the Jewish State* (Cambridge: Harvard University Press, 1961); Arthur Hertzberg, ed., *The Zionist Idea* (Garden City, N.Y.: Doubleday, 1959); Walter Laqueur, *A History of Zionism* (New York: Holt, Rinehart and Winston, 1972); and Howard M. Sachar, *A History of Israel* (New York: Alfred A. Knopf, 1976). Research and analysis of the movement continue, and among the more recent works are Shlomo Avineri, *The Making of Modern Zionism: The Intellectual Origins of the Jewish State* (New York: Basic Books, 1981); and Amnon Rubinstein, *The Zionist Dream Revisited: From Herzl to Gush Emunim and Back* (New York: Schocken, 1984).

The pioneering account of the rise of Arab nationalism is George Antonius, *The Arab Awakening* (London: Hamish Hamilton, 1938), distinguished by its literary quality and its author's personal acquaintance with the Hashemite princes, other Arab leaders, and many British officials responsible for Arab affairs. Some later writers on the subject have questioned certain of Antonius's interpretations, for more or less tacit ideological reasons or to introduce evidence not available when he wrote. Among studies worth consulting are Sylvia Haim, ed., *Arab Nationalism: An Anthology* (Berkeley: University of California Press, 1962); Zeine N. Zeine, *Anglo-Turkish Relations and the Emergence of Arab Nationalism* (Beirut: Khayyat, 1966); Jon Kimche, *The Second Arab Awakening* (New York: Holt, Rinehart and Winston, 1970); and C. Ernest Dawn, *From Ottomanism to Arabism: Essays on the Origins of Arab Nationalism* (Urbana: University of Illinois Press, 1973). Specifically focused on Palestine are Anne Moseley Lesch, *Arab Politics in Palestine 1917–1939* (Ithaca, N.Y.: Cornell University Press, 1979); and a well-researched two-volume study by Yehoshua Porath, *The Emergence of the Palestinian Arab National Movement, 1918–1929* (London: Cass, 1974) and *The Palestinian Arab National Movement: From Riots to Rebellion, 1929–1939* (London: Cass, 1977).

Remarkable for its insight into the psychological reasons for the persistent hostility between the two nationalisms is an essay by a distinguished scholar of the Middle East, recently assassinated on the campus of the American University of Beirut: Malcolm H. Kerr, "The Arabs and Israelis: Perceptive Dimensions to Their Dilemma," in Willard A. Beling, ed., *The Middle East: Quest for an American Policy* (Albany: State University of New York Press, 1973, pp. 3–31). Other writers have discussed the source and ramifications of the Arab-Jewish dispute from a wide variety of viewpoints. Joan Peters, *From Time Immemorial: The Origins of the Arab-Jewish Conflict over Palestine* (New York: Harper and Row, 1984), is a notable example of what can emerge from diligent and rigorously selective research in support of a partisan thesis—namely, that Arabs have no legitimate claim to Palestine. The opposing view is effectively presented in Walid Khalidi, ed., *From Haven to Conquest* (Beirut: Institute of Palestine Studies, 1971), a wide-ranging compilation of published discussions of many aspects of the Palestine issue, with an extended, forcefully argued introduction by the editor. The following scholarly treatment is particularly recommended: Bernard Wasserstein, *The British in Palestine: The Mandatory Government and the Arab-Jewish Conflict* (London: Royal Historical Society, 1978); see also Ritchie Ovendale, *The Origins of the Arab-Israeli Wars* (Chicago: Longman, 1984).

Two historiographical essays are of some interest: Yehoshua Porath, "Palestinian Historiography," *Jerusalem Quarterly*, 5 (Fall, 1977), 95–104; and Tarif Khalidi, "Palestinian Historiography," *Journal of Palestine Studies*, 10/3 (Spring, 1981), 59–76. An important bibliographical reference is Philip Jones, *Britain and Palestine, 1914–1948: Archival Sources for the History of the British Mandate* (New York: Oxford University Press, 1979). Particularly helpful is J. C. Hurewitz, *The Middle East and North Africa in World Politics: A Documentary Record*, 2nd ed., 3 vols. (New Haven: Yale University Press, 1975), notably volume 2, which provides the texts of many of the essential documents with analytical introductions and bibliographical references. Two volumes by George Kirk, issued under the auspices of the Royal Institute of International Affairs, remain indispensable: *The Middle East in the War* (London: Oxford University Press, 1952) and *The Middle East: 1945–1950* (London: Oxford University Press, 1954). Also of great interest for background reference is Howard M. Sachar, *Europe Leaves the Middle East, 1936–1954* (New York: Alfred A. Knopf, 1972). Land ownership, an issue that contributed to the Arab rebellion of the 1930s, is studied in Kenneth Stein, *The Land Question in Palestine, 1917–1939* (Chapel Hill: University of North Carolina Press, 1984). Ylana N. Miller, *Government and Society in Rural Palestine 1920–1948* (Austin: University of Texas Press, 1984), draws on previously unexploited sources to analyze the effects of an emergent state system on Palestinian Arab villagers.

The apparent inconsistencies in the undertakings regarding Palestine given by Britain during World War I to France in the provisional Sykes-Picot understandings, to the Arabs in the Hussein-McMahon correspondence, and to the Zionists in the Balfour Declaration have generated lively controversy and their share of myths. In all likelihood these documents, produced in wartime for tactical purposes, were intentionally phrased to allow more than one interpretation. Significant works in the ongoing discussion of promises to the Arabs, besides the Antonius volume mentioned above, are Harry N. Howard, *The Partition of Turkey: A Diplomatic History, 1913–1923*

(Norman: University of Oklahoma Press, 1931); two works by Elie Kedourie, *England and the Middle East: The Destruction of the Ottoman Empire 1914–1918* (Cambridge: Cambridge University Press, 1956) and *In the Anglo-Arab Labyrinth: The McMahon-Husayn Correspondence and Its Interpretations 1914–1939* (Cambridge: Cambridge University Press, 1976); and Abdul Latif Tibawi, *Anglo-Arab Relations and the Question of Palestine* (London: Luzac, 1977). For decades it was widely believed that Chaim Weizmann took the initiative in persuading the British government to issue the Balfour Declaration. The first scholarly analysis of the evidence then accessible was set forth in Leonard Stein, *The Balfour Declaration* (London: Vallentine-Mitchell, 1961), which, however, cautiously refrains from a forthright statement of the conclusions implicit in the exposition. A useful companion volume, with a somewhat broader context, is Isaiah Friedman, *The Question of Palestine 1914–1918: British-Jewish-Arab Relations* (London: Routledge and Kegan Paul, 1973). Research based on British archival sources for the period suggests that the concept of the Declaration may have taken shape among British officials who—concerned with enhancing Britain's strategic position in the Middle East and with excluding France from a role in Palestine—themselves took the initiative of seeking out the Zionist leaders: see Mayir Vereté, "The Balfour Declaration and Its Makers," *Middle Eastern Studies*, 6/1 (January, 1970), 48–76. This interpretation is not shared by all recent writers on the subject. Ronald Sanders, *The High Walls of Jerusalem: A History of the Balfour Declaration and the Birth of the British Mandate for Palestine* (New York: Holt, Rinehart and Winston, 1984), attributes the decision more to a sentimental empathy between British leaders and the Jews than to imperial self-interest. This assessment is in turn subjected to a rigorous and extended critique in Conor Cruise O'Brien, "Israel in Embryo" (*New York Review of Books*, March 15, 1984).

Among many studies of Palestine affairs under the mandate one remains outstanding for its breadth of view and quality of analysis: J. C. Hurewitz, *The Struggle for Palestine* (New York: W. W. Norton, 1950). The progress of the Yishuv toward statehood is recounted by a prominent diplomat and political advisor to the Jewish Agency: David Horowitz, *State in the Making* (New York: Alfred A. Knopf, 1953). Also of interest is Nicholas Bethell, *The Palestine Triangle: The Struggle between the British, the Jews and the Arabs, 1935–48* (London: André Deutsch, 1979), which draws on the British archives for the period as well as on personal interviews that shed light on the King David Hotel bombing and the *Exodus* incident. The former event receives concentrated examination in Thurston Clarke, *By*

*Blood and Fire: The Attack on the King David Hotel* (New York: Putnam, 1981). Michael J. Cohen's *Palestine: Retreat from the Mandate, 1936–1945* (New York: Holmes and Meier, 1978) and *Palestine and the Great Powers 1945–1948* (Princeton: Princeton University Press, 1982) comprise an able study of the international dimensions of the issue, based on an impressive range of primary sources.

The armed conflict that, in the end, rendered the British position untenable is treated in Menachem Begin, *The Revolt: The Story of the Irgun* (New York: Henry Schuman, 1951), written by the organization's leader and subsequent prime minister of Israel; and in J. Bowyer Bell, *Terror out of Zion* (New York: St. Martin's, 1977). On the much-debated question of why many Palestinian Arabs became refugees during the conflict, two essays independently reach similar conclusions: Walid Khalidi, "Why Did the Palestinians Leave?" *Middle East Forum*, 35/7 (July, 1959); and Erskine Childers, "The Other Exodus," *Spectator* (May 12, 1961).

The mandate ended with the passing of responsibility for Palestine to the United Nations. The UN failed in the attempt to effect an orderly partition, but its role was eventually decisive in negotiating armistice agreements between Israel and its neighbors. The Guatemalan member of the UN Special Committee on Palestine wrote a personal, popular account in which sympathy for the Zionist side is undisguised: Jorge García-Granados, *The Birth of Israel* (New York: Alfred A. Knopf, 1948). A Spanish diplomat who entered the UN's service, Pablo de Azcárate, served as head of UNSCOP's advance mission in Palestine and later as principal secretary of the Palestine Conciliation Commission; his *Mission in Palestine 1948–1952* (Washington, D.C.: Middle East Institute, 1966) is a detailed and objective account of his four years in the area. The UN's first mediator in the dispute is the subject of Sune O. Persson, *Mediation and Assassination: Count Bernadotte's Mission to Palestine 1948* (London: Ithaca Press, 1979), based on primary sources, including Bernadotte's papers.

**The British Perspective**

The British archives for the entire period of the Palestine mandate are open to researchers at the Public Record Office, London. The relevant files are those of the Foreign Office and Colonial Office, which shared direct responsibility for the territory's affairs; the Cabinet Office; the Prime Minister's Office; the War Office; and the Chiefs of Staff. Palestine received sustained attention in Parliament; of particular interest are the records for the years between the Arab revolt of 1936 and the British withdrawal in 1948: *The Parliamentary Debates, House of Commons*, Fifth Series, vols. 317–449 (London, 1936–49); and *House of Lords*, Fifth Series, vols. 103–58 (London, 1936–48).

The vicissitudes of the British government's ultimately unsuccessful effort to harmonize Jewish and Arab interests in Palestine led to reassessments, and published reformulations, of policy. The major documents are the following: *Statement of British Policy in Palestine Issued by Mr. Churchill in June, 1922* (London, 1922: "Churchill White Paper"); Command Paper (Cmd.) 5479, *Report of Palestine Royal Commission, July 1937* ("Peel Report"); Cmd. 5513, *Palestine: A Statement of Policy* (July, 1937); Cmd. 5854, *The Palestine Partition Report* (October, 1938); Cmd. 6019, *Palestine: A Statement of Policy* (May, 1939: the "White Paper"); Cmd. 6808, *Report of the Anglo-American Committee on Palestine* (1946); Cmd. 6873, *Palestine: Statement of Information Relating to Acts of Violence* (1946); and Cmd. 7044, *Proposals for the Future of Palestine: July, 1946–February, 1947* (1947).

Although its scope goes well beyond the limited topic of concern here, Elizabeth Monroe's classic *Britain's Moment in the Middle East, 1914–1971* (Baltimore: Johns Hopkins University Press, 1981) must be highly recommended.

The decision to establish a separate administration in the part of Palestine east of the Jordan was made at a conference of British officials in the Middle East held at Cairo in March, 1921, presided over by Winston Churchill, then colonial secretary. The meeting is the subject of Aaron S. Kliemann, *Foundations of British Foreign Policy in the Arab World: The Cairo Conference, 1921* (Baltimore: Johns Hopkins University Press, 1970).

Several works of interest explore British attitudes toward Jews and Zionism: Col. Richard Meinertzhagen, *Middle East Diary, 1917–56* (New York: Yoseloff, 1960); N. A. Rose, *The Gentile Zionists: A Study in Anglo-Zionist Diplomacy* (London: Frank Cass, 1973); Bernard Wasserstein, *Britain and the Jews of Europe* (New York: Oxford University Press, 1983); Joseph Gorny, *The British Labour Movement and Zionism* (London: Frank Cass, 1983); and Michael J. Cohen, *Churchill and the Jews* (London: Frank Cass, 1985).

Studies of the Palestine mandate before the Labour government came to power in 1945 include William Keith Hancock, *Survey of British Commonwealth Affairs 1918–1939*, 2 vols. (London: Oxford University Press, 1937, 1940); Daphne Trevor, *Under the White Paper* (Jerusalem: Jerusalem Press, 1948); John Marlowe, *The Seat of Pilate: An Account of the Palestine Mandate* (London: Cresset Press,

1959); and Michael J. Cohen, *Palestine: Retreat from the Mandate,* previously mentioned, which describes the frustrations of British policy as well as the debates within the Zionist leadership.

For British government actions and policy respecting Palestine under the Labour government, the central figure is the foreign secretary. He is the subject of a major landmark of political biography, the first two volumes of which appeared in 1960 and 1967; the third, of concern here, is Alan Bullock, *The Life and Times of Ernest Bevin: Foreign Secretary, 1945–1951* (New York: W. W. Norton, 1983). Kenneth Harris, the biographer of Prime Minister Clement Attlee, devotes a chapter to Palestine in his *Attlee* (London: Weidenfeld and Nicolson, 1982). Field Marshal Montgomery participated (on the affirmative side) in the debate within the Labour government over whether to use the military force necessary to impose order in Palestine; his autobiography is thus relevant to this discussion: *The Memoirs of Field-Marshal the Viscount Montgomery of Alamein* (Cleveland: World Publishing Co., 1958). One British member of the Anglo-American Committee of Inquiry was Richard H. S. Crossman, Labour M.P. and assistant editor of the *New Statesman,* who, during the Committee's investigation, became a supporter of Zionism and therefore eventually a Bevin critic. His two books on the issue illuminate one element of the British perspective on Palestine: *Palestine Mission: A Personal Record* (New York: Harper and Bros., 1947) and *A Nation Reborn: A Personal Report on the Roles Played by Weizmann, Bevin and Ben-Gurion in the Story of Israel* (New York: Athenaeum, 1960). The evolution of Britain's approach to the Palestine issue receives searching, meticulously documented analysis in Wm. Roger Louis, *The British Empire in the Middle East 1945–1951: Arab Nationalism, the United States and Postwar Imperialism* (Oxford: Clarendon Press, 1984), part 4 of which is devoted to the Palestine question.

Two major turning points in the Labour government's Palestine policy are discussed in articles by Ritchie Ovendale: "The Palestine Policy of the British Labour Government 1945–1946," *International Affairs,* 55/3 (July, 1979), 409–31; and "1947: The Decision to Withdraw," *International Affairs,* 56/1 (January, 1980), 73–93. Britain's posture in the decisive armed conflict is recounted by the Israeli writers Jon and David Kimche in *Both Sides of the Hill: Britain and the Palestine War* (London: Secker and Warburg, 1960).

**The American Perspective**

The *Foreign Relations of the United States* series has been compiled and published for the applicable years, and supplementary records are available in the National Archives. The papers of the two U.S. presidents concerned are housed respectively at the Franklin D. Roosevelt Library at Hyde Park, New York, and the Harry S Truman Library at Independence, Missouri. The former has custody of the papers of Henry Morgenthau, Jr., Roosevelt's secretary of the treasury, who played an active role in the Zionist movement. The papers of Henry F. Grady, the American co-framer of the abortive Morrison-Grady proposals, are at the Truman Library, as are those of Samuel I. Rosenman, who served as special counsel to both presidents, and Rosenman's successor in this post, Clark M. Clifford. The papers of Justice Felix Frankfurter at the Library of Congress contain a number of letters from Frank Buxton, editor of the *Boston Globe*, shedding light on some aspects of the Anglo-American Committee of Inquiry.

Papers of three of the six American members of the Anglo-American Committee of Inquiry are deposited as follows: Judge Joseph Hutcheson, at the Humanities Research Center, the University of Texas at Austin; Frank Aydelotte, at Swarthmore College, Swarthmore, Pennsylvania; and James G. McDonald, at Columbia University, New York City. A fourth American member of the Committee, Bartley Crum—a San Francisco lawyer, convinced Zionist, and Anglophobe—published a highly colored, perhaps ghostwritten account of the investigation shortly after it was concluded: *Behind the Silken Curtain* (New York: Simon and Schuster, 1947). William Phillips, a former under secretary of state, who also served on the Committee (and whose papers are at Harvard University), gives a contrasting, more reflective account in *Ventures in Diplomacy* (Boston: Beacon Press, 1952).

Among officials of the Truman administration concerned at various junctures with the Palestine issue were David K. Niles, an advisor on minority affairs at the White House, whose papers are at Brandeis University, Waltham, Massachusetts; and James Forrestal, secretary of the navy and the first U.S. secretary of defense, whose papers are at Firestone Library, Princeton University. Parts of the diaries of the last-named are published under the editorship of Walter Millis as *The Forrestal Diaries* (New York: Viking, 1951). Other valuable published documents are John Morton Blum, ed., *From the Morgenthau Diaries, Vol. III: Years of War, 1941–45* (Boston: Houghton Mifflin, 1967); and Thomas M. Campbell and George C. Herring, eds., *The Diaries of Edward R. Stettinius, Jr., 1943–1946* (New York: New Viewpoints, 1975). The vice-president's insights into Truman's thoughts and attitudes are to be found in John Morton Blum, ed., *The Price of Vision: The Diary of Henry A. Wallace, 1942–1946* (Boston: Houghton Mifflin, 1973).

The records of the various American Jewish and Zionist organizations are an essential tool for the study of the U.S. role in the settlement of the Palestine question. The important collections are the American Jewish Committee Archive, the Zionist Archives and Library (which contains the papers of the American Zionist Emergency Council), and the Hadassah Archive, all in New York City; the American Jewish Historical Society collections at Brandeis University (which has the papers of the prominent Zionist leader Stephen S. Wise); and the papers of Abba Hillel Silver, at The Temple, Cleveland, Ohio. The records of the anti-Zionist American Council for Judaism are in the custody of the State Historical Society of Wisconsin, at Madison. The Council's founder, Elmer Berger, a prolific writer, is the author of the following, among other works: *The Jewish Dilemma: The Case against Zionist Nationalism* (New York: Devin Adair, 1946); *Judaism or Jewish Nationalism: The Alternative to Zionism* (New York: Bookman Associates, 1957); and *Memoirs of an Anti-Zionist Jew* (Beirut: Institute for Palestine Studies, 1978). Arthur A. Goren, ed., *Dissenter in Zion* (Cambridge: Harvard University Press, 1982), is a selection of writings by Judah L. Magnes, the California lawyer who became president of the Hebrew University in Jerusalem and a persistent advocate of a binational Jewish-Arab state in Palestine.

The development of Zionism in the United States is treated historically in Melvin I. Urofsky, *American Zionism from Herzl to the Holocaust* (Garden City, N.Y.: Anchor Press/Doubleday, 1976); the same author's *We Are One! American Jewry and Israel* (same publisher, 1978) carries the theme forward into the era of Israeli statehood. Also worthy of mention with respect to U.S.-Israeli relations are Nadav Safran, *Israel: The Embattled Ally* (Cambridge: Harvard University Press, 1978); and Robert Silverberg, *If I Forget Thee O Jerusalem: American Jews and the State of Israel* (New York: William Morrow, 1970). An analytical study of the movement is offered in Samuel Halperin, *The Political World of American Zionism* (Detroit: Wayne State University Press, 1961). More specifically focused on events in Palestine is Dan Kurzman, *Genesis 1948* (New York: World Publishing Co., 1970). Joseph B. Schechtman, the chairman of the Political Committee of the United Zionists-Revisionists of America, is unsparing of criticism of both the White House and the State

Department in his *The United States and the Jewish State Move-ment: The Crucial Decade, 1939–1949* (New York: Herzl Press, 1966). Of particular interest because of its gentile-Zionist author's previous service as under secretary of state and his substantial contribution to passage of the UN partition resolution is Sumner Welles, *We Need Not Fail* (Boston: Houghton Mifflin, 1948), written with the collaboration of the Jewish Agency and published after the outbreak of the first Arab-Israeli war. Mention should be made of the memoirs of Rabbi Stephen S. Wise, one of the most active and promi-nent American Zionist leaders during the years leading to the estab-lishment of Israel: *Challenging Years* (New York: G. P. Putnam's Sons, 1949).

The plight of Jewish displaced persons in Europe at the end of World War II did much to unite a previously somewhat passive Ameri-can Jewish community on the early formation of a Jewish state in Palestine. The origins of the problem, and its handling by the Roose-velt administration, are examined in Henry L. Feingold, *The Politics of Rescue: The Roosevelt Administration and the Holocaust, 1938–1945* (New Brunswick, N.J.: Rutgers University Press, 1970). The re-port of Earl G. Harrison, appointed by President Truman to investi-gate the situation on the spot, was printed in the State Department *Bulletin* on September 30, 1945, and ran in the *New York Times* the same day, thus reaching a broad public. The official response and ac-tion by a variety of civilian organizations are recounted in two well-documented works: David S. Wyman, *Paper Walls* (Amherst: Uni-versity of Massachusetts Press, 1968); and Leonard Dinnerstein, *America and the Survivors of the Holocaust* (New York: Columbia University Press, 1982).

Few aspects of American policy on Palestine have been the ob-ject of such a variety of interpretations as Truman's motivation in ex-tending prompt recognition to the state of Israel, a point on which the primary sources indeed offer conflicting evidence. Ian J. Bicker-ton, "President Truman's Recognition of Israel," *American Jewish Historical Quarterly*, 58 (December, 1968), 173–240, argues that—far from being swayed by domestic politics—the president acted in pursuit of American interests abroad and in support of democracy. John Snetsinger, *Truman, the Jewish Vote and the Creation of Israel* (Stanford, Cal.: Hoover Institution Press, 1974), comes to the op-posite conclusion, that Truman was above all concerned with woo-ing Jewish voters in an election year.

U.S. acts and decisions in the successive phases of the Palestine issue were marked by misunderstanding and a want of coordination among the White House, the State Department, and the American delegation at the UN that, save for the gravity of the problem, would be farcical. The chaos became enshrined in the written record and gave rise to debates that continue today. The president's own memoirs—volume 2, *Years of Trial and Hope* (Garden City, N.Y.: Doubleday, 1956)—presumably set forth the interpretations he desired to establish as authoritative. But his version cannot be reconciled in all respects with the documents in the Truman Library, the National Archives, and successive biographies based in part on them: Jonathan Daniels, *The Man of Independence* (New York: J. B. Lippincott, 1950); Alfred Steinberg, *The Man from Missouri* (New York: G. P. Putnam's Sons, 1962); Margaret Truman, *Harry S. Truman* (New York: Morrow, 1973); Robert J. Donovan, *Conflict and Crisis: The Presidency of Harry S Truman, 1945–1948* (New York: W. W. Norton, 1977); or Robert Ferrell, ed., *Off the Record: The Private Papers of Harry S. Truman* (New York: Harper and Row, 1980).

The consistent opposition to Zionism by the "working" levels of the State Department has drawn rather more *ad hominem* condemnation of the personalities concerned than objective analysis of the U.S. national-interest rationale on which their opposition was based. Philip Baram, *The Department of State in the Middle East, 1919–1945* (Philadelphia: University of Pennsylvania Press, 1978), is based on solid documentation used selectively. Allen H. Podet, "Anti-Zionism in a Key U.S. Diplomat: Loy Henderson at the End of World War II," *American Jewish Archives*, 30/2 (November, 1978), 155–87, carefully draws the necessary semantic distinction between anti-Zionism and anti-Semitism and reaches the conclusion that Henderson was not guilty of anti-Semitism. President Truman often bypassed, ignored, or overruled the Department's recommendations in favor of policies more consonant with Zionist ends. One exception—the dramatic switch to support of a UN trusteeship over Palestine—is examined in Zvi Ganin, "The Limits of American Jewish Political Power: America's Retreat from Partition, November 1947–March 1948," *Jewish Social Studies* (Winter–Spring, 1977), 1–36.

Among general accounts of the U.S. role in the events leading to the birth of Israel, Peter Grose, *Israel in the Mind of America* (New York: Alfred A. Knopf, 1983), closely examines the attitudes of presidents Roosevelt and Truman toward Palestine, the organization of the American Jewish community for political action, and the manner in which its influence was brought to bear on the national leadership. Zvi Ganin, *Truman, American Jewry, and Israel, 1945–1948* (New York: Holmes and Meier, 1979), draws on primary sources to clarify some incidents, such as Truman's reversal of the State Department position on disposition of the Negev, during the UN partition debate. Kenneth R. Bain, *The March to Zion: United States Policy and the Founding of Israel* (College Station: Texas A&M University Press, 1979), draws on official records to discredit some myths, such as the claim that Truman had not approved the plan to defer partition and place Palestine under trusteeship before the proposal was advanced by the U.S. delegation at the UN. Valuable for its background on the State Department and for the author's personal participation in many of the events recounted is Evan M. Wilson, *Decision on Palestine: How the U.S. Came to Recognize Israel* (Stanford, Calif.: Hoover Institution Press, 1979).

**The Soviet Perspective**

As the Soviet Union's archives are not available for scholarly research, Western writers must rely on a variety of indirect sources for analysis of Soviet decision making respecting the Middle East, and other regions of the world. The archives of other governments—notably the United States, the United Kingdom, and Israel with respect to the subject of the present volume—contain much relevant material, as do the Official Records of the United Nations General Assembly and Security Council, which were closely concerned with Palestine during the final months of the mandate. The public posture of the USSR on current issues is enunciated in its press organs, *Pravda* and *Izvestiia*, in the journal *New Times*, and in Moscow radio broadcasts.

For the general Soviet outlook during the period of interest here, Milovan Djilas, *Conversations with Stalin* (London: Rupert Hart-Davis, 1962), is instructive. Two analyses of the USSR's external policies may be recommended: Marshall D. Shulman, *Stalin's Foreign Policy Reappraised* (Cambridge: Harvard University Press, 1963); and Adam Ulam, *Expansion and Coexistence* (New York: Praeger, 1969). The trials of Russia's Jews, which gave impetus to the movement toward a Jewish state in Palestine, are recounted in Yehoshua Gilboa, *The Black Years of Soviet Jewry* (Boston: Little, Brown, 1971). Benjamin Pinkus, *The Soviet Union and Its Jews, 1948–1967* (Cambridge: Cambridge University Press, 1984), includes background material on the period of concern here.

For American policy and Soviet expansionism in the Middle East, the outstanding recent study is Bruce R. Kuniholm, *The Origins of the Cold War in the Near East: Great Power Conflict and Diplomacy in Iran, Turkey, and Greece* (Princeton: Princeton University Press, 1980). An earlier work by André Fontaine, *History of the Cold War from the October Revolution to the Korean War, 1917–*

*1950* (London: Secker and Warburg, 1965), takes a longer historical view; one chapter relates to the subject of Palestine. Two books by Middle East specialist Walter Z. Laqueur are devoted to Communism in, and Soviet relations with, the area: *Communism and Nationalism in the Middle East*, 3rd ed. (London: Routledge and Kegan Paul, 1961); and *The Soviet Union and the Middle East* (New York: Praeger, 1959). Yaacov Roʾi, *From Encroachment to Involvement: A Documentary Study of Soviet Policy in the Middle East* (New York: John Wiley, 1974), assembles some 140 official documents, press articles, and radio broadcasts, mostly from Soviet sources, accompanied by historical commentary and interpretation that not all readers find uniformly convincing. Two symposia may be mentioned: Michael Confino and Shimon Shamir, eds., *The U.S.S.R. and the Middle East* (New York: John Wiley, 1973); and Ivo J. Lederer and Wayne S. Vucinich, eds., *The Soviet Union and the Middle East: The Post–World War II Era* (Stanford, Calif.: Hoover Institution Press, 1974), which contains an essay by Nadav Safran entitled "The Soviet Union and Israel, 1947–69."

Works by contemporary Soviet writers offer useful insight into Moscow's official attitudes, but are otherwise of limited utility. The following were published while the fate of the mandate and Palestine was being decided (I am indebted to Oles M. Smolansky for the listings in this paragraph): I. A. Genin, *Strany Arabskogo Vostoka* (Moscow: Gosizdat, 1948); I. Levin, *Podgotovka voiny na Blizhnem Vostoke* (Moscow: Gosizdat, 1946); V. B. Lutskii, *Angliiskii i amerikanskii imperializm na Blizhnem Vostoke* (Moscow: Vsesoiuznoe obshchestvo po raspostraneniiu znanii, 1948); V. B. Lutskii, *Liga arabskikh gosudarstv* (Moscow: Vsesoiuznoe lektsionnoe biuro, 1946); V. B. Lutskii, *Palestinskaia problema* (Moscow: Vsesoiuznoe lektsionnoe biuro, 1946); and P. V. Milogradov, *Arabskii Vostok v mezhdunarodnykh otnosheniiakh* (Moscow: Vsesoiuznoe lektsionnoe biuro, 1946).

Following the Yalta Conference of February, 1945, unguarded remarks by President Franklin Roosevelt to a Zionist leader generated the impression that Stalin was a firm supporter of Zionism and that he and Roosevelt formally agreed at Yalta that Palestine should be handed over to the Jews. These myths are laid to rest by Joseph Heller in a closely documented essay, "Roosevelt, Stalin and the Palestine Problem at Yalta," *Wiener Library Bulletin*, 30 (1977), 25–35.

Three extended studies have been published of Soviet relations with the pre-independence Zionist leadership and, later, the state of Israel: Avigdor Dagan, *Moscow and Jerusalem* (New York: Abelard-Schuman, 1970); Arnold Krammer, *The Forgotten Friendship: Israel and the Soviet Bloc, 1947–53* (Urbana: University of Illinois Press, 1974); and, particularly well documented and argued, Yaacov Roʾi, *Soviet Decision Making in Practice: The USSR and Israel 1947–1954* (New Brunswick, N.J.: Transaction Books, 1980).

## The Zionist Perspective

For the Zionist outlook on Palestine affairs under the mandate, several archival collections in Israel are of primary importance. These include the Central Zionist Archives and the Israel State Archives, both in Jerusalem; the Weizmann Archives at Rehovoth; the Ben-Gurion Archives at Sde Boker; and the Oral Interview Library, Institute of Contemporary Jewry, Hebrew University, Jerusalem. The publications program of the Israel State Archives has thus far produced four volumes of documents. The first, unnumbered, covers the months immediately preceding statehood: *Israel Documents, December 1947–May 1948* (Jerusalem: Government Printer, 1980). For an appraisal of this compilation, see Michael J. Cohen, "The Birth of Israel—Diplomatic Failure, Military Success," *Jerusalem Quarterly*, 17 (Fall, 1980), 29–39. The numbered volumes begin with May 14, 1948, and thus far cover the period through the armistice negotiations between Israel and the Arab states ending in July, 1949. Annotated companion volumes with summary English translations of the Hebrew documents are being published (New Brunswick, N.J.: Transaction Books, 1980– ).

For insights into Zionist thinking, the memoirs and biographies of the movement's principal figures are of obvious significance. Some works from the pre-1945 era remain of interest from this point of view. The memoirs and diaries of Simon Arthur Ruppin (1876–1943) were edited by Alex Bein and published under the title *Pirke ḥayai*, 3 vols. (Tel Aviv: Am Oved, 1943, reprinted 1947; in Hebrew [I am indebted to Michael J. Cohen and others for guidance respecting works in the Hebrew language]). The journals of Moshe Shertok (later Sharett), who was to become Israel's prime minister in 1953, were published as *The Diaries of Moshe Sharett, 1936–1939*, 2 vols. (Tel Aviv: Am Oved, 1968, 1974; in Hebrew).

Under the general editorship first of Meyer Weisgal, and later of Barnett Litvinoff, the *Letters and Papers of Chaim Weizmann* (*1885–1952*) were published between 1968 and 1980, in twenty-three volumes, the first three by Oxford University Press (London), the rest by the Israel Universities Press, Jerusalem. The memoirs of David Ben-Gurion, senior leader of the Yishuv during the later mandate years and Israel's first prime minister, were printed in forty installments by the *Jewish Observer and Middle East Review* (London, 1963–65), and a volume of *Extracts* appeared a few years later (Cleveland: World Publishing Co., 1970). Supplemental reminiscences are presented in Moshe Pearlman, *Ben Gurion Looks Back in Talks with Moshe Pearlman* (New York: Simon and Schuster, 1965). Biographical studies include Michael Bar-Zohar, *Ben-Gurion: A Political Biography* (Tel Aviv: Am Oved, 1975; in Hebrew); and Dan Kurzman, *Ben-Gurion, Prophet of Fire* (New York: Simon and Schuster, 1983). The autobiography of Nahum Goldmann, *Sixty Years of Jewish Life* (New York: Holt, Rinehart and Winston, 1969), deserves special mention; the author was a member of the Jewish Agency Executive, president of the World Jewish Congress, and a vigorous proponent of the Zionist cause in the United States during the mandate's decisive phase.

Within the pre-independence Yishuv, some minorities pressed alternatives to mainstream Zionism's aim of a Jewish state. The best organized of these were proponents of a binational Jewish-Arab state in Palestine. The movement has received detailed study in a dissertation by Susan Lee Hattis, published as *The Bi-National Idea in Palestine during Mandatory Times* (Tel Aviv: Shikmona Publishing Co., 1970).

The Holocaust and the post–World War II plight of Jewish displaced persons in Europe served as a major catalyst in uniting the Zionists behind the goal of a Jewish state. A detailed and well-researched treatment of this episode is Yehuda Bauer, *Flight and Rescue: Brichah* (New York: Random House, 1970).

A few works addressing individual facets of the later phases of the Palestine question may be noted here. Netanel Lorch, *The Edge of the Sword: Israel's War of Independence 1947–1949*, 2nd ed. (Hartford, Conn.: Hartmore House, 1968), focuses on the Haganah's meticulous military planning that ensured Jewish success in battle. Joseph Nevo, *Abdullah and Palestine* (Tel Aviv: Tel Aviv University Press, 1975; in Hebrew), discusses the subtle posture of Jordan's ruler toward Palestine. Eliahu Elath, *Israel and Elath* (London: Weidenfeld and Nicolson, 1966), is a firsthand account of the negotiations to include the Negev and the port of Elath in the Jewish state; the text was written as a Lucien Wolf Memorial Lecture.

The failure of negotiations among British, Jews, and Arabs and the consequent resort to armed action by the Zionists have received close study. Yehuda Bauer, *From Diplomacy to Resistance: The History of Jewish Palestine, 1934–1945* (Philadelphia: Jewish Publication Society of America, 1970), brings the narrative to the end of World War II. A concise account of the events culminating in Israeli independence is provided in two articles by Joseph Heller: "Anglo-Zionist Relations, 1939–1947," *Wiener Library Bulletin,* 31 (1978), 63–73; and "Neither Masada—Nor Vichy: Diplomacy and Resistance in Zionist Politics, 1945–1947," *International History Review,* 3/4 (October, 1981), 540–64. Among the more extended accounts, two previously noted works are appropriately recalled in this context: David Horowitz, *State in the Making;* and Michael J. Cohen, *Palestine and the Great Powers.* Eliahu Elath, who went on from diplomacy to the presidency of the Hebrew University of Jerusalem, is the author of *The Struggle for Statehood 1945–1948,* 2 vols. (Tel Aviv: Am Oved, 1979, 1982; in Hebrew). Zeev Sharef, *Three Days: An Account of the Last Days of the British Mandate and the Birth of Israel* (London: W. H. Allen, 1962), concentrates on the climactic final events.

**The Arab Perspective**

The official records of the Arab League and the Arab states involved in the Palestine issue at the close of the mandate are not uniformly accessible for research or systematically filed and catalogued. The Institute of Palestine Studies has assembled an archive, now at Geneva, of utmost importance, which includes both official and private documents, minutes of Arab League meetings dealing with Palestine, the resulting decisions and communiqués, and much other pertinent material. The Institute's quarterly *Journal of Palestine Studies* is steadily expanding the data readily available on the mandate era as well as later times. Files of Palestinian and other Arabic press organs for the period of concern here are a valuable supplementary tool.

Several publications of the Arab Higher Committee for Palestine are of particular interest for the Arab viewpoints toward the end of the mandate. These include *A Collection of Official Documents Relating to the Palestine Question Submitted to the General Assembly of the UN* (New York, 1947); *The Palestine Arab Case* (Cairo, 1947); *The Great Betrayal in the UN* (New York, 1948); and *Why the Arab States Entered Palestine* (New York, 1948). A semimonthly *Arab News Bulletin* was published by the Arab Offices in London (1946–49) and Washington (1946–48). The Washington Arab Office published the following pamphlets: *The Problem of Palestine* (1946); *Testimony before the Anglo-American Committee on Palestine by Professor Phillip K. Hitti* (1946); and *Iraq's Point of View on the Palestine Question* (1947).

In view of the important role of Transjordan and the Arab Legion in the evolution of the Palestine issue, the reminiscences of the country's ruler are of interest. *Mudhakkirāt ʿAbdullah ibn Ḥusayn malik al-Urdun* (The Memoirs of Abdullah ibn Hussein, King of Jordan), 2nd ed. (Amman: n.p., 1947) was followed by a sequel: *Al-Takmila min mudhakkirāt Ḥāḍrat ṣāḥib al-jalāla al-Hāshimiya al-malik ʿAbdullah ibn al-Ḥusayn* (Supplement to the Memoirs of His Hashemite Majesty King Abdullah ibn al-Hussein) (Amman: n.p., 1951). A somewhat expurgated English translation of the first volume appeared as *Memoirs of King Abdullah* (London: J. Cape, 1950). The sequel, translated by Harold W. Glidden of the U.S. State Department, appeared as *My Memoirs Completed* (Washington, D.C.: American Council of Learned Societies, 1954). The Transjordan government, following passage of the UN partition resolution, published a statement of its Palestine policy in *Al-Kitāb al-ʾaswad* (The Black Book) (Amman: n.p., 1947). The Hashemite interest in Palestine receives critical examination in Anis Sayigh, *Al-Hāshimiyūn wa qaḍiyat Filasṭīn* (The Hashemites and the Palestine Issue) (Beirut: n.p., 1955).

Other non-Palestinian Arab participants in the intense Arab activity relating to Palestine recorded their experiences. Hazzāʿ Majāli, a Transjordanian, loyal servant of the Hashemites and several times prime minister of Jordan, tells his story in *Mudhakkirātī* (My Memoirs) (Beirut: Dār al-ʿilm lil-malāyīn, 1960). Ṭaha Pasha al-Hāshimī, president of the Baghdad Defense Committee for Palestine before World War II and a wartime premier of Iraq, published his reminiscences—"Mudhakkirāt ʿan Ḥarb Filasṭīn" (Memoirs of the Palestine War)—in the Baghdad daily *al-Ḥāris* (March 1, 1953). Nuri Said attended the December, 1947, meeting of the Arab League Council at Cairo held to discuss military plans and wrote a firsthand account: *Baʿḍ haqāʾiq ʿan qaḍāyā al-ʿIrāq al-akhīra wa Filasṭīn* (Certain Facts about Recent Issues in Iraq and Palestine) (Baghdad: Maṭbaʿat al-shaʿb, n.d. [1948?]). Muḥsin Barāzī, a Syrian diplomat who served as a personal envoy from President Shukri al-Quwwatli to King Farouk and Ibn Saud, published "Mudhakkirāt" in *al-Ḥayāt* (January 16, 1953). Abdullah al-Tall, a Transjordanian army officer, commanded a battalion of the Arab Legion force that asserted Arab control of East Jerusalem during the Palestine War, became civil governor there, plotted against King Abdullah for his "treason" to the Arab cause, fled to Egypt in 1949, and published his recollections, extending to a discussion of the international dimensions of the Palestine issue: *Kārithat Filasṭīn: Mudhakkirāt ʿAbd Allah al-Tall* (The Palestine Catastrophe: The Memoirs of Abdullah al-Tall) (Cairo: Dār al-Qalam, 1959).

Gen. John Bagot Glubb, the British commander of Transjordan's

Arab Legion, provides an authoritative account of the Legion's history and its role in the Palestine War, from the point of view of an outsider sympathetically sensitive to Arab attitudes, in *A Soldier with the Arabs* (London: Hodder and Stoughton, 1957).

As a young student in Baghdad just after World War II, Khalid Kishtainy was drawn to the British periodical the *New Statesman* because of its socialist editorial policy but soon became disenchanted with its consistent Zionist bias; later he undertook an extended content analysis of the journal's Middle East coverage, with particular attention to Palestine: *The New Statesman and the Middle East* (Beirut: Palestine Research Center, 1972).

For background on the Arab League, the focus of inter-Arab activity concerning Palestine, a useful work is Ahmad Mahmoud H. Gomaa, *The Foundation of the League of Arab States: Wartime Diplomacy and Inter-Arab Politics* (New York: Longman Group, 1977). The five Arab Palestinian political parties in existence toward the end of the mandate chose as Palestine's representative at the Arab League during its crucial discussions a political moderate, Musa al-Alami (later to become a respected promoter of economic and agricultural development among Palestine refugees in Jordan). He is the subject of a biography by Geoffrey Furlonge, *Palestine Is My Country: The Story of Musa Alami* (London: Murray, 1969). After the Arab defeat in 1949 Alami published ʿIbrat Filasṭīn (Beirut: n.p., 1949), of which a condensation, "The Lesson of Palestine," appeared in the *Middle East Journal*, 3/4 (October, 1949), 373–405. Among many other reflections by Arab writers on the Arab misfortune the most influential has been Constantine Zurayq, *Maʿnā al-Nakba*, translated by R. Bailly Winder as *The Meaning of the Disaster* (Beirut: Khayyat, 1956).

# Chronology

**1945**

| | |
|---|---|
| August 13 | World Zionist Congress demands that Palestine be opened to 1,000,000 Jews. |
| August 31 | Truman urges British to admit 100,000 Jewish refugees into Palestine. |
| September 14 | Soviet Union demands trusteeship territory in Tripolitania. |
| October 20 | Egypt, Iraq, Syria, and Lebanon warn United States that creation of Jewish state in Palestine will lead to war. |
| November 13 | Britain and United States announce formation of Anglo-American Committee of Inquiry on Palestine. |
| December 6 | American loan to Britain for $3.75 billion. |
| December 20 | Egyptians demand revision of 1936 Anglo-Egyptian Treaty. |

**1946**

| | |
|---|---|
| March 5 | Churchill denounces Soviet Union in "Iron Curtain" speech. |
| March 22 | Britain recognizes independence of Transjordan and concludes Treaty of Alliance. Amir Abdullah assumes title of king. |
| April 2 | Britain announces Cabinet Mission to Egypt. |
| April 15 | French and British troops withdraw from Syria. |
| April 30 | Anglo-American Committee of Inquiry reports recommendations on Palestine. |
| May 11 | Britain announces intended troop withdrawal from Egypt. |
| May 11 | Soviet Union abandons claim to Tripolitania. |
| July 4 | British troops evacuate Cairo. |
| July 22 | Irgun blows up King David Hotel. |
| September | London Conference convenes. Arabs propose Palestinian state. Jews boycott conference. Both Jews and Arabs favor British withdrawal from Palestine. |
| October 4 | Truman's "Yom Kippur" statement calls for bridging of gap between British and Zionist proposals. |
| December 28 | Zionist Congress demands Jewish state. Chaim Weizmann removed from leadership. |

## 1947

| | |
|---|---|
| February 7 | Arabs and Jews reject final British proposal for division of Palestine into Arab and Jewish zones administered as trusteeship territory. |
| February 18 | Britain refers Palestine question to United Nations. |
| May 13 | UN appoints Special Committee on Palestine. |
| May 28–29 | Arab summit meeting at Anshass calls for halt to Jewish immigration and independence of Arab Palestine. |
| June 3 | Britain announces plans for partition of India. |
| June 8 | Arab League Council meets at Bludan and plans economic sanctions against Britain and United States. |
| July 13 | Sterling made convertible. |
| July 18 | *Exodus* Jews denied entry into Palestine. |
| July 30 | Irgun hangs two British sergeants. |
| August 20 | Sterling convertibility suspended. |
| August 31 | UNSCOP majority calls for partition of Palestine. |
| September 26 | Britain announces intention to withdraw from Palestine. |
| October 7–15 | Arab League Council at Aley discusses military action in Palestine. |
| November 29 | UN General Assembly resolution on partition of Palestine. Palestine to be divided into Jewish and Arab states. Jerusalem to be under UN trusteeship administration. Plan is approved by Jews but rejected by Arabs. Anti-American riots in Arab capitals. |
| December 1 | First Haganah-Czech arms contract signed. |
| December 17 | Arab League threatens use of force to block division of Palestine. Raids on Jewish communities begin. |

## 1948

| | |
|---|---|
| January | Units of Arab Liberation Army enter Palestine from Syria. |
| January 15 | Britain concludes Treaty of Alliance with Iraq. |
| January 16 | Riots in Baghdad. |
| March 15 | New Treaty of Alliance between Transjordan and Britain. |
| April 3 | First Czech arms shipment to Jews arrives in Palestine. |
| April 9 | Massacre of Arabs at Deir Yasin. |
| April 13 | Hadassah medical convoy massacred by Arab irregulars in East Jerusalem. |
| April 22 | Jews capture Haifa. |
| May 12 | Jaffa surrenders to Jews. |
| May 12 | Egyptian parliament approves use of regular Egyptian forces in Palestine. |
| May 14 | End of British mandate in Palestine. Israel proclaims independence. United States extends *de facto* recognition. Midnight: Armies of five Arab states cross into Palestine. |
| May 17 | Soviet Union recognizes Israel. |

# Contributors

Wm. Roger Louis is Kerr Professor of English History and Culture at the University of Texas at Austin. His books include *Ruanda-Urundi* (1963), *Germany's Lost Colonies* (1967), *The History of the Congo Reform Movement* (with Jean Stengers, 1968), *British Strategy in the Far East* (1971), *Imperialism at Bay* (1977), and *The British Empire in the Middle East* (1984), all published by the Oxford University Press. With Prosser Gifford he edited *Britain and Germany in Africa* (1967), *France and Britain in Africa* (1971), and *The Transfer of Power in Africa* (1982), all published by the Yale University Press. In 1979 he was awarded the Oxford D.Litt. in recognition of his published works on the history of the British Empire and Commonwealth.

Peter Grose is managing editor of *Foreign Affairs*, published in New York by the Council on Foreign Relations. Before assuming this post, he was senior fellow and director of the Council's Middle East studies program. For the decade 1966–77 he reported the evolution of the Arab-Israeli dispute for the *New York Times*, as diplomatic correspondent in Washington, foreign correspondent based in Jerusalem, and member of the Editorial Board in New York. He served as deputy director of the State Department Policy Planning Staff under Secretary of State Cyrus R. Vance. His other books include *Israel in the Mind of America* (New York: Alfred A. Knopf, 1983) and *A Changing Israel* (New York: Random House, 1985). Son of British historian Clyde Leclare Grose, he holds degrees from Yale and Oxford universities.

Oles M. Smolansky, University Professor of International Relations at Lehigh University, Bethlehem, Pennsylvania, is a specialist in Soviet policy in the Middle East. He is the author of *The Soviet Union and the Arab East under Khrushchev* (Lewisburg, Pa.: Bucknell University Press, 1974) and of numerous articles in professional journals. He has also contributed several chapters to scholarly works.

Michael Joseph Cohen is married, with two children. Born in England in 1940, he took his Ph.D. at the London School of Economics. Professor Cohen has been lecturer in general history at the University of Bar-Ilan, Israel, since 1972. He has been visiting professor at Stanford, Duke, and North Carolina at Chapel Hill universities in the United States, and at the University of British Columbia, Vancouver, Canada. He has published numerous articles in learned journals, and the following books: *Palestine: Retreat from the Mandate, 1936–1945* (New York: Holmes and Meier, 1978), *Palestine and the Great Powers, 1945–1948* (Princeton: Princeton University Press, 1982), and *Churchill and the Jews* (London: Frank Cass, 1985). He edited two volumes of the *Weizmann Letters*, covering World War II, and is currently working on a documentary *History of the State of Israel*.

Walid Khalidi (B.A., London, 1945; B.Litt., Oxon., 1951) was born in Jerusalem, Palestine. During 1951–56 he was university lecturer in Oriental studies at Oxford University, and since 1957 has been professor of political studies at the American University of Beirut, Lebanon. In 1960–61 he was research associate in Near Eastern studies at Princeton University and in 1978–82 visiting professor of government at Harvard, where he is currently research fellow at the Center for Middle Eastern Studies. His books include *From Haven to Conquest* (Beirut: Institute for Palestine Studies, 1971), *Conflict and Violence in Lebanon, Confrontation in the Middle East* (Cambridge: Center for International Affairs, 1978), and *Before Their Diaspora* (Washington, D.C.: Institute for Palestine Studies, 1984).

J. C. Hurewitz, professor emeritus of Columbia University, was director of the Middle East Institute from 1971 to 1984. His books include *The Struggle for Palestine* (New York: W. W. Norton, 1950) and *Middle East Politics: The Military Dimension* (New York: Frederick A. Praeger, 1969). He is completing *British and French Withdrawal, 1945–1967*, the third of a four-volume reference work, *The Middle East and North Africa in World Politics*, for Yale University Press; *European Expansion, 1535–1914* appeared in 1975, and *British-French Supremacy, 1914–1945*, in 1979.

Robert W. Stookey holds a Ph.D. in government from the University of Texas at Austin and is a research associate of the Center for Middle Eastern Studies at that institution. A retired U.S. Foreign Service officer and Arabic language-and-area specialist, he is author of *America and the Arab States: An Uneasy Encounter* (New York:

John Wiley, 1975), *Yemen: The Politics of the Yemen Arab Republic* (Boulder, Colo.: Westview, 1978), *South Yemen: A Marxist Republic in Arabia* (Boulder, Colo.: Westview, 1982), and editor of *The Arabian Peninsula: Zone of Ferment* (Stanford, Calif.: Hoover Institution, 1984), among other publications and journal articles.

# Index

Abdul Aziz, King. *See* Ibn Saud

Abdulilah (Regent of Iraq), 122, 130; hatred of, for Hajj Amin, 112; abrogates Portsmouth Treaty with Britain, 125

Abdullah bin Hussein: made Emir of Transjordan, viii; encouraged by Bevin to take over "Arab Palestine" (1948), 24; negotiates with Zionists (1948), 95–96, 100, 113, 127; territorial ambitions of, 112, 114; cordial relations of, with Zionists, 112; proclaimed king (1946), 114; revives "Greater Syria" project, 114, 115; his army alone could not "overcome Zionists," 127; named supreme commander of Arab forces, 130

Abul-Huda, Tawfiq Pasha, 24, 127

Acheson, Dean, 40, 127

Alami, Musa: recommendations of, to 1944 Arab Congress, 107–108; moderation of, and faith in Britain, 108

Alexander, A. V., 21

Anglo-American Committee of Inquiry, ix, xi, 8–10, 13, 39, 44, 64, 84; report "dismantles" 1939 White Paper, 110

Anti-Semitism, 40; in England, 19, 22, 80; and American diplomats, 57

Arab League, 107, 108, 146, 165; diverging views of, on urgency of Palestine problem (1945), 109; 1939 White Paper cornerstone of its policy, 109–110; 1946 summit calls for halt of immigration, 110; U.S.-Arab dialogue of the deaf, 110–111; secret resolutions of, against U.S. and Britain (June 1946), 111, 117, 119, 123; sponsors new Arab Higher Committee, 112, 118; resolves to provide material aid to Palestinians, 117–118; upholds right of Palestine to be independent Arab state, 119; adopts compromise military measures, 123; efforts of, to persuade Egypt to use regular army, 128–129. *See also* Arab states

Arab Legion, 19, 24, 96, 129, 163–164

Arab nationalism, 149; and question of Jewish state, viii–ix; loss of faith in West, xi; and partition of Palestine, 2; and claim to Palestine, 12; frustrated in Palestine, 23; Roosevelt's view of, 38; and Stalin, 66

Arab states, vii, 24, 26, 69, 73, 75–76, 77n.25, 84, 120; and British evacuation, 90; and UN partition resolution, 92–93; and 1948 war, 95–97; neglect by, of military preparedness, 108; euphoric over U.S. trusteeship proposal, 126

Arms embargo, 70, 73

Wise, Stephen, 81
World Wars I and II, Palestine problem in, vii, ix
World Zionist Organization: pre–World War I rallying of, of support for Jewish state, vii; and Balfour Declaration, viii; and Zionist Congress (1946), 88

Yalta Conference (1945), 64
Yasin, Yusif, 111, 117
Yishuv (Jewish community in Palestine): in conflict with Arabs, vii, ix, 67; and Soviet Union, 66, 70–71, 74–75; and World War II, 82–83; and revolt of 1945–1946, 83–85; and British evacuation, 90; and outbreak of civil war, 95
Yugoslavia, 67

Zionism and Zionists, 33, 34, 41, 144, 146, 148–149, 156–157, 161–162; development of, vii–ix; as threat to Arabs, xi; and Bevin, 1, 80–81; and Creech Jones, 4; and Churchill, 5; use of terrorism by, 10, 14, 21, 80, 83, 91, 96; and Truman's Yom Kippur statement, 11, 87; and claim to Palestine, 12;

and British "UN strategy," 20; and Communism and Soviet Union, 23; and Russian Revolution, 24; and American influence in 1948, 26–27; pressure of, for U.S. recognition of Israel, 52; and Stalin, 64, 66; no choice of, but to seek Soviet assistance, 73; long-term interests of, not complementary with Soviet Union's, 74–75; nature of the campaign of, 79–80; publicity triumph of, with *Exodus* affair, 81; politics of, in America revolutionized by Rabbi Silver, 82; and Palestine revolt of 1945–1946, 83–85; and Morrison-Grady plan, 86; and White House, 88; and UN partition resolution, 90–93; and U.S. trusteeship proposal (1948), 94–95; and Deir Yasin, 96–97; and administrative preparation for new state, 97–98; and "moral imperative" of Holocaust, 100; effectiveness of lobby of, in U.S. and in setting up new state, 101; and shift from British to U.S. sponsorship, 107; military planning of, 127–128